T0330227

States, Banks and Crisis

For Burcu, and my family

States, Banks and Crisis

Emerging Finance Capitalism in Mexico and Turkey

Thomas Marois

Department of Development Studies, School of Oriental and African Studies, University of London, UK

Edward Elgar

Cheltenham, UK • Northampton, MA, USA

Published by
Edward Elgar Publishing Limited
The Lypiatts
15 Lansdown Road
Cheltenham
Glos GL50 2JA
UK

Edward Elgar Publishing, Inc.
William Pratt House
9 Dewey Court
Northampton
Massachusetts 01060
USA

A catalogue record for this book
is available from the British Library

Library of Congress Control Number: 2011942552

ISBN 978 0 85793 857 2 (cased)

Typeset by Servis Filmsetting Ltd, Stockport, Cheshire
Printed and bound by MPG Books Group, UK

Contents

Tables and figures

TABLES

FIGURE

Abbreviations

The acronyms listed below are typically the most commonly used in the literature on Mexico and Turkey.

Abbreviation in use	Name in English	Name in home country language (if applicable)
ABM	Banks' Association of Mexico	Asociación de Bancos de México
AKP	Justice and Development Party	Adalet ve Kalkınma Partisi
ANAP	Motherland Party	Anavatan Partisi
AP	Justice Party	Adelat Partisi
BAT	Banks Association of Turkey	Türkiye Bankalar Birliği
BIS	Bank for International Settlements	
BMV	Mexican Stock Exchange	Bolsa Mexicana de Valores
BRSA	Banking Regulation and Supervision Agency	Bankacılık Düzenleme ve Denetleme Kurumu
BSRP	Banking Sector Restructuring Program	
CBT	Central Bank of Turkey	Türkiye Cumhuriyet Merkez Bankası
CDB	Bank Privatization Committee	Comité de Disincorporación Bancaria
CETES	Treasury Certificates (Mexico)	Certificados de la Tesorería
CHP	Republican People's Party	Cumhuriyet Halk Partisi
CME	Coordinated Market Economy	
CNB	National Banking Commission	Comisión Nacional Bancaria
CNBV	National Banking and Securities Commission	Comisión Nacional Bancaria y de Valores

CNV	National Securities Commission	Comisión Nacional de Valores
DP	Democratic Party	Demokrat Parti
DPTM	State Planning Organization	Devlet Planlama Teşkilatı Müsteşarlığı
DSP	Democratic Left Party	Demokratik Sol Parti
DYP	Doğru Yol Partisi	True Path Party
EOI	Export Oriented Industrialization	
FDI	Foreign Direct Investment	
Fenasib	National Federation of Banking Unions	Federación Nacional de Sindicatos Bancarios
Fobaproa	Banking Fund for the Protection of Saving	Fondo Bancario de Protección al Ahorro
Fonapre	Fund for Preventative Aid for Multiple Bank Institutions	Fondo de Apoyo Preventivo a las Instituciones de Banca Múltiple
FTA	Free Trade Agreement	
G-20	Group of Twenty	
GATT	General Agreement on Tariffs and Trade	
GDP	Gross Domestic Product	
GNP	Gross National Product	
IFI	International Financial Institution	
IPAB	Bank Savings Protection Institute	Instituto para la Protección al Ahorro Bancario
IPO	Initial Public Offering	
ISE	İstanbul Stock Exchange	İstanbul Menkul Kıymetler Borsası
ISI	Import Substitution Industrialization	
LME	Liberal Market Economy	
MHP	Nationalist Action Party	Milliyetçi Hareket Partisi
MoU	Memorandum of Understanding	
MÜSİAD	Independent Industrialist Businessmen's Association	Müstakil Sanayicileri ve İşadamları Derneği
NAFTA	North American Free Trade Agreement	

NIE	New Institutional Economics	
NPL	Non-Performing Loan	
OECD	Organization for Economic Co-operation and Development	
ÖİB	Privatization Administration	Özelleştirme İdaresi Başkanlığı
ROA	Return on Assets	
ROE	Return on Equity	
RP	Welfare Party	Refah Partisi
PAN	National Action Party	Partido Acción Nacional
PNR	National Revolutionary Party	Partido Nacional Revolucionario
PRD	Party of the Democratic Revolution	Partido de la Revolución Democrática
PRI	Institutional Revolutionary Party	Partido Revolucionario Institucional
PSE	Pact of Economic Solidarity	Pacto de Solidaridad Económica
SDIF	Saving Deposit Insurance Fund	Tasarruf Mevduatı Sigorta Fonu
SHCP	Ministry of Finance and Public Credit	Secretaría de Hacienda y Crédito Público
SME	Small and Medium-Sized Enterprises	
SOE	State-Owned Enterprise	
SPP	Secretariat of Planning and Budget	Secretaría de Programación y Presupuesto
TOBB	Union of Chambers and Commodity Exchanges of Turkey	Türkiye Odalar ve Borsalar Birliği
TL	Turkish lira	Türk lirası
TSE	Transition to a Strong Economy	
TSPAKB	The Association of Capital Market Intermediary Institutions of Turkey	Türkiye Sermaye Piyasası Aracı Kuruluşları Birliği
TÜSİAD	Turkish Industrialist Businessmen's Association	Türk Sanayicileri ve İşadamları Derneği

VGM	General Directorate of Foundations	Vakiflar Genel Müdürlüğü
VoC	Varieties of Capitalism	
YTL	New Turkish Lira	Yeni Türk lirası

Acknowledgements

There are not enough words to convey my gratitude for the guidance, knowledge, patience, and inspiration that my teachers, mentors, and friends have generously given me over the years. There are many without whom this book never would have materialized or had the flavor it does. I would like to acknowledge a few of these people. I owe my greatest intellectual debt of gratitude to Gregory Albo who gave form to and encouraged my project from its infancy. Likewise, Leo Panitch and Susanne Soederberg have had an enormous impact on my analytical and academic endeavors. I'd also like to thank Ben Fine, Costas Lapavitsas, and Alfredo Saad-Filho for their input and support while at SOAS. Thanks to my friends and colleagues Dae-oup Chang, Paolo Novak, and Alessandra Mezzadri. A special mention is needed for my friends and colleagues Adam Hanieh and Rafeef Ziadeh for all the marches, intellectual and activist talks, pints, and friendship that we have shared since first meeting at York. Thank you also to Eric Newstadt and Aylin Topal. I am also grateful for the help given by Noemi Levy, Galip Yalman, and Fuat Keyman during my field research trips. There are also those without whom I never would have been a critical academic, including Fred Judson, Joyce Green, and Janine Brodie. It needs mentioning that part of the work contained within the book was carried out with the aid of a grant from the International Development Research Centre, Ottawa, Canada. Information on the Centre is available on the web at www.idrc.ca. This work was also made possible by the support of the SSHRC of Canada. Finally, thanks to my students over the years at York, Queens, and SOAS who have helped me refine and rethink many ideas and concepts.

1. Introducing emerging finance capitalism

The tipping point comes after a period of foreboding economic and political instability associated with the relaxation of financial regulations. The risky ventures of once profitable banks and corporations are exposed, and this breeds financial uncertainty and eventual crisis. The impact is more tremendous than could have been imagined just a few months beforehand. Only massive, immediate, and sustained state intervention will prevent the collapse of the national financial system and stem potential international contagion. The public costs are staggering and austerity measures unavoidable, but government officials assure everyone that the bank rescue is in all their interests and not that of a few wealthy bankers. As the banks return to profitability, state financial managers dedicate their energies to institutionalizing new, costly, and more powerful mechanisms for managing financial instability within their borders. In retrospect, officials say the crisis was an opportunity to put the country's financial house in order. For the bulk of the population, the banks had brought themselves to the edge of the abyss, state rescue had unilaterally pulled them back, and this had come at a colossal social expense. It is an era of emerging finance capitalism.

Many mainstream scholars, analysts, and experts have decided that the interventions of states and governments at times of financial crisis are an unfortunate but necessary feature of contemporary banking and development. Only the degree and design of such interventions remain a matter of debate within and across research paradigms (Ocampo et al. 2007; Demirgüç-Kunt and Servén 2009; Stein 2010; Rogers 2010). The questions of why this is necessary and who benefits from such interventions have been subject to less inquiry. Yet the problems of who benefits and why – that have been played out at different times and in different ways not only in Mexico and Turkey but in most emerging capitalisms since the 1980s – are what have driven me to make a critical assessment.[1] Why do state authorities step in to protect the interests of financial capital when it is so socially costly? Why are they building capacity to do so more comprehensively? If workers as taxpayers are implicated (and there is widespread agreement that they are), how is labor related to the changes between states and banks that enable rescues to occur? Moreover, what is particular and what is general to these banking crises, rescues, and the nature of contemporary development in emerging capitalisms?

Evidently, posing these types of questions begins to take us some way from mainstream assessments that offer technical advice on how best to overcome recurrent banking crises. These assessments refuse to question the underlying unequal and exploitative social relations of power that have arisen with the 1980s transition to neoliberal capitalism, that have assumed a more aggressive finance-led form during the 1990s, and that have now culminated as *emerging finance capitalism* in the current phase of accumulation – an era wherein the collective interests of financial capital principally shape the logical options and choices of government and state elites over and above those of labor and popular classes. This is so even to the extent that state elites at times need to impose restrictions in order to save financial capital from itself, that is from the profit-oriented speculative and volatile practices that lead to crisis.

How can we begin to think of neoliberalism and its progressively finance-led form differently from technical policy assessments? Critical scholars often interpret neoliberalism as not simply a set of market-oriented policies but as a new social form of rule, power, and class discipline specific to the current phase of competition characterized by the internationalization of capital and state (on different aspects of this, see Harvey 2005; Albo et al. 2010; Fine 2010; Marois 2011a). Neoliberal strategies of development are seen as committed to augmenting competitiveness and profitability within emerging capitalisms, but these have come at the expense of organized labor and to the benefit of capital (Bieler et al. 2010; Munck 2010). The collective aim has been first to restore the power of capital over labor and only then to restore profitability. The ideological expression of neoliberal discipline suggests that the indisputable solution to all social, ecological, economic, and political problems is their progressive exposure to world market competitive imperatives and the retreat of the state apparatus. Yet in practice neoliberalism and its finance-led form have required a very active and interventionist state to ensure the conditions of profitability for capital and to enable markets. Finally, critical scholars see how the more universal dynamics of neoliberalism can become institutionalized differently from society to society and need not be reproduced twice in exactly the same way – nor must neoliberalism in order to impart a certain social logic over society (Albo 2005).

Rudolf Hilferding's classic book, *Finance Capital* (reprinted 2006), is useful for understanding current processes and phases of change in neoliberalism and finance, even though his original analysis released in 1910 dealt specifically with the banks in Germany and Austria. In particular, Hilferding instructs us not to look at banks, states, and industry as discrete and historically fixed entities but rather as historically variable institutions that encompass social, political, and economic aspects. Notably, he illustrated how at a particular moment in history 'finance capital' emerged as the new form of capital characterized by processes of change that led to the fusion of bank and industrial capital. The historical structural changes occurred in such a way that the banks assumed predominance and were able to exercise real political influence in society. Finance capital in this specific historical form is not directly transferable to Mexico and Turkey today. However, Hilferding's Marxian methodology allows for historical specificity in banks and in state–bank power relations. This way of analyzing capitalist banking underlies the interpretation here of emerging finance capitalism, which can be seen as a new phase of accumulation flowing out of neoliberal transformation.

This brings us to the question of why we should study states and banks in emerging capitalisms, and specifically in Mexico and Turkey. For one, the state apparatus has always been and continues to be indispensable to the functioning of banks in peripheral countries and emerging capitalisms today. At the same time, and even if all productive financing does not occur through the banks, large banks dominate the financial systems. States and banks are inevitably related in emerging capitalist development and over the last three decades their societies have been penetrated by historically unprecedented flows of money and investment capital. At this time, emerging capitalist societies have come to be more important within the international financial architecture and world market. A few measures are enough to substantiate this uncontroversial claim. The amount of annual direct investment into developing and emerging capitalisms has ballooned from less than $7 billion in 1980 to $149 billion in 2000 to $296 billion in 2010 (reflecting the widening internationalization of capital).[2] Mirroring these flows of money, there has also been monumental growth in the international reserves held by these countries, from $41 billion in 1980 to $83 billion in 2000 to $677 billion in 2010 (reflecting the internationalization of the state). External debt has also grown, from $573 billion in 1980 to $2.37 trillion in 2000 to $5.13 trillion in 2010. Underlining the increasingly finance-led form of neoliberal strategies of development, we can see that while global foreign exchange *daily* turnovers topped a record $1.5 trillion in the late 1990s the figure today is just shy of $4 trillion according to Bank of International Settlements estimates. The point here being that foreign and domestic flows of money have become quantitatively more significant under neoliberalism, leading to a wide variety of qualitative changes globally. This has given rise to a mushrooming finance and development literature that attempts to understand these quantitative and qualitative changes for emerging capitalisms.[3] This book's critical study of Mexico and Turkey seeks to contribute to this literature, but this focus in turn begs the question of why – specifically – Mexico and Turkey.

There are, to begin with, important geographical and current economic markers. Both countries have relatively large landmasses, even though Mexico's (1,943,950 sq. km.) is somewhat larger than Turkey's (769,630 sq. km.), and relatively large populations that are closer in size: Mexico with just over 106 million people in 2008 and Turkey with nearly 74 million. Quite uniquely among emerging capitalisms, Mexico and Turkey each border one of the world's most powerful regions, the US and European Union respectively. Their financial sectors are now larger and more liberalized than ever before, and their societies are tightly integrated with the US and the European Union. Reflecting their rising importance, in 1999 Mexico and Turkey were drawn into the Group of Twenty (G-20) – a high level international body composed of advanced and emerging capitalist countries' finance ministers and central bank governors established in 1999 – and then into the Financial Stability Board in 2009 as G-20 members. The point being that as global financial activity has expanded so too has the importance of emerging capitalisms in relation to financial flows and to the political maintenance of the world market.

However, the emerging capitalisms are not all of equal size and the global importance of a small number overshadows the rest. As is well known, the big four BRICs (Brazil, Russia, India, and China) predominate politically and economically. Nonetheless, Argentina, South Africa, Poland, Indonesia, South Korea, and – the case studies of this book – Mexico and Turkey are also systemically important emerging capitalisms within the international financial architecture (Soederberg 2004; Epstein 2005; Mihaljek 2010). Given Mexico and Turkey's large populations and recovery since crisis in 2008, the chair of Goldman Sachs Asset Management, Jim O'Neill, who originated the term 'BRIC', signaled he wants to expand the BRICs to a wider grouping that specifically draws in Mexico and Turkey as key 'growth markets'.[4] Moreover, while the current prolonged global crisis, which many academics call the 'Great Recession', has hit the Mexican and Turkish societies hard, international commentators have praised the banking sectors for their resilience, which is perceived as the outcome of post-crisis institutional reforms (this is one claim that the book's later chapters challenge). Mexico and Turkey are not the largest but they are among the most important players and, as such, constitute two emerging capitalisms of global significance.

The highlights of their contemporary relevance can be traced on a longer historical trajectory. Peripheral Mexican and Turkish capitalism consolidated in the interwar period of the 1930s that followed early twentieth-century national struggles in each country – the 1910–17 Mexican Revolution and the 1919–23 Turkish War of Independence (Cardero 1984; Knight 1992; Cockcroft 1998 and 2010; Savran 2002; Akkaya 2002). Following World War II authoritarian governments subsequently experimented with different mixed forms of economic liberalism and protectionism as part of their industrialization plans, but state-led strategies of development took effective hold by the 1960s and were formalized in multi-year national development plans. Mexico and Turkey alike achieved noteworthy postwar growth records of 5–7 per cent annually. Workers had made significant workplace gains, including some new rights and organized bargaining power, but great inequality remained between the increasingly powerful domestic family-based holding groups and the vast majority of Mexicans and Turks. In both cases, state authorities facilitated the largest family-based holding groups taking control of the biggest private domestic banks. Contrary to Hilferding's definition of 'finance capital' – where industry and banks fuse interests under the dominance of banks – the Mexican and Turkish industrial and commercial-based holding groups subordinated the banks' operations to the groups' overall interests. By the 1970s Mexico and Turkey's developmental trajectories had become increasingly congruent leading the World Bank to classify the two as 'middle-income' countries, with the OECD reporting comparable levels of GDP per capita – Mexico at $1744 and Turkey at $1246 in 1970 purchasing power terms (the OECD average was $3488). Government developmental policy was actively interventionist, and this too included financial support through the banking sectors.

By the late 1970s state financing of industrialization had hit barriers that were difficult to overcome within a postwar state-led strategy of development that preserved existing capital–labor compromises (Kiely 2007). The subsequent unfolding of the 1980s debt crisis then opened the possibility for capital and advocates of liberalism to press for more market-oriented strategies of development in each country (Cypher 1989; Yalman 2009). The debt crisis was linked to the earlier recycling of petrodollar loans into emerging capitalisms. These foreign loans exploded into unmanageable debt burdens as the 1979–82 US Volcker shock reverberated throughout the periphery in the form of skyrocketing interest rates (from around 3–4 per cent to 17–20 per cent) (Strange 1994 [1988]; Hanlon 2009). In order to preclude collective action by the indebted periphery, the US and international financial institutions (IFIs) restructured the debts on a case-by-case basis. Since then, debt fatigue and structural adjustment programs have resulted in great social costs characterized by more social inequality and poverty (Taylor 2009). By the late 1980s and early 1990s these changes involved more intense financial liberalization measures and debt-led strategies of development (Guillén Romo 2005; Soederberg 2005; Yeldan 2006a). While not the subject matter of this analysis, it must be pointed out that these money flows are not neutral but have been heavily influenced by the international hierarchy of states and US structural power over the evolution of global finance (Konings 2008; Duménil and Lévy 2011).

Organized labor has faced great difficulties in trying to resist neoliberal restructuring. One effect of labor's weakness has been the growing willingness and capacity of the state apparatus to develop and exercise increased institutional and fiscal capacity to absorb mounting financial risks at times of recurrent financial crisis. This socialization of financial risk is most explicit at times of banking rescues (1995 in Mexico and 2001 in Turkey), but it also involves the massive build up of international or foreign reserves to cover the activities of financial capital. Be they traditionally from the left or right of the political spectrum, government parties have facilitated the implementation of IFI guided neoliberal structural adjustment programs in Mexico and Turkey (Rodríguez 2010; Bedirhanoğlu and Yalman 2010). In this regard, the transition to *finance-led* neoliberalism represents an institutionalized victory of foreign and domestic financial capital in Mexican and Turkish society over domestic labor and the popular classes (Marois 2011a).

Nonetheless, while Mexico and Turkey are both OECD members they have been unable to break into the world's advanced capitalist ranks and perennially remain among the 'middle-income' emerging capitalisms. This is not to deny that the two societies have experienced aggregate growth over the last 30 years (see Table 1.1).[5] In GDP per capital purchasing power parity (PPP) terms, Mexico grew from $10402 to $13406 between 1980 and 2008 whereas Turkey grew more dramatically from $5694 to $11932. The annual rate of GDP growth, however, has been characteristically volatile, swinging from negative to very positive growth periods without ever overcoming structural current account deficits. Moreover, aggregate measures of growth are poor measures of inequality between social classes, which has increased almost everywhere under neoliberalism (Wade 2004; Nissanke and Thorbecke 2006; Onaran 2008). Poverty in Mexico and Turkey is on the rise and their populations suffer from among the worst income inequality within the OECD, according to 2011 OECD figures.[6] Furthermore, and with the exception of Chile, inequality has risen fastest in Mexico and Turkey over the last decade. More than 40 per cent of people find it difficult to live on their current income and this has only worsened with the Great Recession.

The growth that has occurred has also been export-oriented and debt-led, and therefore dependent on recurring flows of external finance that are

Table 1.1　Comparative indicators, Mexico and Turkey, 1980–2008

Indicator	Country	1980	1990	1995	2000	2008
GDP per capita, PPP	Mexico	10402	10101	9949	12071	13406
(constant 2005	Turkey	5694	7806	8378	9409	11932
international $)						
GDP growth	Mexico	9.2	5.1	–6.2	6.6	1.8
(annual %)	Turkey	–2.4	9.3	7.9	6.8	0.9
Current account	Mexico	–5.4	–2.8	–0.6	–3.2	–1.5
balance	Turkey	–5.2	–1.7	–1.4	–3.7	–5.6
(% of GDP)						
Exports of goods	Mexico	10.7	18.6	30.4	30.9	28.3
and services	Turkey	5.2	13.4	19.9	20.1	23.9
(% of GDP)						
Total debt service	Mexico	5.8	4.5	9.6	10.3	3.9
(% of GNI)	Turkey	2.5	5.0	6.9	7.9	7.4
External debt stocks	Mexico	30.5	41.1	60.5	26.6	19.1
(% of GNI)	Turkey	29.8	33.4	44.3	44.4	35.3
Domestic credit	Mexico	43.8	37.3	50.0	34.1	37.5
provided by	Turkey	34.5	21.8	29.1	39.3	52.6
banking sector						
(% of GDP)						
Total reserves (%	Mexico	7.3	9.8	10.3	23.6	46.7
of total external	Turkey	17.2	15.4	18.8	20.1	26.6
debt)						

Source:　World Bank, World Development Indicators (April 2010).

far from guaranteed and often very costly. Mexican and Turkish society have also each suffered harsh neoliberal crises. Mexico is often tagged as having gone through the first neoliberal financial crisis in 1995 and Turkey as having suffered one of the most recent, in 2001, at least prior to the Great Recession. In both countries, universal banks are involved in a wide range of financial activities and prevail as the dominant financial institutions heavily involved in servicing public debt requirements. Great political efforts have been made towards financial liberalization before and after each crisis, and foreign bank entry has been significant if uneven in each case. Since the 1980s, external debt to gross national income (GNI) has been in the range of 30 per cent or higher. Mexico has been the notable exception since external debt fell to less than 20 per cent in 2000. This is because the PAN government has privileged internalizing foreign debts and holding them within the large foreign banks that entered Mexico after 2000. One implication of Mexico and Turkey's reliance on debt for development is that each society has had to build up their international reserves as a form of self-insurance against constant financial volatility, which draws national resources from other sectors of society (Rodrik 2006). Whereas total reserves as a percentage of total external debt ranged in the 10–15 per cent mark in the early 1980s, Mexico and Turkey today are compelled to hold reserves in the range of 30–45 per cent as a credible measure of creditworthiness under emerging finance capitalism.

It is important to highlight that these broad historical and structural similarities do not eclipse Mexico and Turkey's specific and interesting differences, which are key to interpreting the changing relations between states, banks, and labor vis-à-vis crisis leading to emerging finance capitalism. For example, Mexico has undergone three rapid structural changes in bank ownership in little more than two decades: from private domestic to nationalized in 1982, from nationalized to private domestic in 1991–92, and from private domestic to largely foreign from 2000–02. By contrast, Turkey has had a long history of large and important state banks, which continue to control about a third of the banking sector today. Private domestic Turkish banks predominate now but their growing influence has been gradual. Only in the past few years have foreign banks taken a more significant stake in the banking sector. This suggests that specific institutional changes in banking, occurring alongside the global convergence towards neoliberalism, have neither occurred at the same time nor at the same pace in Mexico as in Turkey. Further differences are discussed in the chapters that follow.

I would like to pause here to mention my motivations for writing this book, the most significant of which is to fill certain gaps I see in the literature. Comparatively little has been written on banking and development and there is still relatively little known about banking in the emerging world today, as Leonardo Martinez-Diaz recognizes (2009, 4). There is wide agreement that more work needs to be done to understand bank ownership, and increasingly foreign bank ownership, in developing countries (La Porta et al. 2002; Boubakri et al. 2008; Stein 2010). Eswar Prasad and M. Ayhan Kose (2010) also point out that analyses are needed of the current crisis in emerging markets. Much of the content of the book addresses these concerns around emerging capitalist banks, ownership, and crisis. Uniquely, however, it does so from a Marxian-inspired framework (as elaborated on in Chapter 2). Here too I hope to advance Marxian understandings that, according to Hugo Radice (2010, 27), have until recently progressed relatively little on the relationships between banking, finance, and capitalism since Hilferding's *Finance Capital*. The theoretical and empirical content of this book is an attempt to enhance these understandings and, in so doing, to challenge the ways in which issues of banking, finance, states, and development have been framed by the mainstream and understood within Marxian literature. There is one further analytical motivation behind this book. As one reads about the thousands of bank workers laid off at times of financial crisis and the parallel unveiling of harsh austerity programs, the absence of labor and workers in accounts of finance and development becomes glaringly obvious. Coming to empirical and analytical terms with the role of labor in banking has been one of the book's main challenges. This is because labor is not typically integrated into analyses of banking and development by neoclassical, institutionalist, or Marxian political economists. For this the analysis again turns to Hilferding's still original and penetrating insights into the relationship between interest income and labor expenditures, but it also draws inspiration from James O'Connor's (2009 [1973]) classic study on the fiscal crisis of the state.

This comparative project also holds great personal interest. In the past, I was fortunate to participate in academic exchanges in both countries. The first was at the Orta Doğu Teknik Üniversitesi (Middle East Technical University) in Ankara in 1998–99. The second was at the Instituto Tecnológico y de Estudios Superiories de Occidente (ITESO) in Guadalajara in the first half of 2001. While not directly interested in banking and development at those times, I developed a deep and enduring interest in each country's unique and shared experiences with neoliberal restructuring. I have since revisited both countries several times for both personal and academic reasons. Most notably in 2007, 2008, and 2010 I pursued field research into issues of banking. Some of this you will find written into the pages that follow, practically all of which has been influenced by my experiences in the two countries and my interactions with Turkish and Mexican academics and others that have collectively enhanced my understandings of each country's complex historical, economic, political, and social story.

A few words should be shared regarding the intended audience and disciplinary aims of this book. Because the topic relates to seemingly narrowly economic issues of banking, finance, crisis, and development many might think the content geared towards a highly technical and empirical analysis limited to the purview of economists. Yet I suspect those economists who place the burden of proof on positing and quantitatively testing hypotheses with large-scale datasets will find the book disappointing. To be sure, the analysis is grounded in empirical evidence. But such numbers are always assessed historically, qualitatively, and in relation to the political restructuring of state and society. That is, the evidence is used in such a way as to be accessible to all social sciences scholars. I imagine that political economy scholars like myself who are interested in a detailed historical-structural study of neoliberal changes over the last three decades and who engage in interdisciplinary comparative research – be they in economics, finance, politics, geography, sociology, history, or development studies (as I am) – will feel most at ease with the analysis. That said, I imagine that this community of critical social science scholars will be most intrigued by the book's simple core thesis that we can distinguish the current phase of accumulation in Mexico and Turkey as an era of 'emerging finance capitalism': the fusion of the interests of domestic and foreign financial capital in the state apparatus as the institutionalized priorities and overarching social logic guiding the actions of state managers and government elites, often to the detriment of labor.

The argument is developed over seven chapters. Chapter 2 expands on the themes introduced above, explores some core debates, and details the book's four premises of a Marxian analytical framework (namely, that states and banks are social relations and that labor and crisis are vital to emerging finance capitalism). Chapter 3 puts Mexico and Turkey's banking relations in historical and comparative perspective prior to the 1980s. The next four chapters look at Mexico and Turkey in detail from the 1980s debt crisis to the unfolding of the Great Recession today. Chapter 4 begins with a study of Mexico's 1982 bank nationalization process, which paradoxically enabled state elites to take a more direct and aggressive role in making the transition to neoliberalism. Bank privatization followed a decade later, but this deepening of neoliberalism led to an almost immediate banking crisis by 1995. Chapter 5 then turns to the experiences of Turkey and its post-1980s restructuring of state, bank, and labor relations. In this case, state elites used the long-held state banks to channel financing into socially volatile sectors as one strategy to ease neoliberal restructuring, which eventually led to the 2001 banking crisis. Unlike Mexico, Turkey's transition to neoliberalism was not met with the same structural shifts in bank ownership. The next two chapters focus on the turn towards more finance-led forms of neoliberalism and their culmination as emerging finance capitalism. Chapter 6 examines how Mexican state and government elites responded to the 1995 banking crisis by privileging the needs of financial capital. Over time this led to a third structural transformation in bank ownership to foreign control and to the intensification of financial profit imperatives such that Mexican-owned banks no longer need to see themselves in national developmental terms. At the same time, labor has become important to understanding the profitability and stability of the banks in Mexico especially as the forms of financial risk socialization change. The chapter ends with an interpretation of the impact of the current global financial crisis on Mexico. Chapter 7 returns to Turkey and begins with an analysis of the 2001 banking rescue. Far from minimizing the state, the Turkish government restructured the state financial apparatus and bolstered state capacity to manage the crisis, leading to subsequent financial deepening in the market and state. In ways similar to Mexico, the restructuring process internalized new competitive financial imperatives. Special attention is given to the ways in which state managers altered the operations of the Turkish state-owned banks so that these banks began to operate as if they were private, profit-seeking entities. As in Mexico, Turkish workers have played a defining role in the socialization of financial risks and intensification of profit imperatives underlying emerging finance capitalism. I should emphasize that I do not see emerging finance capitalism as something sharply distinguishable from neoliberalism or its finance-led form, but rather more as a historical culmination of processes, institutions, and social relations of power defining the current period.

The final chapter offers a comparative summing up of the experiences of Mexico and Turkey, and comments on the narrow range of alternatives now under consideration by the global financial community. Are these alternatives in fact any alternative at all? I suspect not. Yet in challenging this mainstream orthodoxy I take the opportunity to open a discussion on what does constitute an alternative to emerging finance capitalism. My contribution surely raises as many or more questions than it aims to answer, but this too is my motivation for writing.

NOTES

1. The term 'emerging capitalisms' is used in this book to capture the historical specificity and socially unequal nature of societies located in what some also critically refer to as the periphery, the semi-periphery, and/or the global south. In this way 'emerging capitalisms' is distinct from mainstream terminology, which avoids mentioning capitalism by speaking about emerging markets, the emerging or developing world, and/or middle-income countries.
2. International Monetary Fund (IMF), *World Economic Outlook, February 2011*, ESDS International, (Mimas) University of Manchester.
3. From different perspectives, Soederberg 2005; Stallings 2006; Rodríguez and Santiso 2007; Robertson 2007; Bakır and Öniş 2010; Prasad and Kose 2010.
4. Hughes, Jennifer '"Bric" creator adds newcomers to list', *Financial Times online*, 16 January 2011. The new growth markets also include South Korea and Indonesia.
5. The data provided are meant to be more illustrative than conclusive. Specifics are given as and when required in each chapter.
6. Available from: www.oecd.org/els/social/indicators/SAG.

2. States, banks, and crisis in emerging finance capitalism

This is a book dealing with states, banks, and crisis in emerging finance capitalisms. The bulk of the story is about Mexico and Turkey's transitions to neoliberalism since the 1980s, why neoliberalism took on a particularly finance-led form into the 1990s, and why it has now consolidated as *emerging finance capitalism*. This chapter elaborates on the core concepts used to interpret this history and evidence, on how the book fits within the finance and development literature, and on the book's critical analytical approach. I argue that a Marxian analytical approach concerned with the historical social relations of power and class between states, banks, and labor yields unique and powerful insights into the changing nature of banking, crisis, and development in emerging capitalisms. I argue this by first conceptualizing the period of neoliberalism and how it evolved into emerging finance capitalism. Next, I explore the influential varieties of capitalism and finance debates. I do this in order to situate the book's distinctive contribution, which I lay out in the final section. Here I introduce my underlying Marxian analytical premises – namely, that states and banks can be understood as social relations, that labor is vital to emerging finance capitalism, and that crises have proven to be constitutive of emerging finance capitalism. I follow this by a brief conclusion restating the central arguments of the book.

2.1 CONCEPTUALIZING NEOLIBERALISM AS EMERGING FINANCE CAPITALISM

It should come as no surprise that in countries like Mexico and Turkey states, banks, and labor have existed in definite social relations to one another since the mid-nineteenth century and throughout the early twentieth-century consolidation of capitalism (see Chapter 3 below). Domestic banks helped to fund national development projects premised on industrialization, a deepening monetary economy, and the expansion of wage labor wherein bank owners secured influential positions of power within the nascent state financial apparatus. In essence, states and banks have long since coexisted in relationships geared towards capital accumulation. This is not to say, however, that the specific form and content of these state–bank relationships have remained static. The transition to neoliberalism since the 1980s has brought dramatic changes to the ways in which the state financial apparatus interacts with capital and labor in Mexico and Turkey, and elsewhere. The culmination of neoliberal restructuring has led to a new form of state characterized by its responsiveness to financial imperatives.

As is well known, the Reaganites and Thatcherites of the world championed a political offensive against state-led development and the power of organized labor following the global turbulence of the 1970s. Ideologically, the neoliberal revolution was rooted in the market-oriented neoclassical economics and liberal ideologies of notables such as F.A. Hayek and Milton Friedman. The guiding ideal (which rarely translated into ideal real-world practice) was that whatever the social, political, economic, or ecological problem greater exposure to market competition could resolve it (see Balassa 1982). As Marxist geographer David Harvey contends, neoliberalism offered 'a theory of political economic practices that proposes that human well-being can best be advanced by liberating individual entrepreneurial freedoms and skills within an institutional framework characterized by strong private property rights, free markets and free trade' (2005, 2). Advocates sought to universally institutionalize and generalize neoliberal ideals through policies associated with what has been termed the 'Washington consensus' (Williamson 1990 and 1993) – a compendium of class-based policies advocating privatization, liberalization, deregulation, and so on, which restructured the state's relationship to capital and labor in ways favorable to market-oriented development and accumulation as well as to competitive individualism.

Critical political economists point to the disciplinary effects of neoliberal policies, which have increased inequality and lowered standards of living for the majority of people (Huber and Solt 2004). Marxian scholars Greg Albo, Sam Gindin, and Leo Panitch take it a step further (2010, 28):

> Neoliberalism is not . . . about the extent of deregulation as opposed to regulation, or holding on tenaciously to this or that public policy component. Neoliberalism should be understood as a particular form of class rule and state power that intensifies competitive imperatives for both firms and workers, increases dependence on the market in daily life and reinforces the dominant hierarchies of the world market, with the U.S. at its apex.

Indeed, the experiences of developing countries exemplify how the transition to neoliberalism is not limited to government policy interventions, but entails far-reaching social restructuring of state–society relations (for example, Marois 2005; Taylor 2006; Yalman 2009). In this interpretation, discussed in detail in Chapters 4 and 5, neoliberal transformation processes under way since the 1980s have involved a political assault on organized labor and class solidarity, the result of which has been the reconstitution of class power in favor of capital (Harvey 2005; Glyn 2006). This leads me to define neoliberalism as, at base, *the defeat of organized labor's capacity to resist market-oriented structural adjustment and the rise of capital's power*. This restructuring of postwar class compromises benefited those with access to large amounts of money rather than the general populace, which has lost out on corporate tax revenues and the erosion of public ownership and social provisioning, suffered higher unemployment and debt, and so on.

As a result of the quantitative expansion of capital and the associated qualitative deepening of competitive and financial imperatives throughout society neoliberalism has transformed and become more organized around monetary and financial relations. According to Albo et al., there is a link between neoliberalism and the 'absolute place that finance occupies in overall economic activity' such that today *finance-led* capitalism increasingly shapes the decisions of corporations, affects how people meet their needs, and plays a more determining role in government policy (2010, 28). The point being that under neoliberalism social reproduction has become progressively financialized in ways that reinforce its persistence (Fine 2010). This historical-structural development has given rise to a large and growing literature on the rise of finance, debating important analytical and empirical differences.[1] Yet many of these accounts, and particularly the Marxian ones, are based primarily on the experiences of advanced capitalisms, especially the US.[2] Few begin their analyses based on the specific experiences of peripheral developing countries such as Mexico and Turkey.

This account is also distinguished by framing its understanding of capitalism around the changing form of states in these societies, thus following a more political than economic Marxist interpretation. What are the historical–structural links between neoliberalism and the growing dominance of finance, and how are these institutionalized? The content points to how Mexican and Turkish state financial authorities – such as the bank regulators, bank insurance funds, treasuries, and central banks – have assumed a far greater presence in the management of banking, finance, and development since the 1980s in ways beneficial to financial capital. Following the work of Gerard Duménil and Dominique Lévy (2004 and 2011), I define 'financial capital' as the upper fraction of capitalist owners and the financial institutions under their control that have now attained a dominant position of power globally. Financial capital has reached this position of power because state authorities enabled financial imperatives to penetrate all aspects of state functions as a result of recurrent neoliberal financial crises. That is, the neoliberal project quickly evolved into 'finance-led neoliberalism' during the late 1980s and 1990s as state and government elites in emerging capitalisms developed institutional capacity to absorb and manage the accumulation of risks of foreign and domestic financial capital, and then to lay these financial risks on to society as a whole – especially at times of crisis (Marois 2011a). I understand the continued refinement, deepening, and institutionalization of finance-led neoliberal imperatives within the state apparatus (alongside organized labor's incapacity to halt and reverse this process) as constituting the current phase of emerging finance capitalism in Mexico and Turkey. Put otherwise, the quantitative build up of neoliberal and finance-led changes have led to a qualitative shift and consolidation in capital accumulation strategies. Emerging finance capitalism does not refer to a new form of capital, as per Hilferding, but to a new form of state–society relationship specific to peripheral capitalism. These are defined by *the fusion of the interests of domestic and foreign financial capital in the state apparatus as the institutionalized priorities and overarching social logic guiding the actions of state managers and government elites, often to the detriment of labor.*

This conceptualization of emerging finance capitalism is not the same as but indeed borrows from Rudolf Hilferding's (2006 [1910]) classic analysis of 'finance capital' at the turn of the last century. This 'finance capital', he argued, was the fusion of German banks and industry in such as way that the banks assumed the dominant position of power. Capital had reached its highest and most abstract expression as finance capital. Putting aside the specificity of Germany in the analysis, it is noteworthy that Hilferding did not understand his idea of finance capital as an independent economic category. Rather, finance capital acquired social and political power insofar as it collectively advocated for beneficial and protective policies at home while demanding that state authorities open avenues for the internationalization of capital (compare Carroll 1989). The details are extensive, however, his methodological point about the social forces constituting finance capital and how these social forces defined a specific phase of capital accumulation inform the analysis developed here. To be sure, elements of his particular understanding appear in Turkey and Mexico, especially as commercial and productive holding groups acquire more and larger banks. Yet these banking operations were often subordinate to the larger groups' productive activities (Mexico) or later even separated out from wider commercial activities in order to preserve domestic stability (Turkey). Because the forms of capitalism change historically, there are limits to grafting historically developed concepts onto emerging capitalisms today. Nevertheless, there is much to learn and appreciate in Hilferding's method and analysis that facilitates a compelling Marxian interpretation.

More will be said on Hilferding and the book's Marxian approach in the final section, but I'd like to note that I am not the first to draw on Hilferding's concept of finance capital as an analytical tool to understand the changing relationships between the state and banks in emerging capitalisms like Mexico and Turkey. For example, Russell White's (1992) classic book on Mexico uses Hilferding extensively to provide a class-based interpretation of the 1982 bank nationalization process. By contrast, Clement Henry (1996) uses the idea of finance capital to help explain processes of liberalization in Turkey and other Middle East countries. Quite distinct from Hilferding's Marxian analysis, Henry is concerned with how the greater autonomy of banks from political interference can spur processes of liberal democratization, of which he sees Turkey as a model reformer (Henry 1996, 19). The shared relevance of using Hilferding, then as now, links to the central importance of banks to development in countries like Mexico and Turkey (as in Germany) and the banks' *political* significance. How have more recent debates understood questions of finance and development?

2.2 LOCATING VARIETIES OF FINANCE IN CAPITALISM

Those familiar with the comparative political economy of development literature can see that the story told so far does not coincide well with predominant interpretations, particularly those of the varieties of capitalism (VoC) literature. Many may feel uncomfortable with the general structures, social relationships of power, and class dynamics attributed to 'finance capitalism'. However, these Marxian tools help overcome some of the limitations found in the influential VoC approaches shaped by the work of Peter Hall and David Soskice (2001 and 2009). Without explicitly arguing for the superiority of one model over the other, Hall and Soskice established two different ideal-typical capitalist models based on a range of institutions, labor relations, and productive firms: namely, liberal market economies (LMEs) and coordinated market economies (CMEs). While the original models are based on advanced capitalisms, Hall and Soskice believe their VoC models can be extended to include developing or emerging capitalisms. For our purposes, the VoC distinctions between competing financial systems are most important – distinctions that mirror a second narrower debate in the development literature over market versus bank-based financial systems. These two approaches are discussed in tandem.

On the one hand, Hall and Soskice discuss LMEs in reference to advanced capitalisms such as the US and UK. As an ideal-typical construct, LMEs are defined by the predominance of competitive market-based financial institutions and an aggressive Anglo-American capitalism. Market-based finance differs from bank-based finance because these markets mobilize loanable money capital from an existing pool of savings wherein stock markets play a vital role. The types of financial institutions can include bank-like institutions, for example, smaller micro-credit, community savings, and local development banks, but more significantly also include larger financial institutions such as pension funds, mutual funds, investment banks, and insurance companies. Particularly in the advanced capitalisms, market-based financial institutions have become extraordinarily important since the 1990s and have constituted a revolution in mass investment as people's passive savings, once held in banks, have become converted into active investments managed by institutional investors (Harmes 2001, 4).

Being in a sense more 'market-disciplined', the VoC literature understands LME financial systems as providing more 'impatient' financing insofar as financial investors constantly demand short-term returns on their investments. The types of productive firms found in LMEs and funded by market-based finance can compete internationally because of their fluidity in adjusting to changing market conditions. According to Hall and Soskice, the adaptability and competitive drive found in LMEs encourage development, which is enabled by the state's more liberal institutional environment. Other scholars who advocate explicitly on behalf of market-based models of finance argue that this institutionalized flexibility, transparency, and market discipline allow viable LME firms recurrent access to financing while effectively weeding out weaker, less efficient firms through competitive pressures (Crane and Schaede 2005). In contrast to the more pluralist stance of Hall and Soskice (either LMEs or CMEs can be competitive), neoliberal advocates often favor generalized convergence towards market discipline, believing open markets offer the best hope of raising standards of living and driving national development (Walton 2004; Marini 2005; Bortolotti and Perotti 2007; Mishkin 2009).

On the other hand, Hall and Soskice point to the developmental successes of CMEs in advanced capitalisms such as Germany and Japan. This second VoC is characterized by more collaborative market relationships and bank-based financial institutions. I talk more about bank-based systems below, but what is particular to this CME model is that banks are seen as offering more 'patient' long-term capital to productive firms who are therefore less subject to short-term market discipline. This enables bank-based systems to internalize control and supervision within the firm and bank, which raises the capacity of CME firms to pursue long-term strategies as their particular means of competing internationally. According to Hall and Soskice, the state apparatus plays a more active role in shaping and managing finance and development. On this basis, many Keynesian-inspired and institutional political economists have challenged the idealized role of individual self-interest as an effective financial regulator within LMEs as the only possible or even desirable path to national development (see Ocampo et al. 2008; Stiglitz 2010). Much more policy space should be given for extra-market coordination and the crafting of divergent models of development (Morgan 2007; Stein 2010). Skeptical of the need for global regulatory convergence, critics argue that neoliberal policy reforms have been disappointing as a whole and that governments should opt for a more cautious trajectory. Most recently, it is fair to say that the impact of the Great Recession and the poverty of mainstream economics to predict or understand the current crisis has led many economists openly to question the universalism of self-interested market discipline as the only developmental policy prescription and advocate on behalf of a new post-Washington consensus (see Rogers 2010).

One of the distinguishing features of the VoC literature is the richness of its internal debates. One of the most heated issues involves the explanatory potential of the dualistic LME versus CME ideal-typical model (Hancké et al. 2009). How does one locate individual cases that do not really fit the two models neatly? The US and UK conform to (even define) an LME model and Germany and Japan correspond to a CME model, but the literature acknowledges that other OECD European countries, such as France, Italy, and Spain, are more ambiguous. Some OECD countries outside Europe also pose challenges. Students of Mexico and Turkey would be forgiven some confusion when Hall and Soskice include Turkey in a possible third Mediterranean model alongside France while excluding Mexico altogether because it is still a developing country (2009, 37). Bruno Amable (2003) has responded by developing a grouping of five models that includes market-based, social democratic, Asian, Mediterranean, and continental European models. Soskice too has broken with the original dualism and recently contributed to another new 'hierarchical' VoC model that is particular to Latin America (Schneider and Soskice 2009). However, this too leads to certain analytical problems.

While sympathetic to the VoC approach and welcoming the greater specificity of such new models, Colin Crouch cautions that there is likely more mixing of models in reality than is allowed for in the dualist VoC approach or even by adding more ideal-type models: 'individual empirical cases might well comprise more complex amalgams still of elements from two or more theoretical types' (2009, 90). This raises an important question: at what point do VoC analysts stop modeling real world variety? As other sympathetic critics recognize, the inevitable growth in models has serious repercussions:

> the analytical power and parsimony are sacrificed in favor of a greater capacity for detailed description; and that in an effort to account for the entirety of national political economies, the quantity of variables proliferates but the number of core insights is reduced. (Hancké et al. 2009, 284)

That is, once the parsimony of the VoC dualism is jettisoned it seems more models must beget more models. The hierarchical Latin American model must surely give way to a differentiated Central American model that accounts for such unique cases as Costa Rica (compare Marois 2005). Nothing, as yet, has been said on an African, Middle Eastern, Gulf Region, South East Asian, or Oceanic model and potential varieties thereof. As the empirics build so too must the collection of models. The result of this Xeno-like paradox is that no matter the number of models, the analytical arrow can never quite hit the mark. The varieties seen *in* capitalism, the central object of inquiry, become seemingly unstructured and beyond being understood generally *as* capitalist. The VoC approach erodes into a classic case of missing the forest for the trees (Cammack 1992). There is a second problem that arises in the VoC literature that has immediate relevance. Namely, relatively little analytical import is given to the mounting influence of money and financial capital. Hall and Soskice acknowledge that they are unsure how to interpret the internationalization of finance since the 1980s, fearing that these unprecedented changes might unravel the foundations of their CME model (2009, 66–7). Couched in terms of persistent national autonomy, they nevertheless maintain that global changes towards an LME model will not come to pass if a CME model can protect domestic rates of return. Here too this position is rather too vague, too optimistic, and too dismissive of the structural power of financial capital.

In terms of the changing relationships between finance, the state, and capitalist development in countries like Mexico and Turkey, the VoC approach has great difficulty analytically appreciating that while important and specific institutional and capital accumulation differences prevail, these differences are increasingly subject to wider patterns of determination shaped by financial imperatives. Part of the trouble stems from using ideal-typical models, whether market-based and bank-based or finance-based. As idealizations these hold little real-world application and, if taken too far, produce a false dichotomy. In most advanced and emerging capitalisms banks and stock markets both provide financial liquidity for development, even if one predominates (Kregel 2000; Aybar and Lapavitsas 2001). Moreover, if the actually existing financial institutional make-up differs from the idealization, it is posed as a distortion. How, then, can they interpret Mexico and Turkey's financial sectors, which are basically bank-based insofar as the banks control most assets but also market-oriented and subject to intense competitive discipline? The influx of global banking giants in the late 1990s and early 2000s has upheld the dominance of banks in their societies while foreign bank corporate governance strategies alongside new national competitive strategies have entailed a generalized convergence towards intensified market discipline. Marxian analyses overcome these difficulties by recognizing that each state has a particular form while at the same time being subject to wider social forces and patterns of determination specific to the current phase of capital accumulation (Harvey 2010, 55–6). The mainstream treatment of bank ownership also has difficulty contending with the qualitative changes to banks that are the outcome of the rise of neoliberalism.

2.2.1 Qualifying Neoliberal Bank Ownership and Control

Historically, banks have been among the most important financial institutions in capitalist development. Accordingly, neoclassical, liberal, institutionalist, and Marxian analytical traditions have each grappled with issues of banking vis-à-vis different developmental strategies and historical phases of capitalism.[3] Today, and often alongside and together with the rise in market-based financial institutions, banks remain the dominant financial institution in emerging capitalisms. Given the centrality of private ownership to neoliberal strategies of development, moreover, who owns and controls the banks is a fundamental issue (Rodríguez and Santiso 2007). Yet, as one neoclassical study acknowledges, there has been relatively little research on bank ownership in emerging capitalisms (Boubakri et al. 2008). And the comparative work being done is dominated by liberal and neoclassical-inspired interpretations – interpretations that have great difficulty in qualifying how bank ownership and control have been changed by the transition to finance-led neoliberal strategies of development.[4] This has left a significant gap in our understanding of comparative bank ownership and development. Can we in fact understand Turkish state-owned banks as exactly the same institutions today as they were seven decades ago merely because they remain state-owned? I think not. History also reveals that banks under the control of governments in Mexico and Turkey have been at times the most aggressively neoliberal.

How do mainstream analysts explore bank ownership and what analytical barriers exist to this?

Recently, neoclassical and liberal political economists have renewed their interest in the comparative impact of bank ownership on national development (Barth et al. 2006; Megginson 2005a; Caprio et al. 2004 and 2005). To study bank ownership researchers feed data on dozens of countries and perhaps thousands of banks into large-scale regression models designed to identify patterned and predictable behavior. Rafael La Porta et al.'s (2002) benchmark study of bank ownership in 92 developing countries offers two interlinked conclusions. First, state-owned banks remain pervasive around the world. Second, where states own banks, these countries suffer from weak property rights, low per capita income growth, lower productivity growth, poorly developed financial systems, and interventionist and inefficient governments leading to slower financial and economic development (2002, 290). Subsequently, researchers have followed up by focusing in on two additional core liberal themes: corruption and inefficiency. State ownership enables government officials to use banks to their own ends, and state-owned banks in developing countries are less profitable, more costly to operate, and less efficient than their private domestic and foreign counterparts (Boubakri et al. 2005; Micco et al. 2007). As a rule, the 'politicization' of economic processes results in weaker economic performance and barriers to development (Beck et al. 2006; Boubakri et al. 2008). Having empirically established that there are correlations between state ownership and these economic outcomes, the preferred policy solution is the complete private ownership of banks, for even minority state ownership distorts the benefits of private control. This research follows closely from Hayek (1967 [1944]), wherein private ownership is treated as the *sin qua non* of innovation and efficiency (Shleifer 1998), and from the ideas developed by Edward S. Shaw (1973) and Ronald I. McKinnon (1973) who argue that state interference in finance leads to market atrophy. In this approach, any historical changes in capitalist accumulation strategies and the state are analytically firewalled. Institutional critiques of neoclassical methodology point out, moreover, that the inclusion of widely divergent cases and developmental levels in their cross-country data samples makes it nearly impossible to see any clear relationship between bank ownership and any particular level of economic development or social welfare (Stallings 2006, 11).

It is also important to signal for our purposes that the influence of neoclassical empiricism has manifested in a relatively common commitment to a quantity theory of bank ownership within mainstream circles. This appears usually as a 'fifty per cent plus' rule, which defines a bank's majority ownership and, by extension, characterizes the bank's operations (see, for example, Andrews 2005; Caprio et al. 2005; Megginson 2005b). As we will see, such a methodological approach fails to appreciate that while private bank ownership is a *sufficient* condition for a bank to be profit- and market-oriented in emerging capitalisms today, private ownership can no longer be convincingly said to be a *necessary* condition. State-owned and nationalized banks have been and are equally profit- and market-oriented. Neither, then, can it be said that domestic bank ownership constitutes any necessary or direct relation to national development. Neoliberal restructuring changed matters such that state financial regulation and competitive imperatives now compel all banks, regardless of ownership, to operate as if they were profit-seeking banks without institutionalized regard for national development. Only a political break in the social relations and institutionalizations of class power defining state, bank, and labor relationships can lead to substantive alternatives (Chapter 8).

There is a second neoclassical-inspired approach dealing with bank ownership and development, namely new institutional economics (NIE). NIE has attempted to compensate for certain neoclassical methodological limitations by drawing on aspects of institutionalism. Therein, the work of Douglass North has been especially important to NIE: 'That institutions affect the performance of economies is hardly controversial. That the differential performance of economies over time is fundamentally influenced by the way institutions evolve is also not controversial' (1990, 3). Maintaining a hardcore faith in private ownership and capitalist markets, North argues that the most important state institutions should enhance the state's capacity to enforce private property rights because this encourages development (North 1981, 21). As NIE scholar Stephen Haber (2005a) argues in the case of Mexico, to help avoid crisis and to ensure banking stability better institutions are required, but ones that specifically create incentives that enhance respect for the rule of law and private property rights in the banking sector. Viewed in its own terms, NIE appears compelling. Increasing state capacity to minimize the social and political risks capitalists face is sure to further investment and profit for capitalists, arguably leading to development (when understood as the extension of the market). Yet according to Adam Przeworski (2004), the NIE 'institutional' form of causality is also too narrow and offers no alternative trajectories once set, leaving ontologically unanswerable the possibility of endogenous change.

In relative contrast to neoclassical-inspired interpretations, the institutionalist and Keynesian-inspired literature on banking and ownership offers more historically detailed and case study-oriented research critical of universal market-oriented solutions to banking and development (Stallings 2006; Carvalho 2009–10). These accounts draw on postwar developmental themes that argue that because capitalist markets are relatively unstable and inefficient, they require the active role of the state (Gerschenkeron 1962; Shonfield 1969 [1965]).[5] In practice, state regulation, control, and sometimes ownership in the banking sector allowed postwar Mexican and Turkish governments to do what the private sector refused to do, thereby facilitating national capitalist development. With the transition to finance-led neoliberalism, the terms of reference have shifted. Many reflect Keynesian themes as developed along the lines of Minsky's financial instability thesis, or the idea that 'from time to time, capitalist economies exhibit inflations and debt deflations which seem to have the potential to spin out of control' (1992, 1; also see 1994). Because capitalist development remains unstable, the state needs to absorb certain risks to stabilize growth. Strong domestic institutions can overcome most problems associated with either public or private ownership, market or government failure (Stallings 2006; also see Weizsäcker et al. 2005). The role of extra-market and institutional coordination in banking and finance is advocated over free market determinacy (McKeen-Edwards et al. 2004). Contrary to orthodox 'shock-therapy' approaches, bank privatization and financial liberalization are less problematic where state authorities adopt an appropriate pace and sequencing of market and competition-enhancing institutions (Neiman Auerbach 2001; Öniş 2003; Garrido 2005). Looking at the experiences of neoliberal transformation, the wrong policies for states to pursue vis-à-vis the banking sector are unfettered neoliberal policies (Vidal et al. 2011). In line with the VoC literature, developing-country banking sectors can be internationally competitive, and in a variety of ways. The greatest challenge today, however, is not state or private ownership. Rather, the problem is how state authorities can maintain national developmental policy *autonomy* given mounting foreign bank control and the power these banks can wield over developing economies (Correa 2004; Bakir and Öniş 2010; Marshall 2010). Here, too, there is an often explicit commitment to a quantity theory of bank ownership (see Martinez-Diaz 2009, 7).

Where does this leave us in terms of qualifying bank ownership under neoliberalism and in emerging capitalisms? Neoclassical regression studies can only point out that there is some correlation, but they have no historical argument as to why there is any relationship between this type of bank ownership and that level or form of capitalist development. Indeed, their evidence may even hide more than it reveals as data samples often fail to distinguish the performance and operational strategies of rescued *cum* nationalized private banks from the performance of long-held state-owned banks (you see this in, for example, Andrews 2005 and Caprio et al. 2004). The NIE approaches are more historically nuanced, but only insofar as they elevate the legal and private property rights of private bankers above all other social, political, economic, environmental, and collective rights, and then see how these deviate historically in given countries. Merely drawing domestic property rights institutions into the NIE analysis, however, cannot overcome the failure of its deeply rooted neoclassical exchange-based methodological individualism, which fails to explain persistent power inequalities and developmental discrepancies (Ankarloo and Palermo 2004; Albo 2005). Finally, the more critical Keynesian and institutionalist-inspired approaches are committed to lessening the inequality of neoliberal development (Wade 2003 and 2004). But in doing so they nonetheless share with neoclassical economics and liberal political economists a normative orientation towards establishing the conditions necessary for capitalist accumulation and development (Allegret et al. 2003). A notable critic of neoliberal convergence theories, economist Dani Rodrik, grants as much when he notes that the end goals of competitiveness, enhanced property rights, market integration, efficiency, and so on are not in question, but only whether 'these ends can be achieved in a large number of different ways' (2008, 1). Rodrik thus affirms what more radical critics of the VoC and mainstream literature claim, namely that advocates of national 'divergence' have already embraced the competitiveness criteria of neoclassical 'convergence' accounts to the extent that state intervention, collective bargaining, and inter-firm collaboration need not distort market efficiencies (Panitch and Gindin 2003/04, 9; compare Coates 2005). Mainstream neoclassical and institutional approaches to bank ownership differ in the *forms* of competitive capacity in capitalist banking but share an impoverished reading of the structural changes in the social relations of states and banks in Mexico and Turkey that are defined more by newly institutionalized financial and competitive imperatives than by timeless understandings of ownership. This suggests that there is room in the literature for a more historical-structural Marxian interpretation.

2.3　FOUR PREMISES OF A MARXIAN ANALYSIS OF EMERGING FINANCE CAPITALISM

This book's political Marxist analytical approach fundamentally differs from the mainstream in its epistemological commitment to investigating and exposing the underlying exploitative and unequal social, economic, and political forces constituting different phases of capitalism, and in its normative orientation towards ending this inequality (Devine 1988; Poulantzas 2000 [1978]). Issues of power, class, state, and struggle are internalized within an analysis of capitalism, which is understood as a social system constituted as both an abstract-formal object and as diverse historical forms in time and space (Albo forthcoming 2012). What seems to be an apparent contradiction in fact enables Marxian scholars to look at capitalist society as a whole without sacrificing historical specificity. According to Bertell Ollman, one of Marxism's hardcore ideas is that each part of society ontologically incorporates 'in what it is all its relations with other parts up to and including everything that comes into the whole' (1993, 35). Little interpretative currency is given to mainstream categories that formally separate, for example, micro- versus macroeconomics or states versus markets. Instead, states, markets, capital, and money are conceptualized as social relations and as such are treated as parts of a social *totality* – a 'logical construct that refers to the way the whole is present through internal relations in each of its parts' (1993, 37). Ollman continues to say that the 'very idea of attributing an ontological priority to either individuals, class, or the species assumes an absolute separation between them that is belied by Marx's conception of man (*sic*) as a social relation with qualities that fall on different levels of generality' (1993, 59). It follows that historical and structural change is a product of interrelated individual, collective, and class agencies mediated by a pre-existing contextual rationality – a context, however, that is not of any one person's own choosing (Marx 1959, 320). In this, individual and collective agents are endowed with consciousness and tend to act deliberately towards goals. But their actions may well entail unintended consequences and are subject to the structured contingency of capitalist social relations (Engels 1959 [1888], 230). As such, a major contribution of Marxian comparative analysis is its capacity to contextualize human rationality and institutions *within* a structural logic and sets of institutionalized power relations historically specific to capitalism and specific to distinct national social formations. Neither individuals, nor classes, nor institutions, nor markets are taken as autonomous or determinant factors in themselves so as to capture the complex dynamics of history, institutionalized relations of power, and change (Lipietz 1997; Greenfield 2004). Accordingly, Colin Leys writes the following on the nature of Marxian research on development (1996, 55):

> A genuinely historical theory will allow us to analyze the process of combined and uneven development of capitalism on a world scale, as it has been experienced . . . in particular countries, and hence as it presents itself to any one of them now, in the form of class struggle conducted in the framework of a particular inherited structure of productive relations, forms of exploitation and exchange relations, and a particular structure of relations of political and ideological domination, internal and external, etc.

A Marxian-inspired comparative approach is well positioned to capture the diversity of Mexico and Turkey's experiences in a unified understanding. The methodology draws from Philip McMichael's (1990) incorporated comparison research strategy that integrates multiple and singular comparative forms. The multiple form recognizes that Mexico and Turkey exist within a continuously evolving historically singular process as time- and space-differentiated instances. The singular form allows one to investigate a cross-section or variation in or across space within this historical process. The two comparative forms can be combined as mutually conditioning, with the multiple form seen as a generalizing thrust and the singular as a particularizing one. According to McMichael, the incorporated comparison approach integrates theory and history such that both abstract individuality and abstract generality are avoided so as to 'try to perceive the unity in diversity without reifying either' (1990, 395). To this end, I interpret the experiences of Mexico and Turkey based around four underlying Marxian analytical premises dealing with states, banks, labor, and crisis. These premises by no means exhaust the range of Marxian theory, but they do go some way to enabling a distinct and historically sensitive interpretation of emerging finance capitalism in Mexico and Turkey. Substantiating historical and empirical content follows in subsequent chapters.

2.3.1 Premise One: States are Social Relations

The history of peripheral capitalist development and the transition to neoliberalism in Mexico and Turkey illustrates how and why state managers and the state apparatus have always been involved in the constitution, enabling, and restructuring not only of markets but also the banking sector specifically. Of course, bank-like institutions pre-dated many modern states and banks (Itoh and Lapavitsas 1999). Yet in modern Mexico and Turkey, state authorities were the primary agents who organized and enabled their modern banking systems in collaboration with capitalist elites within their borders. In this sense, states always have been involved in banking and banking always involved in state formation, and indeed this remains so. Quite contrary to the idealizations of liberal political economy, the state is perhaps the most vital institution to capitalism, with even neoliberal strategies of development powerless to eliminate the state's functions (Wood 2003, 139–40; Jessop 2010). In fact, emerging finance capitalism has entailed the constant widening of administrative, regulatory, and materially supportive units within the state. Yet states are not uncomplicated 'actors' that simply 'act' at the behest of capital, let alone bankers.

Nicos Poulantzas (1974; 2000 [1978]) reminds us that capitalist states are social formations, and as such they comprise historically specific institutionalizations of class struggle and power that are malleable but also momentarily fixed and formative. In this sense, states are institutionally organized political arenas that appear relatively separate from markets as the form of state–society relations specific to capitalism (Poulantzas 2000 [1978], 17–19).[6] According to Poulantzas, this relative separation is 'two expressions of a single pattern of relations between State and economy under capitalism . . . [and] are rooted in the hard core of capitalist relations of production' (2000 [1978], 19). This means that the state apparatus has an intertwined economic role within the totality of capitalism and in class struggle alongside an enduring socio-political role in the reproduction of capitalist society and the world market. As such, states are not reduced to individual governments, which are typically more transitory, collective, party-based organizations composed of executive agents of change within the state apparatus. Neither are states seen as formally autonomous from market forces, and thus outside patterns of determinacy specific to capitalism. To say this is not to suggest economic determinism in state policy but rather to claim the ontological interrelation of politics and economics. In Mexico and Turkey, some of the individual and collective agents struggling to shape the institutions of state and its relationship to banks have involved state managers and political parties alongside (and sometimes comprised of) the ruling classes and domestic and foreign capital but this is never to the complete exclusion of organized labor and popular classes. The presence or relative exclusion of different social forces in the state varies in different places and according to different phases of capitalism. The result of such social struggles can be conceived of as institutionalizations of power relations, and these institutionalizations form the social logic of the state apparatus and its regulatory and distributive framework. Under emerging finance capitalism the interests of financial capital have become the dominant institutionalized interests within the state.

The changing form of the capitalist state has also had much to do with the intensified integration of state and society into the world market over the last three decades. The reproduction of capitalism involves a potentially unlimited market, or *world market*. For Marx, '[t]he tendency to create the *world market* is directly given in the concept of capital itself. Every limit appears as a barrier to be overcome' (1973, 408; emphasis in original). As capital overcomes expansionary barriers, often facilitated by new state regulations and openings, this intensifies the pressure capital can exert on other capitalists, labor, and states, thus altering pre-existing balances of economic and political forces (Jessop 2010, 40). In this framework, the world market is conceived of as a real abstraction, meaning that the world market has taken shape in the historical context of capitalism, is in essence composed of universal and abstract flows of money, credit, and capital, and maintains a material reality in itself (see Himmelweit and Mohun 1981). In this, the world market exerts very real pressures on actually existing people, firms, states, and societies: 'The form of value (money, capital) and the law of value (the market) impose a particular logic upon people and make a particular form of rationality plausible to them – a pressure that takes effect behind the backs of the subjects' (Nachtwey and ten Brink 2008, 45). This extended sphere of market exchange and capital circulation is, nonetheless, state-organized while being international in scope, thereby forming an all-encompassing international context of capitalist competition (von Braunmühl 1978, 167). Thus, while the institutional forms of states vary in time and place relative to local specificities, power relations, and patterns of accumulation, all states remain party and subject to world market competitive and capital accumulation imperatives (involving, as we will see, both the internationalization of capital and the state apparatus). It follows that individual and collective agents are to be understood in their own context of class divided societies and contending domestic social forces, but at one and the same time as they exist within a wider constellation of interstate and the capitalist world market relations (Alavi 1982; Poulantzas 1974).

As constituents of the world market and interstate relations, states are also spatially defined. Yet like states, 'space' in Marxian terms is also socially constructed and produced by the social practices and practical interrelations between subjects and their surroundings (Lefebvre 1991). In other words, space is not intrinsic or inherent because people produce space in historical conditions. State borders are politically constituted and contingently delineate one's internal space in hierarchical relation to the interstate system and the world market (Peck and Tickell 2002). This also pertains to the regional and urban inequalities produced by capitalism within state boundaries (Myrdal 1963 [1957]). Under capitalism, the institutions of state help to organize these inside and outside social spaces as spheres of accumulation. To facilitate such organization, powerful agents within states discursively frame the legitimate roles of the state apparatus (Hay 2002; Poulantzas 2000 [1978]). Discourse is critical to gathering domestic social support and legitimacy for change, as well as to influencing the way people will act within and interpret their social contexts. For example, it has been through the discourse of financial crisis that Mexican and Turkish state managers, government elites, and business leaders have framed these moments as conjunctural, requiring a break with the past, and in need of popular austerity measures. This conceptualization allows one to preserve the uniqueness of each state's history while understanding

that the structural processes and characteristics of capitalist development are always mediated by differing, territorially-bound state–society
formations (Albo 2003, 90).

2.3.2   Premise Two: Banks, too, are Social Relations

In contrast to mainstream methodologies, the ways in which firms such
as banks act is not historically fixed but rather is socially and historically
constructed and therefore must be understood within a given set of social
and material relationships (compare McDonald and Ruiters 2006, 15). In
other words, banks are institutionalized social relations that reflect historically specific relations of power and reproduction between the banks,
other firms, the state, and labor in general, and within the banks between
those who own and control money capital and labor. Conceived as such,
this allows for the qualitative integration of agency and power struggles
into an analysis of how change occurs at the level of banking institutions.
At the same time, banks as institutions must be located within the wider
social relations of capitalism and money (Hilferding 2006 [1910]).

As a historically specific mode of production and social reproduction,
capitalism has evolved into the most developed form of market economy.
The reproduction of capitalist social relations is structured by competitive
imperatives: capitalists are incessantly compelled to compete and accumulate money capital or cease to exist as capitalists (Guttmann 1994, 19).
Money is fundamental to this competitive reproduction insofar as money
takes on a powerful role as a unifying force that integrates disparate
competitive activities (Itoh and Lapavitsas 1999, 57–8). For the present
purposes, two forms of money are important. First, money exists 'as
money', as a medium of exchange, as a measure of value, as a means of
payment, and as means of saving (Lapavitsas 2003). Second, money exists
'as capital', which in this form means money is mobilized in the production of surplus-value to generate more money. Banks and financial capital
specialize in money dealing and interest-bearing capital, that is, making
money from money, whose functions have evolved into modern day credit
systems.

What are some of the core functions of capitalist credit systems (see
Harvey 1999 [1982], 262–72)? At base, the credit system mobilizes all
money savings as capital. By pooling everyone's money and lending it out
for interest, this credit function permits capitalists to overcome investment
barriers. No longer do their own limited money resources bind individual
capitalists. This function is vital to the creation of large fixed capital
projects such as buildings, factories, production centers, and so on. But it
has led to the creation and circulation of greater and greater amounts of

fictitious capital: that is, a capitalized claim to or share of future revenue (Hilferding 2006 [1910], 128). In other words, fictitious capital is a flow of money capital not backed by any commodity transaction, but which is created whenever credit is advanced against future labor (Harvey 1999, 265–6). This means fictitious capital is not pure speculation (except in the most fraudulent cases): instead it is integral to the productive and exploitative processes of capital accumulation. Hilferding also pointed out that the shares held in joint-stock companies are a form of fictitious capital because shares do not represent existing productive capital but a share of future revenue (2006 [1910], 111). Likewise, state bonds are a form of fictitious capital because the bonds do not represent actual existing resources but claims to the state's future annual tax yield convertible into money. In the fulfillment of this core credit function, Harvey also shows that the credit system reduces barriers to the flow of capital between different spheres of production and circulation, thereby facilitating the expansion of capitalist markets and social relations of production. Competition, moreover, drives capital from spheres of production and circulation with lower profit rates to spheres with higher profit rates, and these capital movements are made possible by the credit system. As a whole, the development of the credit system increases the flexibility and power of those agents who own and control money. Moreover, as Harvey emphasizes, the credit system has become a 'major lever for the extraction of wealth by finance capital from the rest of the population' (Harvey 2010, 245). That is, the basis of the credit system is to accumulate money not necessarily to fulfill any ideal-typical function. The banker does not wake each day thinking what ideal role s/he plays or fails to play, but about how better to increase her or his wealth.

As the most developed market society, the owning and controlling of money represents not only wealth but also the power to act and to discipline within capitalist society. Financial capital has taken on an increasingly hegemonic position. This suggests that conflicts can and do erupt between different fractions of capital, given the ever-greater power of financial capital, as well as between financial capital and all manner of popular classes and state authorities in different historical conjunctures, as later chapters will illustrate. However, the interests of financial capital increasingly represent the common interests of all capitals. Since the late 1980s financial capital has taken the lead in disciplining states so that they fall into line with neoliberal restructuring, the central target of which has been organized labor within their societies. A key aspect of financial capital's power has been the granting, pricing, and/or withholding of credit. Governments have responded by bolstering the power of central banks, which have in turn developed ways to guarantee the creditworthiness of individual banks within their borders and, by extension, the credit-worthiness of the country. Because central banks exist within a hierarchi-cal interstate system and world market, the power of any central bank is constrained both by its state's relative position (for example, the Central Bank of Turkey sits much lower than the US Federal Reserve) and by the nature and actions of the financial intermediaries within its borders (for example, Citibank in Mexico exerts greater power than the much smaller regional Banco Amigo). As such, individual banks find themselves embedded within a series of relationships ranging from the customers they offer credits to, to other stronger and weaker banks, to central banks, to powerful external institutions like the IMF and US Treasury. These are all intertwined and related to capitalist social relations of production and accumulation in the world market, which are increasingly subject to and facilitated by financial capital flows.

By this point it should be clear that from a Marxian perspective capi-talist finance is not neutral or classless. At its very foundation the credit system is based on socializing many people's money for use by a few in order to overcome the barriers that individual private property poses for capitalist production (Hilferding 2006 [1910], 180). Because banks and financial institutions have evolved historically, and their practices are institutionalized in the state apparatus, individual capitalists today are not bound by their own savings but can draw on the money savings of everyone to invest and to earn profit. In this way the banking and credit system integrates individual workers, peasants, landlords, capi-talists, governments, and so forth together as generic 'savers' who save money in return for interest payments (Harvey 1999, 263). However, workers' savings or even shareholdings have not given workers new rights, made workers associates of capitalists, or allowed labor organiza-tions to control most firms (de Brunhoff 2003, 149; also see Soederberg 2010b). The class divide between the role of labor and the role of capital remains intact. According to Harvey, class 'is a role, not a label that attaches to persons. We play multiple roles all the time . . . The role of the capitalist is to use money to command the labor or the assets of others and to use that command to make profit, to accumulate capital and thereby augment personal command over wealth and power' (2010, 232). By and large, workers remain confined to using money as money, that is, to consuming what they earn in order to survive (food, clothing, shelter). Increasingly, neoliberal austerity has compelled workers to turn to financing these basics through consumer credit. At the same time, financial capital has managed to restructure the state so that a more burdensome role is placed on labor in sustaining profit-oriented financial accumulation processes.

2.3.3   Premise Three: Labor is Vital to Emerging Finance Capitalism

Labor matters to banking and finance, and indeed to emerging finance capitalism. As Tom Bottomore emphasizes in his introduction to Hilferding's
Finance Capital, the escalating power of finance is 'fundamentally detri-
mental to the working class – increasing the power of employers' organization, raising the cost of living, imposing a heavy burden of taxation,
weakening democracy . . .' and so on (2006 [1910], 9). For present purposes, I can highlight three ways in which labor is constitutive of emerging
finance capitalism. First, labor creates value in production from which
financial capital can earn interest. Second, labor in general provides the
base income tax revenue upon which the state apparatus can socialize
financial risks at times of crisis. Third, labor is also important because
bank workers constitute the operational foundations of banks. This suggests that banks and labor are socially and economically linked at the level
of capitalism in general, at the level of the state, and at the level of the
banking institutions.

At the most general level, how can we link labor to an understanding
of emerging finance capitalism? As is well known, Marxian labor theory
of value analyses begin with an understanding of capital not as a thing
or institution alone, but as an exploitative and unequal social relation
that exists between capital and labor and that is historically specific to
capitalism (Fine and Saad-Filho 2004). Marx (1970, 1005) writes:

> Capital is not a thing, any more than money is a thing. In capital, as in money,
> certain specific social relations of production between people appear as rela-
> tions of things to people, or else certain social relations appear as the natural
> properties of things in society. Without a class dependent on wages, the
> moment individuals confront each other as free persons, there can be no pro-
> duction of surplus-value; without the production of surplus-value there can be
> no capitalist production, and hence no capital and no capitalist!

In this framework, *surplus-value* is the monetary form of the social
surplus product expropriated by capitalists – that is, the difference between
the value produced by a worker and the value of his or her own labor
power. The value created by labor is realized if and when the commodities
produced are sold in *markets*. Contrary to neoclassical accounts, capitalist markets are not neutral mechanisms of voluntary exchange because
markets reflect the underlying and unequal power relations of capitalism
to the benefit of capital. Under capitalist social relations so-called 'free'
workers are compelled en masse to sell their labor power for money wages
to survive (their role as worker is structured by their need to earn a wage).
There are three implications of a Marxian account worth pointing out here

that distinguish it from liberal understandings based on ahistorical human nature, voluntary exchange, and methodological individualist theses. First, capitalist social relations have arisen historically as a result of processes of primitive accumulation that gave rise to a class of capitalists and a class of workers (Brenner 2007).[7] Second, the rise of capitalism is therefore a result of the reorganization of social relations and the way in which these are crystallized in state–society formations (Poulantzas 1974; 2000). Third, capital accumulation does not result from the abstinence or thrift of individual capitalists but from and through class exploitation (compare Wilkin 1996; Harvey 1999). As such, it is misleading to speak about bank capital without bringing labor and workers into the analysis.

Following Marx, Hilferding roots his understanding of the reproduction of banks and financial capital in a labor theory of value (2006 [1910], 156, 170, 173, 183). The earnings of banks derive from the profits expropriated by capitalists in production. That is, the profits banks earn are not in a strict sense the same as profits earned in production. Rather, bank earnings come from the interest received on the capital loaned out (Hilferding 2006 [1910], 172). Interest, therefore, is a deduction from the average social profit and claim on the surplus-value created in the production process. This understanding ontologically contradicts mainstream analyses that posit a dualism between the so-called real productive economy and a speculative financial economy. Rather, as Albo et al. emphasize, 'capitalism rests on the production of commodities not just their circulation . . . [m]oney capital, bank capital, credit and speculative capital are all necessary moments in the circuits of capitalist production and exchange' (2010, 33–4). In this way the reproduction of finance and banking is linked to labor in production at the general level of capitalist social relations. In simpler terms, bankers and financial capital produce nothing (Christophers 2011).

The specific form that the state has taken under emerging finance capitalism is also closely linked to questions of labor and revenue. The state's institutional capacity to act and reproduce itself depends on revenue generation, which authorities can do in three ways: by creating new state-owned enterprises or by increasing their productivity to produce surpluses; by issuing debt bonds by borrowing against future tax revenues; and by raising or introducing new taxes (O'Connor 2009 [1973], 179). The transition to neoliberalism has entailed the shedding of SOE capacity through privatization, increased state borrowing, and the reconfiguration of tax revenues around income tax and VAT, which fall disproportionately onto the working majority while minimizing corporate taxation. On the one hand, privatization weakens organized labor's power within the state apparatus while, on the other hand, the other two sources of revenue depend disproportionately on labor's capacity to work, create value, and pay taxes. At the same time, as the state increases its reliance on debts this increases the state's dependence on financial capital. In these ways, the very form of the state has shifted towards its being organized in the interests of financial capital rather than the interests of labor.

The strengthening of state authorities' capacity to socialize mounting financial risks is one of the most significant manifestations of this shift in capital–labor power relations within the state. This is most evident at times of crisis when the socialization of financial risks is demanded to avoid systemic collapse. Thus, as the Bank of England Governor, Mervyn King, so bluntly put it, the price of 'financial crisis is being borne by people who absolutely did not cause it'.[8] Even mainstream economists cannot help but acknowledge that state-led financial rescues represent a transfer of resources from present and future taxpayers to bankers (Haber 2005a, 2342; Furceri and Mourougane 2009). Interpreted under a Marxian lens, this form of socialization represents a struggle over the allocation of present and future social resources (insofar as state bonds, or fictitious capital, help cover the costs of rescue) collected by and distributed through the state apparatus. According to J.S. Toms, the growing power of capital in society has enabled capital to build state institutions capable of transferring aspects of their risks onto weaker groups in society (2010, 97, 101). Moreover, when financial crises strike, the state-led rescues are usually undertaken without democratic deliberation and often managed by an independent, unaccountable, and technocratic state financial apparatus whose institutionalized imperatives are to protect the financial system's health. Unambiguous democratic complications arise insofar as future generations must pay for the new debts incurred – debts over which they have had no say, either then, now, or later. Yet the transfer of social resources and the creation of fictitious capital occurring outside the sphere of democratic accountability have constituted the linchpin of government and state elites' capacity to overcome recurrent financial crises since the 1980s, which depends on a laboring population. As we will see, there are other forms of socialization that have become important since the 1990s and in response to crisis, such as the build-up of foreign reserves as a form of financial insurance. The state's institutional capacity to socialize risks has helped to constitute emerging finance capitalism to the benefit of financial capital and to the detriment of labor.

Finally, and in addition to the role of labor in capitalist reproduction generally, there is a need to look at labor at the level of individual banking institutions to understand emerging finance capitalism. Interestingly, most banking analyses, Marxian or otherwise, do not seriously account for the role of labor in bank profits. For example, Susan Strange's classic analysis of the financial structure of states and markets explicitly excludes bank labor as a factor in bank profitability (1994 [1988]). Yet the private and state banks in Mexico and Turkey have all manipulated employee levels at times of crisis and their overall staff costs are exploited as strategies to restoring and increasing profitability. The centrality of bank labor to a bank's earnings was, however, captured by Hilferding. According to Hilferding, a bank's gross profits come from the interest rate difference between what a bank borrows capital at and what it can earn from lending capital out. Net profit or the banks' 'bottom line', however, comes from the banks' gross profits less their operating costs (Hilferding 2006 [1910], 172). As the balance sheet of any bank reveals today, operating costs are a major factor in overall profitability. What is tagged as operating costs are diverse, but typically include physical infrastructure such as bank branches, technology, and other day-to-day costs of doing business, many of which are not easily adjusted. The most significant operating cost, and incidentally the most 'flexible', however, is staff (labor) costs. A bank's staff costs can account for as much as 40–50 per cent of a bank's after tax profits. The manipulation of staff costs has become a central aspect of bank crisis and recovery, as well as their long-term profitability strategies in ways consistent with neoliberalism.

2.3.4 Premise Four: Crises are Constitutive of Emerging Finance Capitalism

Marxian accounts situate crises as integral to capitalist social relations of production and competition insofar as they constitute an *internal* disruption (Devine 1987, 19). Because capital must constantly accumulate within a competitive environment, the coercive law of competition imposes stresses upon capitalists and leads to periodic breakdown (Marx 1990, 433). Marx also states:

> We thus see how the method of production and the means of production are constantly enlarged, revolutionized, how division of labor necessarily draws after it greater division of labor, the employment of machinery greater employment of machinery, work upon a large scale work upon a still greater scale. This is the law [of competition] that continually throws capitalist production out of its old ruts and compels capital to strain ever more the productive forces of labor for the very reason that it has already strained them – the law that grants it no respite, and constantly shouts in its ear: March! march! This is no other law than that which, within the periodical fluctuations of commerce, necessarily adjusts the price of a commodity to its cost of production. (Marx 1849)

In other words, crises are inherent to capitalism. However, not all crises are the same. Minor crises, for example, can cause the periodic revamping and readjusting of capitalist reproduction and social relations (Lipietz 1997, 262–4). Major crises, by contrast, can cause formerly institutionalized compromises and strategies to be no longer viable: 'struggle' wins out over 'unity'. This can result in the complete breakdown and separation of existing relations; the formation of new sets of relations; or the renewal of existing relations newly institutionalized and under a different model of accumulation. The tendency towards crisis, however, can be offset by counter-tendencies such as labor intensification, the opening of new markets, the discovery of new resources and technology, state intervention, and so on. Nonetheless, the ways in which minor and major crises are resolved, or not, is historically contingent on domestic social affairs, state institutional capacity, relative balance of power between capital and labor, and global pressures. In this sense, while crises are a structural feature of capitalism, so too are they specific to given state–society formations. For these reasons there is a strong relationship between crisis and social change, but no necessary or automatic outcome. That is, no economic or financial crisis in capitalism is necessarily so deep that the those who benefit disproportionately (capital and increasingly financial capital) cannot find ways to recover from it so long as workers acquiesce by, for example, absorbing the brunt of crisis through austerity, unemployment, falling standards of living, worsened working conditions, higher taxes, the socialization of financial risks, and so on.

The resurrection of capitalist social relations in these ways has been witnessed time and again in emerging capitalisms. The 1995 Mexican and the 2001 Turkish state-led bank rescues left their societies responsible for servicing, respectively, $100 billion and $47 billion in financial risks gone bad. These and other major banking crises during the 1990s delivered a message that emerging capitalisms would be *unable* to sustain the idealized Washington consensus market-oriented strategies of development characterized by minimal state supervision and a belief in individual self-interest as effective self-discipline without risking full-scale global financial collapse. The crises led to changes within capitalism. At the level of IFIs, this gave rise to the so-called post-Washington consensus seen in the World Bank 1997 and 2002 Development Reports, which legitimized the idea that institutions matter at the level of states. In this regard, the resolutions to crises are rarely simply a domestic affair but occur within a hierarchical interstate and world market context. A range of international and foreign agencies support and even press for market-oriented changes often framed discursively as these countries' best hope of escaping underdevelopment and poverty. The most important agents include the US government and the European Union as well as major IFIs like the International Monetary Fund (IMF) and the World Bank. Through these international links, Mexico and

Turkey have received technical advice on how to transition to neoliberal-ism and have accessed billions of dollars to support neoliberal restructuring and crisis management. To this day, both countries remain major clients of the IMF and World Bank, which act as 'external anchors' rooting each society's market-oriented development trajectory. This is not to imply that the complex social changes involved in the neoliberal restructuring of states, banks, and labor have been simply imposed by IFIs and foreign states amidst crisis. Rather, there is always a context of contingent collaboration between foreign and domestic capitals as well as between foreign and domestic state and financial agencies (compare Ercan and Oguz 2006).

Finally, integrating crisis into our understanding points us towards one of the most important paradoxes of emerging finance capitalism. Market-oriented restructuring over the last thirty years has given rise to recurrent financial volatility and crisis in such a way that crisis has become a regular feature of neoliberal strategies of development. Yet instead of challenging the social rule of neoliberal capitalism and the mounting power of finan-cial capital, the resolutions to crises have institutionally fortified financial interests within capital accumulation, social reproduction, and the state (compare Albo et al. 2010, 35). Indeed, the growing centralization and concentration of financial capital gives financial capitalists an interest in strengthening the power of the state to intervene on its behalf at times of crisis – power that is also augmented by subordinating the interests of all classes to its own (compare Hilferding 2006 [1910], 337). Mainstream analyses question crisis resolution only to the extent, or not, that the responses have resuscitated, revived, and/or enhanced capitalism (but without questioning its unequal social relations) (Martinez-Diaz 2009; Acemoglu 2009). By contrast, this book takes as a premise of its analysis that the building of state capacity to manage recurrent financial crises – before, during, and afterwards – is a deeply class-based affair that has institutionally privileged the power of financial capital. In this way, crises and the ways in which states and banks have resolved crises have proven to be constitutive of emerging finance capitalism.

These four Marxian analytical premises – states as social relations, banks as social relations, labor as vital to, and crisis as constitutive of emerging finance capitalism – are not a priori concepts of the kind found in neoclas-sical and liberal analyses that support hypothetical deductive investiga-tions. Rather, the premises are grounded in a historical understanding of capitalism that builds on Marxian abstractions that are revised in light of concrete and complex real world events. In this regard, the premises do not cloud the specificity of Mexico and Turkey's experiences but help to reveal underlying historical-structural processes.

2.4   RESTATING THE ARGUMENT OF EMERGING FINANCE CAPITALISM

Before moving on to the case study chapters, it is worth restating the book's core argument presented earlier. In its simplest form the book argues that the post-1980s transition to neoliberalism and to its progressively finance-led form since the 1990s in Mexico and Turkey has culminated in a qualitatively new phase of accumulation and development – emerging finance capitalism. This phase of emerging finance capitalism is defined by a new form of state that represents *the fusion of the interests of domestic and foreign financial capital in the state apparatus as the institutionalized priorities and overarching social logic guiding the actions of state managers and government elites, often to the detriment of labor.* This interpretation penetrates beneath surface level policy analyses and helps to explain the underlying dynamics of why the banks in Mexico and Turkey have shown relative resilience amidst current economic and social disparity stemming from the Great Recession. This line of argument also engages two interrelated debates. First, in contrast to the convergence versus divergence polarities found in the mainstream literature, the historical culmination of emerging finance capitalism in Mexico and Turkey is typified by the *dual aspects of universalization around competitive financial imperatives as differentiated by the historical specificities of each society.* In this way the analysis captures both the specific complexity and the generality of historical change. Second, and in contrast to quite rigid quantity theory of bank ownership debates, the book suggests that *while private bank ownership remains sufficient to explain a bank's profit- and market-oriented operational strategies, private ownership is no longer necessary under emerging finance capitalism.* Neither a return to state bank control nor a revival of domestic bank ownership on their own constitutes a break with the class-based social imperatives of neoliberalism and, today, emerging finance capitalism. As the concluding chapter suggests, any substantive alternative to emerging finance capitalism will not be defined by, for example, bank ownership changes but by a social and political break in the class relations and institutionalizations of power constituting the state and emerging finance capitalism as integrated in the world market.

NOTES

1. For example, see Ertürk 2003; Epstein 2005; Stockhammer 2008; Foster 2008; Orhangazi 2008; Martinez-Diaz 2009; Lapavitsas 2009; Evans 2009; Fine 2010.
2. For example, Guttman 1994; Harvey 1999 [1982]; Gowan 1999; Duménil and Lévy

2004 and 2011; Panitch and Gindin 2004, 2005). In terms of both finance and 'finan-cialization', so to speak, there has been relatively little Marxian research dedicated to the particularities of emerging capitalisms (the few notable exceptions include White 1992; Soederberg 2004, 2005; Bello 2006; Lapavitsas and dos Santos 2008). For a review of Marxian debates on finance, see Marois forthcoming 2012.

3. Some of the more important works include Hilferding 2006 [1910]; Gerschenkeron 1962; Shonfield 1969 [1965]; Shaw 1973; McKinnon 1973; Itoh and Lapavitsas 1999.

4. It should be said that I focus primarily on the commercial retail and universal banks found in Mexico and Turkey. These banks pool local deposits and take foreign loans to lend to individuals, firms, and public bodies (involving both consumptive and some productive lending). Universal banks undertake a wide range of financial services and are often part of a larger holding group, often family-based, or global banking network (for example, Citibank). National developmental banks, investment banks, and other market-based financial institutions are not generally explored.

5. There can be, of course, a certain amount of crossover and ambiguity between research approaches, particularly between neoclassical influences in NIEs, institutionalism, and the now hegemonic post-Washington consensus (compare Rogers 2010). This is evident in Hall and Soskice's VoC work but also in, for example, the work of Ocampo et al. (2008), who argue for extra-market coordination but more in line with neoclassical market-oriented development imperatives.

6. On the question of the relative autonomy of the state, see Miliband 1974 [1969]; Jessop 1990, 1982; Carnoy 1984; Knutilla 1987; Clarke 1988a.

7. For analyses drawing on ideas of 'primitive accumulation' in Mexico and Turkey, see Morton 2010 and Karadag 2010.

8. Inman, Philip, 'Bank of England governor blames spending cuts on bank bailouts' *Guardian online*, 1 March 2011.

3. States, banks, and the history of postwar development in Mexico and Turkey

Two pre-capitalist societies, colonial Mexico and the Ottoman Empire, existed worlds apart. The vast majority of Mexicans and soon to be Turks knew little of each other. Yet within the first two decades of the twentieth century their societies would share national revolutionary upheavals with far reaching consequences. Within a couple more decades Mexico and Turkey would also have in common an expanding wage labor workforce, an integrated and domestically controlled banking system, and a state apparatus geared towards national capitalist development. Specific and important differences characterize each society's historical consolidation of capitalism and the evolution of their state–bank relationships. Nonetheless, this chapter explores how by the late 1970s both societies had become subject to the power of money and credit as never before. The newly institutionalized relationships between the state apparatus and banks set the historical backdrop against which one can interpret the 1980s debt crisis and subsequent turn towards neoliberal strategies of development. Section 3.1 below looks at Mexico and Turkey's historical consolidation and Section 3.2 considers the expansion within both countries of state-led development and banking. Section 3.3 then explores the breakdown of these state–bank relationships during the 1970s and following the impact of the US-authored Volcker shock. This is followed by a brief conclusion.

3.1 CONSOLIDATING CAPITALISM IN MEXICO AND TURKEY

3.1.1 Mexico

In colonial Mexico most Mexicans survived on subsistence-based production and lived outside any sort of a generalized wage labor or money economy (Cockcroft 1998). Wealth was highly concentrated among a small number of emerging commercial capitalists, large *hacendados* (estate land owners), and the Catholic Church. Political rule was unstable and marked by a series of authoritarian governments and violent struggles. Domestic capital formation was weak and nationally integrated markets undeveloped. Still, regional markets had emerged around urban centres of power. Mexico City became a base for the old Spanish elite, and this was followed by Veracruz, Monterrey, and Guadalajara for the nascent merchant free-traders. Banking and credit barely existed and what did exist was institutionally thin. With independence in 1821 the new Mexican governments gained greater access to foreign capital resources. Official foreign debt quickly rose and soon became costly to service, even though interest rates were in the range of 4.5 to 6 per cent (Adamson 2006, 199). When the government defaulted in 1827 foreign credit dried up until the mid-1880s – offering an early lesson in debt discipline.

It was the early industrial capitalists who established the first private banks in Mexico. They did so in order to service their own capital needs, which precipitated both the spread of credit relations and the establishment of their financial power base in Mexico. For instance, the Banco de Avío y Minas was founded in 1784 to 'form, conserve, and augment' mining capital. Foreign capital later established the most important commercial banks. English investors during the brief reign of Hapsburg emperor Maximillian (1864–67) created the first private commercial bank in Mexico, the Banco de Londres, México y Sudamérica in 1864.[1] But it was the Mexican dictator President Porfirio Díaz (1876–1911) who really took a leap forward in the organization of credit by promoting foreign investment and by consolidating the institutionalized power of elites. Díaz passed new laws promoting foreign investment and joint-stock company formation, reorganized public debt, eliminated internal trade tariffs, and modernized the banking and credit laws (Haber 1992, 11). In the banking sector, instability arising from a crisis in 1884 drove new reforms intended to stabilize credit relations. The ruling government forced two recently established banks to merge into one, the Banco Nacional de México, whose ownership structure included significant Mexican participation (including that of President Díaz).[2] The merged bank then served as a de facto central bank that put control of the Mexican banking sector in private hands. The reforms then institutionalized a privileged position of power for private bankers within the Mexican state financial apparatus. Those who owned and controlled money in Mexico had established themselves at the top of a desperately unequal social hierarchy and had begun to integrate their interest within state formation processes.

By the twentieth century the nature of the intensive exploitation and oppression of the Mexican population had resulted in widespread social discontent, animosity, and resistance. The Wall Street panic in 1907 then had the effect of weakening the power base of Mexican bankers and that of President Díaz, both of whom were tightly linked to foreign capital interests. In this context, the long-oppressed peasantry and proletariat ignited the Mexican Revolution in 1910–11. According to James Cockcroft, the revolution was an 'explosive confrontation between social classes that pitted peasants and workers against landlords and capitalists' (2010, 13). By 1914 the revolutionary forces of Villa and Zapata had united against the liberal Constitutionalists. In response, and in return for access to Mexican oil for American interests, the US navy occupied the port of Veracruz to help ensure a Constitutionalist victory and US access to Mexican resources.

Control over the banks played an important role during the revolution. Between 1915 and 1916 the Carranza Constitutionalist government seized the Mexican banks and took possession of their reserves to finance the military campaign against Villa and Zapata. Nationalization did not, however, deter New York bankers from providing the additional war credits needed to secure victory (Adamson 2006, 199–200). Domestically, while Carranza's banking decrees alienated him from some sectors of the wealthy, he drew in some popular support from those not aligned with the revolutionary forces and increased his power base. As one worker wrote in a letter to Carranza about the banks, 'Señor, don't forget the fact that the majority of the capitalists are rich men who are political enemies of the government' (in Richmond 1987, 294). This passage gives some insight into the 1915 split between the urban workers and the peasant alliance, when the former accepted a deal with the Constitutionalists. By incorporating workers the Constitutionalists undermined the revolution's radicalism and potential victory, the outcome of which saw a defeated peasantry, a weakened and corporatist proletariat, and a victorious bourgeoisie led by industrialists, landowners, and regional *caudillos*. A relatively progressive constitution nonetheless emerged.

The new 1917 Constitution included male suffrage, limitations on church power, agrarian reform, state ownership of all minerals, oil and sub-soils, and among the most progressive labor legislation in the world at the time (Cockcroft 1998, 106; Hellman 1978, 20–1). To the benefit of domestic and foreign capital, the 1917 Constitution also institutionalized the protection of private property and provided a legal framework for presidents Carranza, Obregón, and Calles – the so-called northern 'Sonora gang' of capitalists from 1917 to 1935 – to better institutionalize Mexican capitalism and quell enduring societal opposition by force. The Mexican tradition of authoritarian political power congealed in 1929 in the new Partido Nacional Revolucionario (PNR; National Revolutionary

Party) – the precursor to the Partido Revolucionario Institucional (PRI; Institutional Revolutionary Party), which was established in 1946 and maintained one-party rule until 2000. Political organization took the form of co-opting social resistance by drawing the capital, labor, and peasant sectors into the state apparatus and by promoting Mexican nationalism over class conflict (Richmond 1987; Knight 1992).

With the assassination of Carranza in 1920 the Sonora gang became increasingly conservative, pro-capitalist, and increasingly concerned with consolidating the power of state and capital over Mexican society. One strategy involved better institutionalizing the generalized role of money in Mexican society. To do so, the Sonora gang established the Comisión Nacional Bancaria (CNB; National Banking Commission) and the Banco de México (BdeM; Bank of Mexico) in 1924 and 1925 to facilitate overall financial and monetary coherence and to exert regulatory control over the national currency, exchange rates, and interest rates. The new institutions also helped to integrate Mexico into the growing complexities of international finance. The Sonora gang then restructured state power to reside in the president's office and to flow through the financial apparatus, most notably the Secretaría de Hacienda y Crédito Público (SHCP: Ministry of Finance and Public Credit), the BdeM, and the state development banks. Finally, to elevate the place of capital domestically meant finding ways to mobilize scarce domestic resources for development. To this end, Mexican state agencies helped to reorganize the collapsed banking sector and re-establish Mexican bankers in the banks. Moreover, the PNR incorporated Mexican bankers directly into the BdeM administrative council in such a way that the government shared the power to determine monetary and financial state policy with domestic capitalists (Cardero 1984, 22). The foundations of state–bank relations had been institutionally set, and the power of bankers figured prominently.

The socially progressive aspects of the 1917 Constitution by and large remained dormant until President Lázaro Cárdenas (1934–1940) broke with the conservative Sonora gang and implemented policies intended to consolidate capitalism but without further alienating the majority of Mexico's peasantry and workers. Cárdenas's move was more pragmatic than the result of a benevolent or autonomous state. Mexican society was at the time again at the brink of civil war amidst the Great Depression. People continued to suffer as the peasant-based economy was thrust into capitalism, threatening its consolidation. To avoid risking another revolutionary uprising, Cárdenas had to establish some form of class compromise between the majority of Mexicans who worked and produced wealth and the rich minority who appropriated the wealth but who controlled great resources and had the most influence among state elites. Cárdenas did this by formally organizing capital, labor, and peasant sectors under state regulation and within capitalist relations of power (Hellman 1978, 40). The corporatist and state-led form of capitalism was framed as a defense of the Mexican Revolution and state legitimacy came to be based on post-revolutionary principles such as (limited) political democracy, (limited) social justice, domestic economic development, and the defense of national sovereignty (Crespo 1992; O'Toole 2003). As one example of this balancing act, Cárdenas focused on agrarian reform. Whereas in 1930 there were three peasants without land for every small farm producer, by 1940 a one to one ratio had been achieved through land redistribution and the spread of communal lands (*ejidos*) (Arregui Koba 1990, 20–21). Unlike his predecessors, Cárdenas refused to use force to suppress all labor strikes and did not allow foreign capital a free hand in Mexico (Hellman 1978, 35–6).

Cárdenas's political intent was to nail down a national development project shaped around state-led capitalist growth and redistributive principles as tied to post-revolution efforts to minimize foreign ownership. This led the government to nationalize the railroads, expropriate foreign oil reserves and companies, and form dozens of new state-owned enterprises (SOEs). It also led the government to channel state resources into infrastructure projects that supported the profitability of large Mexican capitalists. Both strategies involved establishing domestic extra-market control over the commercial banks, but not direct ownership. For example, the BdeM reserve requirements enabled state managers to use the money resources controlled by private Mexican banks to fund domestic development projects. Together with the state development banks (the most important being the Nacional Financiera), the BdeM directed financial resources into priority sectors (Frieden 1981, 418; Bennett and Sharpe 1980, 175). This was not a case of crowding out the private sector – the ahistorical explanation preferred by present-day neoliberal advocates. Rather, state funds filled the gap where private *financieras*, or investment-type banks, were unwilling or unable to develop markets or infrastructure, or facilitate growth in agriculture, rural areas, and mortgages. National development also entailed greater international market integration via trade and portfolio capital borrowings (if not more direct foreign investment) by Mexican and American capitalists. Nacional Financiera was responsible for negotiating with foreign finance on behalf of domestic firms, both public and private.

Money became a central feature of national capitalist development and from the earliest foundations of the banking sector the disciplining of bank workers was important to state authorities that feared organized labor exercising any control over the banking sector. Indeed, quite early on Mexican bank workers had tried organizing into unions to achieve better working conditions (Cardero 1984, 22). Their efforts resulted in modest workplace gains in 1937 under Cárdenas, but so too were significant compromises negotiated. In one instance, the minister of the SHCP asked bank workers to minimize their demands 'in national solidarity' to confront the current financial crisis. The government then banned any collective action by bank workers that might interfere with banking transactions and granted Mexican bank owners full control over hiring and firing conditions. By the end of Cárdenas's six-year term, his administration had secured a Mexican controlled bank-based financial system in support of state-led capitalist development around an idea of national solidarity over class-consciousness. Capitalist social relations of power, production, and money had consolidated in Mexico.

3.1.2   Turkey

The history of power, banking, and capitalist development in modern Turkey has its own particularities. The conquest of Constantinople in 1453 had marked the definitive ascent of the Ottoman Empire (1300–1922), but also the decline of the city as a centre of Genoese and Venetian banking and financial innovation (de Roover 1971, 7). Under Ottoman rule Islamic injunctions against usury were strictly interpreted and enforced. This inhibited the spread of western interest-bearing forms of capitalist banking, but early credit and banking services remained available through non-Muslim communities within Ottoman territories. By the nineteenth century the Ottoman Empire had begun to decline and this spurred the 'Tanzimat' period of state reorganization from 1839 to 1876 (see Lewis 1961; Tezel 2010). One strategy involved the modernization and Europeanization of monetary and banking relations, which at the same time meant the subordination of Ottoman finances to foreign powers. For example, the founding of the Ottoman Bank in 1856 was important because it internalized a western colonial form of banking within Ottoman society, and therefore the power of interest-bearing credit, debt, and discipline. British capital (later joined by French and Austrian capital) owned and controlled the Ottoman Bank, which kept its head office in London. The bank served as the intermediary between the debt hungry Ottoman state and foreign capital and, moreover, opened the empire's borders to the entry of new foreign banks. An 'Agreement' in 1863 augmented the Ottoman Bank's power over the Ottoman state, for example, by authorizing the Ottoman Bank to issue currency. However, the bank fell short of acting as a central bank since it could not control the liquidity and credit volume of the economy. The agreement also stipulated that the Ottoman state hold all income in the Ottoman Bank, as well as channel all expenses and issue all bonds through it. In return, the Ottoman Bank was obliged to provide the state with short-term credits. Because of the weak financial and political position of the Ottomans, the Ottoman Bank gained the right to supervise the state budget. This odious 'Debt Administration' subordinated the Ottoman state's finances to European capitalist powers.

Unsurprisingly, this colonial-like situation led to social discontent focused on the Ottoman Sultanate and state as well as on the foreign powers exercising enormous influence over them. The 1908 Young Turk movement challenged the situation (see Hanioğlu 2001). The Young Turks, however, did not represent a popular insurrection but a top-down, power-centralizing bourgeois revolution aimed at defining private property rights and restricting pre-capitalist Ottoman state power by re-establishing parliament, which had been suspended by Sultan Abdul Hamid II in 1878. Yet the movement did spark wider multi-ethnic social demonstrations and labor activism, which erupted in the wake of the 1908 revolution and in response to worsening economic conditions (Akkaya 2002, 130). The ruling Committee of Union and Progress government responded by enacting oppressive regulations in 1909 that allowed state forces to suppress worker militancy. Political and social turmoil persisted through the period of World War I. The 1919–22 national liberation struggles against foreign occupation represented the zenith of the fight to control the area known as Turkey today, but also resulted in the suppression of ethnic and worker identities to a new national Turkish identity that came with the founding of the Republic of Turkey in 1923.

Mustafa Kemal ('Ataturk') assumed the first presidency, and among the first orders of state was to centralize government power within the Cumhuriyet Halk Partisi (CHP; Republican People's Party) and to establish Ankara as the capital city. The Turkish state thus came to life not under multi-party democracy but under an authoritarian single-party regime – one that attempted to forestall class struggle by claiming that Turkish society was untouched by class differentiation. The CHP attempted to formalize this around nationalist 'Kemalist' sentiments. At the time, it should be recalled, the capacities of the state apparatus were modest and the domestic economy was largely subsistence-based agriculture organized around small villages. Most people lived outside of any generalized money relations and formal wage labor. Only a few small agrarian firms grew export commodities. Local production did not have extensive credit requirements because techniques were traditional. Foreign capital invested in Turkey, but mostly in large ventures such as railroads and mining. Turkey's economy was dependent on imports for most manufactured goods and capital flows. The 1923 İzmir Economic Congress aimed to change this by crafting a mixed capitalist economy. The Kemalist developmental strategy involved nurturing a national Muslim–Turk bourgeoisie and tight capitalist relations with state elites. The Turkish state apparatus assumed an active role in supporting private sector development by offering public tenders, public–private partnerships, subsidized credits and inputs from new SOEs, and easy access to foreign exchange. The Kemalist strategy also involved the government actively mediating tensions between the wealth *producing* classes (the popular masses including workers and the peasantry) and the wealth *appropriating* classes (the state elite and domestic capitalists) (Yalman 2002, 26–7). The specific class compromises embedded in Turkey's particular development strategy precluded any serious land reform as seen in Mexico, and this would lock in persistent patterns of unequal rural–urban development.

One of the chief concerns of the Kemalist government officials, state managers, and the representatives of agriculture, trade, and industry present at the İzmir Congress was the need to shake off colonial financial imperialism by organizing a domestic banking system. Between 1908 and 1923 a nascent wave of pre-republic Ottoman capitalists, based largely in İstanbul and Ankara, had established a couple of dozen local banks. Yet despite favorable state policy, the small local banks could not compete with the larger foreign banks. If Turkish state formation and a domestic capitalist class were to thrive, it was thus agreed at the İzmir Congress that the Turkish private sector alone could not establish strong enough banks (BAT 1999a; also Yılmaz 2007). The new Turkish state would have to take an active role in financing development, displacing the power of foreign capital, and creating domestic markets.[3] For example, commercial capital rallied around establishing a major commercial bank, which Kemalist cadres helped to establish as a private domestic bank, Türkiye İş Bank, in 1924. İş Bank also took the lead in financing state-led infrastructure investments, which demanded more official international credits while drawing heavily on domestic resources (Eres 2005, 321). The Türkiye Sanayii ve Maadin Bank then opened in 1925 as the first development bank to grant credits and offer technical advice to industrial capital. To support and expand agricultural development the government changed the status of Ziraat Bank, which was initially formed as a state agriculture bank, into a private joint-stock company in 1924 following an injection of capital from the state (BAT 1999a). In 1927, the government established Emlak Bank with the mandate to offer home mortgages and real estate loans. New private domestic banks were by no means barred from entry, and Turkish capital began to create smaller banks to service its own short-term credit demands (Cosar 1999, 125).

The CHP government also pursued new strategies to help institutionally consolidate capitalist markets and finance national development. For one, the CHP created the Türkiye Cumhuriyet Merkez Bankası (CBT; Central Bank of Turkey) in 1931. The CBT assumed responsibility for and expanded the banking system functions previously performed by the Ottoman Bank, such as printing money, controlling the value of the Turkish lira, balancing liquidity, lending money to other banks, and so on. The CHP did not initially establish the CBT as a state-owned institution but rather as a joint-stock company. Then in 1936 the new banking law set reserve requirements at 15 per cent of all bank deposits, which the CBT then channelled in national development priorities. The impact of the Great Depression, however, led to the recognition by state managers that industrialization would require more stable sources of capital resources. This material constraint on national development led the government to create more Turkish state-owned banks with institutionalized 'duties' to subsidize specific sectors of the economy. For example, in 1933 the CHP established Sümerbank to finance SOEs and Belediyeler Bank to support the infrastructure needs of municipalities. The CHP then created Etibank in 1935 to finance mining, mineral marketing, and power supplies and Halk Bank and Halk Sandıkları in 1938 to offer small trade credits. Ziraat Bank kept on subsidizing crop prices and credits to small farmers throughout the 1930s, but in 1937–38 the CHP converted Ziraat back into a state-owned bank and, again, increased the bank's capital base to finance agricultural expansion. With these state-led efforts under one-party rule, the Turkish financial sector solidified as a bank-based financial system that operated in the service of national capitalist development. Unlike in Mexico, however, Turkish state authorities assumed a major presence in the sector in ways that constituted different social relations of power in banking.

Three further changes that occurred in and around the Great Depression should be noted for their importance to the consolidation of capitalism in Turkey (Savran 2002, 8–9). First, much as in Mexico Turkish state managers crafted a legal framework in support of the rule of law and private property. Second, the Kemalist government adopted 'westernization' as official ideological and cultural policy. Third, state managers and Turkish capitalists transitioned from a commerce-based to an industrial-based capital accumulation model because the depression of the 1930s had exposed the vulnerability of the primary goods-based developmental model. As a result, a state-led model of development took hold and was characterized by the growth of large-scale production units and the promotion of a national capitalist class. State authorities established SOEs to complement private capital formation, and state development projects

targeted areas where domestic capital was unable and unwilling to participate, including infrastructure, electricity, railways, and iron and steel. The
Kemalist state-led strategy of development rejected free market competition as the core organizing principle of capital accumulation but, again
much as with Mexico's state-led strategy, in a way that was by no means
anti-capitalist (Yalman 2002, 29–30). The CHP enacted a series of labor
laws and prohibitions that severely curtailed the rights of workers to strike
and to collective organization on the basis of class. What worker organization the CHP allowed was channelled through the state apparatus as a
form of corporatism. The Turkish economy would 'modernize' and grow,
but it is difficult to imagine this growth as anything but dependent on the
formation of a disciplined working class and a cadre of elite state managers committed to supporting a national capitalist class.

By the end of World War II, society in both Mexico and Turkey had
radically transformed from a non-capitalist subsistence production basis
operating without generalized money or wage labor relations and/or an
effective state apparatus to capitalist societies defined by these social
relationships exercised in the service of capital accumulation.

3.2   THE POSTWAR EXPANSION OF CAPITALISM AND BANKING IN MEXICO AND TURKEY

In peripheral countries such as Mexico and Turkey, postwar governments often pursued some variation of state-led strategy of development.
Prevailing into the early 1980s these strategies focused on production
for the domestic market and the sequenced expansion of manufacturing
capacity to replace imports. The development of manufacturing capacity
typically began with lower value non-durable consumer goods such as
processed foods, tobacco, beverages, cotton textiles, and the like. A next
phase established the manufacture of durable consumer goods such as
household appliances, automobiles, simple chemical goods, and cement.
In larger peripheral countries, state-led strategies established some production of steel and capital goods. State-owned enterprises assumed a
great deal of responsibility for providing infrastructure, industrial inputs,
and basic goods, including but not limited to air travel, ports, roads,
telecommunications, water, sanitation, electricity, oil and mineral extraction, and steel. In many cases, the state apparatus took a lead position in
organizing development finance and credit through differing central bank,
state development bank, and commercial bank relationships. In unique
ways, both Mexico and Turkey conformed to this relatively stable pattern
of state-led development and finance until the mid-1970s.

3.2.1 Mexico

The Mexican postwar strategy of state-led development was intended to limit the market determination of long-term investment decisions and the capacity of foreign capital to maximize profitability without concern for long-term social interests (Cypher 1989, 65). The strategy was politically shaped under authoritarian one-party PRI rule, corporatist social control, and the context of World War II. The latter facilitated the consolidation of Mexico's domestic industrialization strategy as a result of the rise of postwar tariff protections and fears of communism that stimulated US aid to Mexico. A state-led development path was formalized in 1945 when the PNR (soon to be PRI) government signed an IMF adhesion protocol integrating Mexico into the new Bretton Woods system. The 1946 Law of Executive Authority in Economic Matters then centralized institutional power on economic matters within the federal executive, from price controls and trade barriers to creating SOEs across most sectors. The newly formed SOEs produced inputs that supported private capital development, often in sectors that domestic capital would not or could not enter but that were vital to overall industrialization. The PRI brokered capital–labor comprises that established a limited social safety net for the growing Mexican labor force. Yet, relations of power within the Mexican state apparatus were in constant flux. Intra-state conflict played out through successive presidents trying to gain control via centralization and then decentralization of state authority that resulted in various levels of authority, sources of enrichment, and niches of political power (MacLeod 2005, 41). Nonetheless, gross domestic product (GDP) growth was strong into the 1950s at just under 6 per cent per annum while the public deficit and external debt remained manageable at just over 1 per cent and 11 per cent of GDP respectively (OECD 1992, 14). Via this pattern of development Mexican elites hoped to break into the world's industrialized ranks.

In the early 1950s a sudden decline in the external terms of trade triggered the 1954 peso devaluation. The PRI, supported by state managers and domestic capitalists, responded to the instability with a renewed industrialization strategy that included tariff protections, price subsidies, and financial aid. This initiated the period of 'stabilizing development' characterized by high aggregate economic growth and low inflation (Solís 1997). The SHCP and BdeM regulated the banking system and helped guide the flows of bank capital into key sectors via obligatory reserve requirements, quantitative controls on credit, a system of selective loans to priority sectors, and the regulation of saving and loan interest rates. The state financial apparatus sterilized and controlled excessive liquidity and foreign currency liabilities. The period typified the height of Mexican state-led development finance wherein the domestic private banks alongside the state development banks helped to finance new industrialization efforts. In return, the bankers were rewarded with overall sector growth, high profits, and a seat at the table of state financial policy formation (FitzGerald 1985, 213).

The number of financial institutions grew rapidly alongside postwar industrialization. While the Mexican state owned a few significant development and investment banks, commercial banking was left to Mexican capital. Whereas in 1940 fewer than 40 private banks existed in total, the number more than doubled to 105 in 1971; the number of branches ballooned from 265 to 1777 over the same period (Bátiz-Lazo and Del Angel 2003, 344). From 1940 to 1950 alone the number of banks with countrywide service more than doubled from six to fourteen (Cardero 1984, 38). At the time, private banks dominated the financial system controlling about 70 per cent of all financial assets. However, *financieras*, or investment-like banks, also emerged as more relaxed state regulations enabled the *financieras'* asset control to expand from about 16 to 30 per cent by the mid-1960s (Aubey 1971, 26). As such, the Mexican financial system consolidated as bank-dominated and Mexican-owned, but not without developing other market-based financial institutions. The informal integration of bank and market-based financial integration had been loosely in play since the 1930s but this accelerated in the 1950s and 1960s as commercial banks channeled more resources through their non-bank financial affiliates to escape regulation and boost their market power (Del Ángel-Mobarak 2005, 46). Mexican financial capital illustrated patterns of increased concentration and centralization. By the mid-1960s most large commercial banks owned or had acquired one or more *financiera*. The six most powerful financial groups controlled 72.9 per cent of all financial sector resources (as compared to 40 banks controlling about 75 per cent in 1950) and just over 85 per cent of all bank capital assets (Aubey 1971, 26). These same six groups owned 44 commercial banks and 21 *financieras*. Mexico's large family-based holding groups benefited from this structure since they could use a bank's money savings to service the capital requirements of the group's associated commercial, manufacturing, and industrial enterprises – a form of finance capitalism specific to peripheral capitalisms (compare White 1992). The presence of Mexican bankers in the state apparatus was reflected in favorable state regulations, which restricted foreign competition and promoted the domestic ownership of bank capital by reserving investment in banking, insurance, and finance for Mexican capital alone.

Contrary to liberal and neoclassical accounts that see almost any state action as by definition sub-optimal and repressive, the postwar state regulation of finance did not stifle financial growth in Mexico but enabled it. Bank assets expanded from less than 10 per cent of GDP before 1962 to almost 20 per cent by the early 1970s, achieving annual growth of over 5 per cent (Del Ángel-Mobarak 2005, 46). Nor did regulation repress bank profitability. In recent testimonies Mexican bank owners – who lost their banks with the 1982 nationalization – lauded the postwar financial structure, which generated high profit levels while allowing the banks to manage financial risk and promote stable development via the so-called more gentlemanly banker model (Legorreta 2005, 58; Aguilar 2005, 64). The point being that postwar financial regulation was a necessary, if not sufficient, condition of capitalist state, class, and market formation. State and domestic elites wanted money capital to flow into what at the time was an uncertain and unstable process of capital formation. The liberalized financial arrangements of today were simply impractical, even impossible, given the 'risks' involved. More importantly, the postwar state financial apparatus had yet to develop anything near the institutional capacity needed to rescue financial capital should it enter into crisis and threaten the overall stability of the postwar developmental project.

The pattern of national capitalist development tends to proceed unevenly, and flows of money and capital can facilitate this unevenness (Harvey 1999; Smith 2010 [1984]). For example, Mexican bankers responded to the mounting capital and credit needs of urban industrial and commercial capital thus enabling capitalist expansion in and around urban settings. Yet the strategy used to fulfill urban capital requirements involved drawing on the banks' rural savings accumulated from the agricultural sector. In other words, money flowed from Mexico's already capital-poor rural areas to the already capital-rich urban centres (Aubey 1971, 31). The government's state-led development strategy likewise supported urban production and population concentration thereby reinforcing existing uneven patterns of capital accumulation and centralized services, especially financial capital concentrated in major cities (Guillén Romo 2005, 198–200). The BdeM's reserve requirements and state development banks did little to offset this uneven concentration of capital and labor power, which centered first around Mexico City, followed by Monterrey and Guadalajara. At the same time, urban workplace mobilization led to industrial working-class organization and some price protections (for example, corn, tomatoes, and so on) to ensure real wage gains (Cardero 1984, 31). But these urban worker victories often came at the expense of rural workers as a consequence of the agricultural price limits. The dynamic created an uneven pattern within the domestic terms of trade between agriculture and industry. Mexican peasants followed the spatial accumulation patterns by migrating from rural agriculture and mining to the urban industrialized mega-cities. To mitigate such uneven rural–urban development, President Díaz Ordaz (1964–70) tried to draw industry away from Mexico City through tax incentives but this had only limited decentralization effects. To this point, aggregate growth and capitalist expansion had remained steady but structural barriers like the rural–urban divide, growing financial problems, and persistent social inequality pointed towards mounting problems and the developmental limits of Mexico's state-led development strategy.

3.2.2 Turkey

Turkey's postwar state-led strategy of development has parallels with Mexico's. It was historically shaped by national independence struggles, pre-war production patterns, and the desire to limit the power of foreign capital over long-term domestic interests. During the war years a new Turkish commercial bourgeoisie, composed of rich landlords and merchants, took shape by dealing in black market goods (Aydın 2005, 27). Beginning in the mid-1940s commercial capital pushed for more market-oriented strategies of development than seen in Mexico, which held some influence until 1960. This accompanied demands for more political power from pro-market political elites, students, intelligentsia, and other social forces as well as from fractions of commerce, banking, and agricultural capitalists. Building on this discontent the newly formed Demokrat Parti (DP; Democratic Party) broke with CHP leadership in 1946 and established links to these groups. Although only implicitly so, Islamic support was also important to the success of the DP (Gunter and Yavuz 2007, 289). In 1950 the DP won the general election and then spearheaded an early liberal experiment, although the political and economic differences between the DP and CHP should not be overplayed (Yalman 2002, 33–4). At the time, both official parties campaigned around forms of liberalization and the DP maintained continuity with Turkey's authoritarian state form. The CHP–DP split entailed neither a major break between different fractions of capital nor the ascendancy of working-class power. The post-1945 liberalization and anti-state discourse was more about creating a development strategy that centered on private capital accumulation. Still, rather than wanting any real independence from the Turkish state, domestic Turkish capital wanted to prosper alongside an effective capitalist state. In this way domestic elites believed Turkey could achieve relative growth and industrial expansion in the postwar period.

To kick-start its development program the new DP government accepted official bilateral aid framed by the American military Truman Doctrine and the economic Marshall Plan. This aid entailed institutionalizing some forms of western-oriented world market integration. The DP built on Turkey's 1947 membership in the IMF and International Bank for Reconstruction and Development (soon to be World Bank) by establishing membership with the International Finance Corporation in 1956 and with the OECD in 1960. The DP reduced some trade barriers and accelerated the internationalization of Turkish capital by promoting trade in goods and services. Government and state managers worked to systematically organize state–capital relations in the service of market expansion and capital accumulation. As one illustration, the government established in law the Türkiye Odalar ve Borsalar Birliği (TOBB; Union of Chambers and Commodity Exchanges of Turkey) in 1950 as the representative of domestic capitalist interests to Turkish state managers and government elites. As another example, the 1958 Banking Act also established the Türkiye Bankalar Birliği (BAT; Banks Association of Turkey) as the official representative body of all banks operating in Turkey. As state and government elites built capacity to manage capitalist development in Turkey, so too were they establishing institutionalized means of incorporating the voice of domestic capital into official policy formation.

The 1958 Banking Act also sought to put the growing banking sector on more solid footings domestically. Postwar capitalist consolidation had meant more investment and production, greater aggregate wealth, a larger population, and urbanization – all of which created greater demands for credit, especially from domestic capitalists. The newly founded state banks could not immediately service these credit requirements so Turkish capitalists established smaller private banks to provide credits to themselves. At the same time, inflation during the 1950s, and the more liberal regulatory framework, had the effect of drawing capital into the banking sector to take advantage of speculative opportunities. More than 30 private banks were established from the 1940s to 1960s, but many of these were unstable and soon collapsed (BYEGM 2005). The 1958 Banking Act aimed to stabilize and boost domestic credit supplies by allowing banks held within large Turkish holding groups to extend unlimited credits to their associated firms – so long as the group controlled 25 per cent or more of the bank's shares. The banking act in this way encouraged holding groups to acquire private banks and then to grant credit, first and foremost, to its own shareholders. Owning a bank thus became a powerful lever of accumulation.

Despite the goals of the DP government Turkish postwar trade continued to be marked by the unequal exchange of Turkish primary goods for imported foreign manufactures. When Turkish primary goods exports commanded high world market prices, importing foreign manufactured goods did not pose insuperable trade imbalances for Turkey (Eres 2005,

323). Foreign financial aid through the late 1940s and 1950s also helped to avoid problematic trade imbalances. But the DP government's more liberal industrialization plan began to collapse when poor harvests and limits to agricultural expansion created a crisis in investment financing by the mid-1950s. In response, the DP government relied more and more on CBT credits to compensate. Postwar European agricultural recovery simultaneously led to a fall in demand for Turkish exports, triggering a foreign exchange crisis in 1958 (compare Maxfield and Nolt 1990, 71). As with Mexico's 1954 crisis, the DP responded by devaluing the Turkish lira to restore competitiveness. The IMF responded by initiating a stabilization program, but the plan to drive up exports and drive down inflation was unsuccessful and limited short-term credit availability. This only worsened the balance of payments problem. The DP-led postwar liberalization experiment had increased foreign debt without diversifying the Turkish economy beyond primary commodities, and this led to a break in the liberalization experiment. Moreover, the 1958 crisis exposed underlying power conflicts in Turkish society. 'Modernizing' fractions of urban industrial capital began to square off against the rural majority tied to more 'backward' ruling class fractions (Savran 2002, 10–11). Social and class tensions flared, marked by widespread student mobilizations. The turbulence culminated in the 27 May 1960 military coup orchestrated by young military officers.

Out of the social unrest and coup rose the 1961 Constitution, which attempted to institutionally balance the conflicting social struggles in Turkey. One element involved emphasizing liberal pluralist freedoms as well as social and economic rights to help diffuse power across Turkish society (Cizre Sakallığlu 1991, 57–8). To this point in time, workers' representation had largely been co-opted, controlled, and coerced to stay out of political affairs. In 1961, however, the possibility of a democratic state opened for the first time because a legal framework was established, in the words of Galip Yalman, 'for the dominated classes to establish their own economic and political organization, albeit within limitations' (2002, 34). Previously suppressed social dissent exploded with the ascent of the workers' movement alongside student, peasant, and Kurdish radicalization.

State and government elites also undertook strategies to ease social tensions following the 1960 coup, which involved mitigating the fears of Turkish capitalists. While the 1961 Constitution represented a relative shift away from the free market orientation of the DP, the government created new five-year state development plans to complement the Turkish private sector (Aydın 2005, 34–5). The Devlet Planlama Teşkilatı Müsteşarlığı (DPTM; State Planning Organization), established in 1961, was charged with managing the plans, initially under the watchful eye of the military. The first five-year plan lasted from 1963 to 1967, the second from 1968 to 1972, and the third from 1973 to 1977. The political intention was to bolster the mixed economic framework wherein private sector interests were served by Turkish state-owned services and production. The state apparatus assumed majority ownership in the riskier ventures, for example in iron, steel, sugar, paper and board, and textile production. The political support for domestic over foreign controlled industry was apparent as was support for restricting international flows of money in favor of domestic control of credit.[4] For example, the January 1970 Central Bank Act enabled monetary policy to be set in line with the five-year plans. The CBT could finance industrialization priorities up to 15 per cent of the total budget and the government could adjust bank deposit and lending rates according to developmental priorities in sectors such as agriculture, crafts, and certain manufacturing industries. The success of the five-year plans depended upon exerting extra-market political coordination.

The protected domestic market and state support shielded Turkish capitalists from world market competition – another then necessary condition for capitalist expansion. A small number of increasingly monopolistic national family-based holding groups took advantage of this by aggressively pulling together many different stages of production and distribution by buying up smaller import and export firms (Cokgezen 2000, 528–30). State-subsidized loans facilitated this process of capital centralization and concentration, but the state could not service all the needs of capital. Far from 'repressing' bank capital during this period, Turkish state authorities encouraged the centralization of banking as a means of accelerating private sector investment (BAT 1999a). As a result, the acquisition of banks by holding groups accelerated into the 1970s. Holding groups found that without controlling a bank the cost of credit for their groups remained high. All smaller local banks have consequently disappeared in Turkey. There has also been increased concentration of bank assets within specific private banks. By the early 1970s nearly 75 per cent of all private bank assets were controlled by just three Turkish banks, İş Bank, Yapı ve Kredi Bank, and Akbank (Tonge 1974, 221). The private domestic banks, however, were unable or unwilling to take control of more than 27 per cent of banking assets prior to 1970. Rather, eleven state-owned banks dominated the sector and controlled on average well over half of the banking assets, and corresponding investments underpinning industrialization (BAT 1971 (1963–2010)).

Turkey, like Mexico, displays a tendency towards the uneven spatial concentration of banking capital. The regions around İstanbul, Ankara, and İzmir emerged as clearly dominant and accounted for about three-quarters of all deposits and credits in the postwar era (BAT 1965 (1963–2010)). The remaining seven regions experienced very little growth in credits and savings. This uneven distribution of bank assets is linked to the rise of the large Turkish holding groups, which concentrated their activities and resources around these three core regions with İstanbul at the heart (Cokgezen 2000, 530). This in turn has helped to create and reproduce Turkey's historic regional disparities. The state banks more or less duplicated this pattern of uneven regional development, although one can see a modest redirection of money capital from rich to poor areas through the state banks (that is, they mildly counteracted market forces).

The postwar period saw an increase in inter-bank competition, which was characterized by the 'need of the banking sector to increase its geographical presence' (BAT 2009c, 103). Within a context of state regulated interest and exchange rates and limited access to international funds, the banks had to capture more domestic deposits to lend more interest-bearing capital. This involved building and acquiring new branches and hiring more staff. From the 1960s to the 1980s, all banks, regardless of ownership, steadily grew as bank branches increased nearly fourfold, or from about 1500 branches to about 6000 (BAT 2009c, 104). Bank employee numbers rose from about 40 000 to over 130 000. Under the protection of the 1961 Constitution, the situation of bank workers improved as civil liberties expanded during this period (Cosar 1999, 127–8). Bank labor unions formed and won improvements in working conditions, hours, salaries, vacations, fringe benefits, and some social and medical rights.

Rather than (erroneously) grafting the neoclassical assessment standards of profit-seeking private banks today onto the Turkish state banks in the postwar era, it is important to contextualize their different mandates and goals. At the time, the state banks' operations were organized around legally mandated development strategies that were not profit-oriented (duties). Even so, the Turkish state banks do not post losses, on average, in the postwar period and were only marginally less profitable than the private banks (BAT 2009c, 183). Both state and private banks earned ROA profits of around 1 per cent.[5] This rate was average for that phase of capitalism and reflects the higher fixed costs of a multi-branch competitive strategy (today the banks earn nearer to 2 per cent). The state bank ROE and ROA measures, however, declined steadily in the 1970s. With the US recession unfolding so too did the world economy enter a recessionary phase. In Turkey, the costs of financing SOEs grew and the state banks began to accumulate losses and suffer waning profitability following the 1976 Turkish crisis. In contrast to neoliberal responses, the knee-jerk reaction was not to displace the crisis onto workers by dismissing large swaths of state bank employees, and this retention of state bank employees goes some way to explaining weaker profitability. Moreover, during this period of crisis the state banks channeled money resources back into the Turkish economy in the form of government-authored subsidized duties, loans, grants, and transfers to other SOEs and sectors of the economy. At base, these duty losses represent a postwar class compromise and a means of state managers facilitating the stability of capitalist development through value transfers. This extra-market coordination internalized significant control over domestic money resources within the state form, which had the effect of moderating the balance of power between capital, labor, and state authorities. It was not until this compromise dissolved under neo-liberalism in favor of capital that the state bank duty losses became an economic problem for Turkish development.

For their part, the private domestic banks' ROE increased almost three and a half fold during the 1960s and 1970s, signaling a turn to more risky and speculative profit-making strategies (and foreshadowing the increasing volatility of the late 1970s and 1980s) (BAT 1999a). Much as with the state-owned banks, it should be noted that the actual utility of the private banks, at this time, is difficult to gauge based on isolated profitability measures. Most private banks formed part of larger holding groups wherein the banks enabled the group itself to be more profitable by providing credits to the group's productive and commercial affiliates (without this necessarily being reflected in bank profitability). This practice was encouraged by state policy and contributed to the expansion and concentration of capital within the holding groups as part of Turkey's national development strategy.

As postwar Turkish capitalism expanded, so appeared new forms of inter- and intra-class conflict. The interests of Turkish holding groups changed as they expanded in size and power. For one, the presence of İstanbul holding groups within the Turkish state clashed more and more with the interests of the Anatolian small- and medium-sized enterprises (SMEs). TOBB had served as the only official representative organization of Turkish business since 1950, and it had become dominated by rural SMEs. The large holding group fraction split from TOBB in 1971 and formed the still powerful Türk Sanayicileri ve İşadamları Derneği (TÜSİAD; Turkish Industrialist Businessmen's Association). Since then, TÜSİAD has become known as the representative body of the İstanbul bourgeoisie, dominated, as it was, by six large holding groups whose families resided there (these were Koç, Sabancı, Doğus, Tekfen, İş Bank, and Çukurova). Tensions arose not only between TÜSİAD and TOBB but also between Turkish capitalists and labor more broadly as the limits to state-led development became more apparent in the 1970s. Turkish capital refused to compromise and accept the emergence of a working-class movement enabled by the 1961 Constitution – despite Turkey's relative economic prosperity and growth. Certain elements within the state apparatus and the working class constituted a real threat to the power of Turkish capital (Yalman 2002, 37). This led to the 1971 military intervention, which failed to re-establish what Turkish capital believed ought be an unchallengeable position of power and social rule in Turkish society. The 1971 intervention nonetheless heralded the more violent 1980 coup – again supported by Turkish capitalists – that would successfully open the way for an authoritarian neoliberal revolution.

3.3   THE BREAKDOWN OF STATE-LED BANKING AND DEVELOPMENT

Mexico and Turkey's development efforts and economic (if not political) stability were internationally praised into the late 1960s and early 1970s. Industrial production had reached record levels, with significant levels of investment, strong domestic sales, and improving agricultural output. Experts predicted annual growth to continue within the 5–7 per cent range. Yet many workers, students, and peasants in Mexico and Turkey did not share this optimism and engaged in struggles that mirrored popular unrest and socialist aspirations internationally. This popular dissent presaged the nearing economic disorder.

3.3.1   Mexico

By the time incoming Mexican President Luis Echeverría Álvarez of the PRI took office on 1 December 1970 it had become clear to state authorities that underlying industrialization problems had to be dealt with and that Mexico's spectacular growth (7.5 per cent in 1970) would not continue indefinitely. Shortly thereafter matters worsened as the US recession in the early 1970s began to impinge on Mexico through a widening trade deficit, current account imbalances associated with expenditure increases, and inflationary pressures. These social and economic problems threatened PRI political legitimacy and pressured state managers to find ways of accommodating the contradictory demands of Mexican capital and labor. In response, the PRI aimed to revive the existing state-led strategy of 'national' capitalist development. This involved revitalizing state oil exploration and large-scale fertilizer production, renewing agricultural infrastructure investment, and offering social compensation in the form of food subsidies, improved urban services, and improvements in health and education. The PRI government also renewed its promotion of domestic capital goods industries and large infrastructure projects with public investment. The May 1973 Foreign Investment Law (or so-called 'Mexicanization' Law) captured the political intentions of the time.

The 1973 Mexicanization Law, while allowing foreign investment to enter in ways that could contribute to national development, privileged state-sponsored financing for Mexican capitalists to invest in fixed assets, job creation, technological development, and so on, as well as enabling the buy out of firms with majority foreign ownership. To promote Mexicanization, the 1973 law limited foreign ownership to 49 per cent control in many cases and often prohibited foreign capital from assuming ownership and control of failing firms, thus stemming foreign capital control in Mexico as intended (compare Newfarmer and Mueller 1975). The 1973 law also succeeded in supporting Mexican capitalists. However, this was not necessarily in ways that led to greater economic diversification or the overcoming of existing developmental barriers. Instead, a select group of Mexican capitalists directly benefited from state support 'by virtue of the extraordinary and unjustifiable quantities of public resources channeled to them – in the most varied ways – with a view to favoring and accelerating the process of capital concentration and centralization' (Delgado Wise and Del Pozo Mendoza 2005, 73).

There were also significant unintended consequences of the 1973 law. For their part, Mexican capitalists were unwilling to prop up failing firms and often refused to undertake investments in partnership with foreign capital (Bennett and Sharpe 1980, 180). The limits placed on foreign capital, and private domestic reticence, increased pressure on the PRI to nationalize failing private firms or risk destabilizing capitalist development in general due to social discontent. The law gave a pretext for doing so, thus relieving capital of unwanted businesses in Mexico. As a result the number of SOEs expanded to 504 by 1975 and then peaked at 1155 by 1983 (the epitome being the 1982 bank nationalization discussed below). State spending correspondingly grew from 24.8 per cent to 37.9 per cent of GDP while SOE expenditures rose from 13.4 per cent to 17.8 per cent of GDP from 1971 to 1976 (Rogozinski 1998, 43). Mexicanization *cum* socialization put extraordinary pressure on state borrowing needs, which gave rise to a burgeoning conflict between PRI officials, state elites, and Mexican financial capital because the expanding SOE sector was financed via the BdeM official reserve requirements, of which privately owned Mexican banks were the source. By the mid-1970s the state sector was absorbing about two-thirds of all private bank assets, up from about a fifth from 1947 to 1966 (FitzGerald 1985, 227). State-led development strategies had begun increasingly to creep into more and more areas of the economy, and this was unwelcomed by domestic capital.

The financial limits that now appeared had already presented themselves in the course of capitalist development and had by the late 1960s spurred changes in the Mexican financial sector, culminating in a new bank law. Prior to 1970 specialized private domestic credit institutions had been functioning at the margins of financial legislation by setting up informal relationships with larger banks where not formally permitted, gradually increasing the size and power of financial capital in society (White 1992, 58–66). Coordinated policies across separate financial institutions helped to expand profit-making opportunities and to service the needs of domestic capital by offering a single grouping of deposit, savings, finance, mortgage, and fiduciary institutions (antecedents to the universal bank). The December 1970 Credit Institutions and Auxiliary Organizations Law (the Bank Law) institutionalized change by allowing these loose relations to crystallize as formal financial associations. In return, the banks within a financial group now had to follow a coordinated policy of reciprocal guarantees among its members to cover any losses to the overall capital base of the group (CNBV 2004 (2001–10), 11). But this also put the power of financial capital on much stronger footings in Mexican society. The 1970 Bank Law – far from repressing the interests of financial capital – encouraged bank mergers by favoring already existing financial groupings over smaller banks and independent firms. Larger financial groups received preferential interest rates, easier guarantee requirements, and automatic renewal of lines of state credit (Guillén Romo 2005, 232). A period of bank capital centralization and concentration ensued. From 1970 to 1977, 225 financial intermediaries merged into 87 (OECD 1992, 170). Big Mexican financial groups became bigger and further concentrated their market power, but this did not immediately lead to greater competition and a squeeze on bank profits. Given supportive state regulations the banks remained highly profitable and stable with few bankruptcies and low systemic risk (Del Ángel-Mobarak 2005, 52–4). Average ROE profits rose to around 20 per cent in the 1960s and 1970s, which is a modest increase from the 17 per cent range in the 1940s. Non-performing loan ratios remained quite low into the 1970s.

More and more, however, US-trained and ideologically committed market-oriented state financial managers became vocal advocates of financial liberalization during this period (Babb 2005). Many wanted to diversify the financial products available to SMEs and to make investment less dependent on private commercial bank loans (compare Guillén Romo 2005, 230). The 1975 Securities Market Law formed the backbone of change and signaled Mexico's opening turn to developing forms of more market-oriented finance (Lukauskas and Minushkin 2000, 708). The 1975 law also pulled together the previously regional Guadalajara, Monterrey, and Mexico City stock markets to centralize all operations in the Mexican Stock Exchange. Then in March 1976 the SHCP altered the national banking regulations to allow the formal establishment of universal banks out of the financial groups that had been established previously. These new institutions, according to the CNBV, 'continued with the tendency to incorporate new financial services, and this time they did it through their participation in the capital of non-bank financial intermediaries: broker-age houses, leasing *financieras*, factoring companies, insurance, etc., which allowed them to be "shareholders" of these entities' (2004 (2001–10), 12; author's translation). Most barriers to the domestic consolidation of private commercial, investment, and non-bank financial operations within universal banks had been removed. In this same period the PRI enabled new patterns of capital flows in and out of Mexico to support develop-ment and capital accumulation. In 1974 legal changes granted Mexican banks the right to enter international markets by opening branches and participating in foreign institutions' capital bases. Some banks began operating internationally through their own accounts while others formed consortiums (Bustamante 2000, 261). The internationalization of Mexican banks did not entail the reciprocal *internalization* of foreign bank capital, however. In fact, foreign bank branches were prohibited from operating in Mexico with Mexican residents' money in 1978. However, the López Portillo administration (1976–82) allowed foreign portfolio investment in Mexican firms through the 'Mexico Fund' – a closed-end mutual fund that continues to be listed on the New York and London stock exchanges.

On average, Mexico's postwar state-led developmental strategy attained significant levels of capitalist industrialization. Nevertheless, state-led development had tended to produce substitutions between different types of imports rather than substitutions of imports (Guillén Romo 2005, 194–5). This was most striking in the capital goods industries, which remained dominated by foreign ownership, technology, and equipment. Long-neglected agricultural investment, speculative real estate dealings, internal migrations, and persistent class and social inequalities exacer-bated these imbalances. Attempts to break through the barriers of state-led development in the 1970s, however, demanded more money capital from an increasingly unwilling and hostile Mexican banking sector. Rather than putting bank capital into expanding the state's role in the economy, Mexican bankers pulled their money out of Mexico. Between 1976 and 1977, $5 billion in capital flight left Mexico (a massive amount when compared to the $7 billion earned with the same year's exports) (FitzGerald 1985, 227). This was the largest capital exodus since the 1938 oil nationalization – one that would be repeated from 1981 to 1982, leading to bank nationalization. The significant outflows and loss of financial capitalist confidence triggered the 1976 economic crisis, at which point the PRI government decided to float the peso. This ended over twenty years of fixed exchange rates and involved a major devaluation (Levy 2003, 165).

In effect, the crisis situation reflects the process of Mexican financial capital struggling to redefine its relationship to the Mexican state, society, and development. Market advocates argued that the crisis brought an opportunity to push back against López Portillo's state-led developmental initiatives and to further restructure the economy around efficiency and competitive imperatives (Solís 1997, 30). The post-crisis IMF intervention, mounting Mexican debt held in US banks, and the militancy of foreign and domestic bank capital bolstered the ascendancy of neoliberal 'technocrats' within the state apparatus. At base, the desired changes reflected a shift in the social relations of power within capitalism. As E.V.K. FitzGerald puts it, 'the external pressure to reduce the expansion of the Mexican state was effective to the extent that it supported particular domestic groups with a similar strategy' (1985, 229). Yet it cannot be supposed that the turn to neoliberal policies with President de la Madrid (1982–88) was a foregone conclusion at the time (Marois 2008). Two years into his presidential term López Portillo put in place his National Development Plan (1978–82), which reflected a structuralist interpretation of Mexican developmental barriers. Far from releasing 'market forces', the NDP was a clear statement of Portillo's intent to use oil revenues for continued state-led development, especially of heavy industry, using energy as a basis to build cost advantages. However, external debt mounted, trade imbalances worsened, and inflation grew as the 'petrolization' of Mexico created new speculative opportunities and economic volatility (Rodríguez Araujo 2010, 42). At the same time, the 1976 peso devaluation had increased prices on a wide range of goods and services as López Portillo held down wage increases below the rate of inflation to insulate the profitability of domestic capital. As a result, few social benefits emerged from the brief oil boom in the late 1970s. Indeed, the NDP would ultimately collapse as the US Volcker shock unleashed the 1980s debt crisis, Mexico's default, and a decisive turn towards neoliberalism.

3.3.2 Turkey

The breakdown of Turkey's postwar state-led strategy of national development shares many similarities with Mexico's but also demonstrates specific differences, particularly in bank ownership structures. From the 1960s Turkish GDP growth averaged over 6 per cent annually, domestic savings grew consistently at over 20 per cent, inflation was manageable at less than 10 per cent, and diversification away from a primarily agricultural base advanced (World Bank 1990, 549). Many experts read the 1971 Association Agreement with the European Economic Community as a sign of enduring developmental success. Indeed, the fiftieth anniversary of Turkey in 1973 was seen as a marker of Turkey's break with earlier patterns of underdevelopment. In spite of this optimism Turkey remained the poorest of all the OECD countries. Meager postwar income levels meant that Turkey's sustained growth was still insufficient to make a significant impact on the average Turk's standard of living (Öniş 2006, 243). Moreover, social and economic inequalities continued between classes, while uneven regional development persisted between east and west, rural and urban, Turk and Kurd.

Turkey's state-led developmental strategy had, like Mexico's, emphasized domestic control and state ownership of industry and finance. By the implementation of the third five-year plan from 1973 to 1977, the Turkish state controlled about a third of industrial production and was scheduled to finance 49 per cent of manufacturing investment. This put significant pressure on state and government agencies to secure recurrent sources of finance capital. Domestic price controls had also begun to create losses for the SOEs, adding more to the state deficit. The development plans, moreover, had yet to tackle foreign exchange dependence (Yalman 2002, 37–8). Aside from the limited contributions of tourism and workers' remittances, Turkish society could not generate additional foreign exchange because the scale and technological limits of domestic industry were not as developed as in Europe and other advanced industrial states. As the US economy declined and the world recession unfolded in the early 1970s, the pressure on foreign currency shortages increased and exacerbated an increasingly unstable social and economic situation. The CBT had borrowed heavily on short-term and low interest recycled foreign petrol dollars. From 1972 to 1978 Turkey's deficit to GDP ratio grew from 1.67 to 3.34 per cent (Duman et al. 2005, 123). At the same time the Turkish current account balance shifted from a surplus of 0.11 per cent of GDP to a deficit of 4.57 per cent. Foreign debt exploded from an average 1.4 per cent of gross national product (GNP) from 1972 to 1976 to 14.5 per cent from 1977 to 1980 (Boratav and Yeldan 2002, 51). This explosion in foreign debt was punctuated by the 1976 foreign exchange crisis.

It is in this context of expanding markets, mounting debt burdens, and structural instability that changes in bank ownership structures began to occur. The dominance of Turkey's state-owned banks waned throughout the 1970s while that of private domestic banks increased. State bank control fell from nearly 65 per cent of assets in the 1960s to just over 40 per cent by the late 1970s. Private bank control, by contrast, went from about 27 per cent to just over 42 per cent (BAT 1999a). Foreign banks continued to play a relatively minor role, controlling only 2.5 per cent of bank assets. The shift to greater private domestic control corresponds to a new willingness of Turkish capital to assume larger financial risks and of state authorities to relinquish control over the allocation of money and credit. The large family-based holding groups, which had become the most powerful owners of banks, benefited most. By the 1980s four large holding groups, Sabancı, Doğus, İş Bank, and Çukurova, owned most private banks and together controlled about a third of all domestic deposits and credits (Cokgezen 2000, 530). Bank ownership carried on conferring important competitive advantages on the controlling group (Gültekin-Karakaş 2008). Corporate managers could direct the collective money savings of Turkish society into their private group's wider profit-oriented operations – often to the exclusion of rival Turkish firms. This motivated holding groups to draw in as many banks as possible. Turkish state authorities supported this process by, for example, restricting the number of new bank licenses and by reserving any new licenses granted for Turkish capital alone. The political intention was to augment domestic credit supplies under private domestic bank control. Despite the instability of the 1970s the Turkish private banks remained profitable following the 1976 crisis averaging 0.9 per cent ROA and 34.7 per cent ROE profits from 1976 to 1980 (BAT 1999a). The relatively high ROE profit measure suggests the private banks were engaged in increasingly leveraged activities in support of the wider holding groups. Nonetheless, without state and society addressing the fundamental power imbalances between capital and labor in Turkey the government's efforts to sustain state-led capitalist development were bound to hit insuperable barriers. In 1978 the Turkish government defaulted on interest payments and in June 1979 the IMF intervened with a bailout package attached to a series of market-oriented structural reforms. The US Volcker shock only intensified a social context of political and economic disorder in Turkey, which would lead to the 1980 military takeover and neoliberal restructuring.

3.3.3 The US Volcker Shock

The 1979 to 1982 US Volcker shock was the death knell of state-led strategies of banking and development. Mexico and Turkey exist within the context of an expanding world market and by the late 1960s and 1970s doubts surfaced, particularly in the US, over America's Keynesian expansionary policies, which had been giving rise to escalating inflation, downward pressure on profits, collapsing investment, and increasing unemployment (Brenner 1998). These problems became global as a result of the growing US commercial deficit, President Nixon's decision to end the fixed gold-dollar standard in 1971, and the 1973 oil crisis with its associated rise in circulating petrodollars and mounting peripheral country debts. At the same time large corporations based in the advanced capitalisms internationalized as they sought to regain falling profit levels by going abroad (Strange 1997a [1986]). Unemployment rose and wages fell in the US and Western Europe, as well as in the periphery (Kapstein 2000, 365). The 'stagflation' that occurred in the 1970s resulted from a *balance* of class forces domestically and internationally wherein workers had effectively demanded better wages and conditions to their benefit, not that of capital (Clarke 1988b, 86). The Volcker shock, resolutions to the 1980s debt crisis, and IFI sponsored structural adjustment programs all aimed at reversing workers' gains. The 1980s thus opened a new phase of market-oriented neoliberal accumulation premised on defeating organized labor's collective capacity and on supporting the ascendancy of capital. While the global details of this shift cannot be explored here (each case is explored in later chapters), the structural changes ought to be understood as the sum total of a wide range of political, economic, and social processes of internationalization with material, institutional, spatial, and discursive dynamics that take place both at a global level and from within individual nation states (Cerny 1999; Panitch 1994; Beaud 2001; Marois 2011a).

The Volcker shock was an especially decisive catalyst to the forcefulness with which neoliberal restructuring and the power of financial capital took root in peripheral societies because of the debt crisis it sparked. Notably, Paul Volcker, the US Federal Reserve Chair, caused US interest rates to skyrocket to help 'tame' inflation and restore US competitiveness. One result was further recession-induced high unemployment in the US and abroad. Another was a dramatic spike in interest rates globally, which also encouraged firms to channel profits into financial institutions and accumulation, bolstering the material force of financial capital. Then there were the peripheral countries' debt crises. The interest rates on peripheral countries' petrol dollar loans exploded from 4 or 5 per cent to near 20 per cent. Their societies' inability to pay back the loans and subsequent defaults led to the mostly US banks being rescued via US Treasury 'aid' packages and a revitalized IMF, which has since helped to sustain debt-led and financially-disciplined growth strategies internationally. Since this time private loans and development assistance have been replacing official bilateral debt as the main source of development finance in many middle-income developing countries. The US Federal Reserve, for its part, has assumed leadership for managing an anti-inflationary interest rate for a world market based on the dollar. This in turn led to the political 'triumph of central banking' of a particularly American hue, which has privileged the needs of financial capital (Panitch and Gindin 2004; Sarai 2009). At the same time the 1980s crisis allowed global overproduction to be liquidated and new class compromises crafted (read: the defeat of labor) thus paving the way for renewed capital accumulation and the economic boom of the mid-1980s under the hegemony of the US (Clarke 1988b; Bonefeld 1999).

In these ways the Volcker shock facilitated the 'debt crisis as opportunity', as so succinctly put by the critical economist James Cypher (1989). Neoliberal structural adjustment and new financial imperatives have risen in tandem with the new class-based accumulation strategies designed simultaneously to reconstitute US power and the power of capital globally (Gowan 1999; Patomäki 2001; Soederberg 2001). On consecutive waves of state-authored liberalization measures financial capital has rushed to peripheral areas marked by the highest profits and least protection for capital flows. The result has been more intense inter-state and inter-firm competition of a type that brings more aggressive forms of financial speculation and economic volatility while increasing the structural power of financial capital (Strange 1997a [1986] and 1998; Glyn 2006). The US government has been a major protagonist of liberalization measures in ways meant to retrench US power, the crux of which lay in seigniorage – the privilege of not being held to the same balance of payments constraints that other states incur due to America's ability to swing the price of the dollar under the pure dollar standard (Gowan 1999, 24–5). Peter Gowan refers to this as the 'Dollar-Wall Street Regime' (DWSR) wherein the centrality of the US dollar directs people towards Wall Street for finance and the strength of Wall Street as a financial center reinforces the dollar as an international currency. Integral to its reconstituted hegemony the DWSR allows the US, as the dominant power, to make up many of its own rules by deciding the price of the dollar and, therefore, to have overwhelming influence on the evolving dynamics of international financial relations. Within the context of this global shift towards neoliberal strategies of development and the reconstitution of US power, the ways in which peripheral societies such as Mexico and Turkey act and react can vary significantly in detail while they remain party and subject to the generalizing thrust of neoliberalism.

3.4   CONCLUSION

The twentieth century witnessed a remarkable transformation of Mexican and Turkish society. From peripheral countries in which wage labor, money, banking, and even the state apparatus had relatively marginal roles in most people's day to day lives, these social relationships became institutionalized as capitalist social relations and assumed an undeniably important influence over everyone's lives and their society's developmental trajectories by the late 1970s. Moreover, while relatively insulated by state-led strategies of development, Mexico and Turkey had also integrated into the world market, and this would have important consequences as postwar developmental strategies began to break down in the lead up to the Volcker shock. The universalization of capitalist social relations and the growing influence of money and financial capital, nevertheless, were shaped by the particularities of each society's already-existing political, economic, and social relations. In Turkey, the state banks were central to the nature of state–bank–labor relations in national development whereas in Mexico private domestic bankers held far greater significance. These differences, too, would influence the shape of neoliberal transformation to come.

It is important not to read the relative stability and growth seen during the postwar period of state-led development and finance as a glorification or vindication of the so-called strong or developmental state thesis. Mexico and Turkey's postwar capitalist development experiences were premised on highly exploitative productive, political, and social relations that disproportionately benefited wealthy family groups, even if organized labor made relative distributional gains. Too often developmental state approaches overlook this dark side of capitalist social relations by accepting that development can, perhaps even should, take shape out of authoritarian, anti-democratic, and repressive regimes seeking to solidify capital–labor relations (see Chang 2009 for a critique of the developmental state). I find this position morally untenable, even if such relations might yield aggregate growth. Moreover, such positions sidestep the ways in which state-led development and the increasing importance of financial capital established the conditions making possible the post-1980s turn to neoliberalism.

NOTES

1. This bank later became Banca Serfin and then the now Spanish-owned Santander Serfin.
2. This bank later became Mexican owned Banamex and then US owned Citibank-Banamex.
3. Even with the establishment of state banks, the embryonic Turkish financial system could not immediately do away with foreign dependence and foreign banks continued to service domestic commercial capital requirements into the mid-1940s. Unlike in Mexico, foreign banks were never banned in the postwar period and did not become a major factor again until after the 2001 banking crisis (Chapter 7).
4. In the postwar period foreign banks maintained a relatively minor presence in Turkish banking, controlling only between 2 and 4 per cent of all banking assets. These British,

Italian, Dutch, American, French, Libyan, and Kuwaiti sources of foreign bank capital were largely geared to financing export markets.

5. Return on assets is a measure of how much profit a firm earns relative to the total money value of its assets ((ROA) = (Annual Net Income/Total Assets)). Assets include cash reserves, accounts receivables, property, equipment, and so on. Return on equity measures how profitably a firm's management employs investors' money ((ROE) = (Annual Net Income/Average Shareholders' Equity)). Both are ratios that measure a firm's capacity to profit from investments. The key difference involves debt. If a firm has no debt, ROE will be the same as ROA. If ROA shows a positive return and debt levels are reasonable, a strong ROE is a sign that firm management is generating positive returns from shareholders' investments. But if the ROA is low and/or the firm is carrying a lot of debt, a high ROE may give a false impression that the firm is on good footing. In other words, the ROA is the fundamental measure of a firm's core situation, while ROE shows what happens when management leverages the firm's fundamentals by taking on debt. If ROA is falling and ROE increasing, then a firm is likely headed for crisis.

4. Neoliberal idealism, crisis, and banking in Mexico's state-led structural transformation, 1982–94

By the 1980s the Mexican state apparatus had grown to an unprecedented size supported by an equally unprecedented bank-based and predominantly private Mexican-owned financial system. State-led strategies of development, however, had begun to absorb significant financial resources, organized labor had grown stronger, and Mexican capital wanted more access to areas of the economy previously developed and owned by the state apparatus. This led to social, economic, and political instability and the weakening of Mexico's postwar class compromises. The breaking point came with the 1979–82 US-based Volcker shock, which sent global interest rates through the roof instigating the 1980s debt crises in the periphery and the rollout of neoliberal structural adjustment programs. What followed in Mexico and elsewhere left the once predominant state-led strategies of development in ruins and a state apparatus restructured towards facilitating capital accumulation.[1]

The transition to neoliberalism in Mexico, however, should not be interpreted just as a top-down process of imposed structural adjustment that led to the withering away of the once strong state apparatus. Rather, I argue that advocates of neoliberalism within the Mexican state and society actively pursued changes that led to the restructuring and strengthening of the state's capacity to support capital accumulation. This occurred in contradictory ways. Notably, while intended by the outgoing López Portillo administration to revive state-led capitalism amidst the 1982 debt crisis, the 1982 bank nationalization decree unintentionally handed the incoming Miguel de la Madrid administration a powerful financial tool with which to take charge of neoliberal state and market restructuring. This chapter explores this by first examining bank nationalization and Mexico's state-authored transformation of the state and banks. Section 4.2 then looks at the process of bank privatization and the structural transformation in bank ownership. The final section examines how Mexico's attempt to approximate the ideals of neoliberalism led to the 1994 crisis. This is followed by a brief conclusion.

4.1 THE 1982 DEBT CRISIS, BANK NATIONALIZATION, AND NEOLIBERAL TRANSFORMATION

At the height of the 1980s debt crisis in Mexico the López Portillo PRI administration was not yet committed to the same neoliberal structural adjustment programs enforced under the military rule of the likes of General Pinochet in Chile or General Evren in Turkey. Rather, Portillo attempted to revive Mexico's state-led strategy of development – the underlying logic of which led to the 1982 bank nationalization decision in response to the instability caused by 1982 debt crisis in Mexico. The debt crisis came as a result of the Volcker shock, which made it nearly impossible for the public and private sectors to service their foreign debts (Dussell Peters 2000, 47–8).

By the second half of 1981, in the lead up to crisis, the Mexican economy was suffering from high inflation and dependency on petrol income amidst falling world market oil prices. Public debt expanded to compensate both for lost oil revenues and for the earlier waves of 'Mexicanization' (see Chapter 3). Those with money in Mexico began to lose faith in the future value of their peso resources sparking a massive conversion of pesos into US dollars, which drained Mexico's international reserves. Nearly half of the $60 billion in public debt accumulated prior to 1982 went to financing capital flight (Buffie 1989, 155). External financial capital also began to lose faith in Mexico, and suspended credits, making it impossible for the Banco de México (BdeM) to respond to demands for foreign exchange. No matter how profitable it was to hold pesos under rising domestic interest rates the demand for dollars was insatiable. At one point international reserves were only capable of covering three weeks of imports. The PRI government had seemingly lost all capacity to stabilize the economy. Unemployment had climbed to nearly 10 per cent and real wages began to fall. In late August 1982 Finance Minister Jesus Silva-Herzog announced that Mexico could no longer service its largely US-owned foreign debt and requested a 90-day moratorium during which Mexico would make interest-only payments. Then on 1 September 1982 President López Portillo erected a system of exchange controls to stem the outflow of capital. Most famously, he nationalized the Mexican-owned commercial banks (also see White 1992).

According to Carlos Tello, who acted as an architect of the nationalization decree while serving as the governor of the BdeM, in the months preceding the bank nationalization decree Portillo had asked key advisors to present possible options for ending the problem of the peso and its value relative to the US dollar (Tello 1984). Four orthodox economic policy options were offered: to pursue a new and stronger peso devaluation; to allow the value of the peso to freely float; to impose exchange controls; and to allow the February 1982 devaluation more time to work. However, a so-called 'fifth option', bank nationalization, emerged as that chosen by Portillo. At the time, Portillo had asked a small inner working group to prepare a roadmap for bank nationalization. The working group suggested five conditions under which bank nationalization should take place, and these were subsequently followed.

First, for nationalization to work the BdeM's administrative council had to be revamped because it was dominated by Mexican bankers who were 'judge and jury' of the Mexican financial system (Tello 1984, 11). Since the mid-1920s state elites had incorporated Mexican bankers directly into the BdeM administrative council thus institutionally sharing the power to determine monetary and financial state policy (Cardero 1984, 22). Bank nationalization involved altering pre-existing institutionalized state to bank relationships of power. Second, the government instituted state controls over capital flight to help manage the possibility of large-scale bank withdrawals. In practice, the controls proved somewhat ineffectual. Third, the working group recognized the need to manage a possible backlash from Mexican industrial capital, which the government mitigated through a series of financial and exchange rate measures. Fourth, the working group identified the need to woo bank workers. In consequence, the government granted them the right to unionize, which led to the formation of bank worker unions (see Bouzas Ortíz 2003). Finally, the only foreign bank, the US owned Citibank, had to be left alone in order to avoid any possible repercussions from the US government. This is not necessarily unique to Mexico, as other major foreign banks have also been left alone where bank nationalizations have occurred elsewhere in the periphery (Maxfield 1992).

Portillo's bank nationalization decision represented a pragmatic attempt to rescue capitalism in Mexico. Because the banks had reached a point of technical bankruptcy there was enormous pressure on government elites to stabilize the private banking sector or risk Mexican capitalism collapsing into itself. At the same time bank nationalization reassured US financial capital that their loans would be repaid whatever the social cost to Mexican society. If the Mexican state owned the foreign debt obligations, then debt repayment was effectively guaranteed backed, as it was, by Mexican society and the government's sovereign promise to pay. In national discourse, however, Portillo justified the bank nationalization decree as a defense of the Mexican Revolution against a powerful and corrupt banking elite. This carried significant resonance among the poor and destitute of Mexico and, much to Portillo's surprise, the Zócalo in

Mexico City filled with popular supporters showing solidarity against what they believed to be a long-held banking oligarchy.

Having anticipated a more favorable resolution to the debt crisis than nationalization, the now ex-bankers but still powerful Mexican capitalists reacted with alarm. The post-revolutionary social pact between national capitalists and the Mexican state had suffered a fracture at the expense of Mexican bankers (Ramírez 1994, 21). In the three-month political lag between the outgoing Portillo administration and the incoming de la Madrid administration (December 1982) the bankers and others who opposed nationalization argued that the decision was an abuse of the Mexican presidency. Yet their opposition was more deeply rooted. As Martin Hart-Landsberg writes, '[t]he fact that the state was willing and able to pursue stabilization at the expense of private property rights intensified business determination to pursue a new economic strategy based on neoliberal principles' (2002, 17). Nationalization had hardened Mexican capital's resolve to break with postwar state-led strategies of development.

The continued instability of the economy did not help matters for Portillo as his hopes for an unorthodox 'developmentalist' exit to the crisis never materialized. As Friedrich Engels once reminded us, while individual and collective agents are endowed with consciousness and tend to act deliberately towards goals, their actions and decisions may well entail unintended consequences (Engels 1959 [1888], 230). When President de la Madrid took office his administration made an abrupt about-face to actively bring about the market-oriented transformation of Mexican state, capital, and labor relations. According to Judith Teichman, this involved immediate structural stabilization, liberalization, and austerity measures along with a longer-term commitment to overall neoliberal restructuring (1992, 91).

The main policy vehicle for this restructuring was de la Madrid's Programa Inmediato de Reordenación Económica (PIRE; Immediate Program of Economic Reorganization) – a structural adjustment program sponsored by the IMF to ostensibly restore economic and financial stability. The PIRE called for severe public sector austerity; restrictive credit polices; the devaluation of the real exchange rate; liberalization of subsidized prices; trade liberalization; General Agreement on Trade and Tariffs (GATT) membership; the internalization of foreign capital; export promotion through maquiladoras; and the dramatic reduction of state-owned enterprise (SOE) numbers by 40 per cent. That is, the PIRE reflected a more or less standard Washington consensus-like package of desired changes. The subsequent public expenditure cutbacks created dramatic results, especially within SOE spending. The primary fiscal balance, excluding interest payments, improved from a 5 per cent deficit in 1983 to a 5 per cent surplus by 1987 – 80 per cent of which derived from reduced state expenditures (Ortiz Martínez 1993, 257). Market reformers also celebrated the 1985 entry of Mexico into GATT as the formal end to state-led development in Mexico and as the beginning of an export-oriented industrialization (EOI) strategy. All in all, the changes meant a decisive turn towards new market imperatives characterized by reduced benefits for workers and peasants and greater state support for capital.

High inflation and interest rates, however, thwarted state elites' austerity efforts as domestic imbalances grew alongside the collapse in oil prices, the shortage of foreign credit extended to Mexico, and the transfer of domestic resources abroad through debt service. These problems culminated in the 1987 Mexican stock market crash, itself tied to the October 1987 US stock market crash. According to Ministry of Finance and Public Credit (SHCP) manager Guillermo Ortiz Martínez (1993), the crisis reversed many of the austerity-induced gains for Mexican capital and the state. The fiscal deficit grew to over 16 per cent of GDP, inflation increased to nearly 160 per cent, and capital flight resumed.

The US government, however, had a deep interest in safeguarding the overall integrity of the capitalist world market, which instability in Mexico and elsewhere was threatening (see Glyn 2006; Duménil and Lévy 2011). To help restore global stability US state authorities crafted the 1985 Baker Plan and 1989 Brady Plan to help bridge the global transition to neoliberalism by re-organizing the early 1980s debt hangover and to streamline future debt discipline. The 1985 plan involved high-level debt restructuring efforts by the IMF and World Bank to encourage surplus countries (like Japan) to lend more to peripheral debtor countries (like Mexico and other Latin American countries) while pressuring debtors to re-orient domestic production towards exports (in order to earn the foreign currency required to pay back the loans). In 1987 through a myriad of private and official lenders' rescheduling agreements, Mexico received nearly $13 billion in new credits. The Brady Plan, nevertheless, proved incapable of resolving the instability and growth problems of the 1980s 'lost decade'. The US subsequently unveiled the 1989 Brady Plan to provide further long-term debt restructuring, conditional on governments implementing more market-oriented restructuring. Mexico's $97 billion in debt became the test case for the new Brady Plan's capacity to encourage foreign capital inflows, the repatriation of Mexican capital, a decline in domestic interest rates, and to cultivate export-oriented growth strategies. While there appears to be no evident relationship between the debt restructuring and renewed growth,[2] both the Baker and Brady plans helped to underwrite and legitimize the globally volatile transition to neoliberal strategies of development to the benefit of financial capital. This, however, came about as a result of the state managing the debts on behalf of financial capital in order to avoid a break in neoliberalism. Not until 2003 did Mexico retire its Brady bonds.

About this time PRI President Carlos Salinas de Gortari (1988–94) assumed power through what most believe were fraudulent elections (Salinas had gained a slim majority during a period when the vote counting system crashed). His illegitimately gained political project subsequently led to the intensification of neoliberal restructuring (Morton 2003). Salinas's National Development Plan (NDP; 1989–94) outlined specific market-oriented policy goals, which included increased economic efficiency, mini-mized public expenditures, and SOE privatization, adding that Mexico must achieve stability and modernization (BdeM 1991 (1990–2006), 163). Yet Salinas's crowning achievement, discussed below, would be the signing of the North American Free Trade Agreement (NAFTA) with Canada and the US. Consistent with the underlying tenets of neoclassical economics and neoliberal ideology, Salinas's NDP did not aim at crafting equitable growth for all Mexicans. Rather, Salinas premised Mexico's neoliberal developmental strategy on increasing the already unequal rela-tions of power between Mexican workers and capital (be it domestic or foreign) to the benefit of capital (see Kus and Ozel 2010). For example, the government undertook efforts to promote and intensify maquiladora production in the north. This form of export-oriented production – itself a strategy meant to facilitate the repayment of foreign debt – demands a surplus of cheap Mexican labor, which all subsequent governments have promoted as one of Mexico's main competitive advantages (Soederberg 2002). Maquiladora production also militates against effective labor unions as the owners massively exploit the labor market base (women, in particular) (Guillén Romo 2005, 207). Indeed, the comparative advantage of Mexican capitalists and their ability to compete internationally in trad-able goods depends on cheap labor, which the PRI facilitated via govern-ment authored wage freezes below the rate of inflation (Ramírez 1994, 26; Cypher 2001, 29).

In response, organized labor engaged in collective resistance and threatened a general strike, which won some modest wage recovery by the late 1980s (Álvarez Béjar and Mendoza Pichardo 1993, 34). Yet the policy guidelines for continued neoliberal transformation became formal-ized in state-authored capital–labor–campesino (peasant) compromises. The first of these involved the December 1987 to November 1988 Pacto de Solidaridad Económica (PSE; Pact of Economic Solidarity), which was later reworked as the Pacto para la Estabilidad y el Crecimiento Económico (PECE; Pact for Stability and Economic Growth) in December 1988. In discourse, the compromises involved battling against inflation and strengthening capital–labor relations. In practice, organized Mexican labor (perhaps more rightly said its leadership) had subordinated its collective interests to those of capital in Mexico. President of the Congreso de Trabajo (Labour Congress), Lorenzo Duarte, argued that the structural changes being undertaken were necessary and even noble. In essence, however, government elites and state managers along with domestic and foreign capital had already formed a common front over how to restore Mexican competitiveness and profitability – intensified world market competition, they argued, left no other option but to crack down on the cost of labor. The 'pacts' institutionalized these ideas, which in turn subordinated all social forces to the anti-inflationary neoliberal restructuring program (Álvarez Béjar and Mendoza Pichardo 1993, 35). Add to this the restructuring of the privatized SOEs and associated layoffs, and the weakened bargaining position of Mexican labor unions becomes apparent. Yet it was not only the pushing of SOEs and state workers into the private sector that changed state–capital–labor relationships of power in Mexico. So too did Mexico's state-led financial transformation, which involved the operational restructuring of the nationalized banks.

4.1.1 State-Authored Financial Transformation

The 1982 bank nationalization unintentionally facilitated neoliberal transformation in Mexico by increasing the power of state managers to shape society. Why? Prior to the 1980s the Mexican-owned banks had been relatively profitable and stable. What is more, those who owned banks could channel money capital into their associated commercial, manufacturing, and industrial affiliates in such a way as to escape regulation and to boost their group's power (Del Ángel-Mobarak 2005, 46). State regulation had also restricted foreign bank competition. Any attempt to approximate neoliberal strategies of development in Mexico (as it has everywhere) would challenge these institutionalized relationships. If not exercising outright resistance, the bankers undoubtedly would have struggled to shape neoliberal changes to their benefit. The 1982 bank nationalization unintentionally, but effectively, eliminated the need for government and state elites to negotiate with the Mexican bankers over neoliberal and financial liberalization processes while simultaneously gaining complete control over the financial system. At the time the Mexican banks controlled about 53 per cent of all bank assets and the state development banks about 28 per cent (Guillén Romo 2005, 231). Bank nationalization therefore brought about 80 per cent of all domestic banking sector assets under the power of Mexican state elites, and the PRI was unafraid to exercise this to restructure the state and banks around market-oriented imperatives.

The PRI began by making some regulatory changes to support neoliberal restructuring. From 1982 to 1987 the BdeM reserve requirements were reduced from 50 per cent to 10 per cent of bank savings (Guillén Romo 2005, 233–4). However, this did not necessarily free up bank resources for domestic re-investment and private sector loan making. Rather, state-mandated obligatory investment ratios rose from 25 per cent to 65 per cent of bank savings and up to 45 per cent of this ratio could be directed towards loans for SOEs and the federal government. In other words, in a context where leadership refused to increase the contribution of capital to national development through such tools as taxation, the nationalized banks became an important source of financing public expenditures (like oil investment) and foreign debt servicing in ways that smoothed neoliberal transition. State managers also set new interest rate and credit policies that helped the nationalized banks to increase profits and build up reserves with the view to later privatization (OECD 1992, 175). The growing tendency to profit from servicing state debts would become an enduring and lucrative source of revenue for the banks, be they Mexican or foreign. State authorities did not, by contrast, restructure the banks to finance national developmental priorities.

The PRI then instigated a process of rationalizing the nationalized banks according to market-oriented tenets. This first meant immediately liquidating and closing nine banks by 1983.[3] This left 49 nationalized banks. Over the next three years, state managers centralized the operations and capital of these 49 into 18 core banks. The process was complex and uneven, but focusing on a few examples will help to illustrate (I draw on the examples of Banamex, Serfín, and Banorte here and throughout the Mexican case). In 1982, Banamex was, as it still is, one of the largest banks in Mexico. State managers did not fold Banamex's operations into any other banks. Yet with Serfín, another large bank, state managers pushed many different banks into it and at different times. By contrast, the medium-sized Banorte was subjected to only one merger. The bank mergers formed part of the SHCP strategy to create a more uniform and market-oriented sector. Overall, the strategy anticipated six national banks to finance large public and private domestic investment projects as well as to support and develop external commercial operations, seven multiregional banks to direct credit activities towards areas of concentrated economic activity, and five single region or local banks to support economic decentralization and channel resources to local market and client needs. The SHCP designated Banamex and Serfín to operate at the national level and Banorte at a regional level. It is important to highlight the remarkable speed with which state managers were able to undertake sector-wide restructuring. Such extensive and rapid market-oriented rationalizations would have been, in all likelihood, impossible without the state owning the banks (for example, Turkey's process was much longer and arduous). Then, to help internalize a market-oriented logic within the nationalized banks, the de la Madrid administration re-established some private share ownership. In 1985 the PRI amended the Bank Law to create a new set of state bank ownership shares, which the PRI began to sell in early 1987 as part of a recapitalization strategy (OECD 1992, 175). All but three of the eighteen nationalized banks acquired some non-voting private share participation by 1990. However, Mexican capitalists were not as interested in acquiring non-voting shares as they were in regaining owner-ship and control of the now larger, restructured, and rationalized banks.

While enabling banking sector reorganization, bank nationalization also allowed the PRI to mobilize the banks as agents of SOE privatiza-tion and, by extension, of neoliberal state restructuring in ways otherwise unlikely or impossible. The de la Madrid administration framed privati-zation, at first blush, as a defense of the 1917 Constitution. According to Jacques Rogozinski, head of Mexico's Office of Privatization from 1989 to 1993, the public resources liberated by privatization would permit the government to 'focus on activities of true strategic importance to national development' while boosting economic efficiency (1998, 50). With this aim the de la Madrid NDP proposed privatization in two phases. The first phase was intended to develop the state's institutional capacity to privatize and to win public acceptance and confidence and was aimed at privatiz-ing the smallest SOEs first. The second phase was to begin in 1986 and target larger SOEs (but would be pursued most forcefully by the Salinas administration after 1988). The results were spectacular: the number of SOEs fell from 1155 in 1982 to 737 in 1986 to 280 in 1990 (OECD 1992, 89). As a reflection of the smaller size and importance of the initial SOE sell-offs, first phase revenues reached only about $2 billion from 1984 to 1989 (SHCP 1994). What is important, though, is that the relationship of power between the state, labor, and capital had begun to change signifi-cantly. The PRI had removed the state apparatus and state workers from many areas of productive capacity, including such things as bottled water, textiles, cement, automobiles, and pharmaceuticals, and transferred them into the private sector. The process also restructured the Mexican state by amputating some of its productive capacity and associated commitments to state workers.

The nationalized banks, ironically perhaps, served as powerful agents of Mexico's privatization process. Once the government and state managers identified an SOE for sale, the SOE was reassigned to the SHCP, which then assigned a nationalized bank as the sale agent (Rogozinski 1998, 88; SHCP 1994, 16). The agent banks then developed privatization strategies together with the Office for Privatization, helped to analyze bids, and made recommendations on the offers while profiting from the privatization commissions. Rogozinski underscores that the agent banks gained experience with each sale, which improved institutional learning and expertise thereby making it possible to privatize more Mexican SOEs more rapidly (1998, 91–2). World Bank experts have praised the nationalized bank-led Mexican privatization model as one of the most effective techniques available (Guislain 1997, 163). Bank nationalization thus enhanced the government and state's capacity to effect neoliberal restructuring while the nationalized banks and bank workers internalized market imperatives in practice.

The 1982 bank nationalization also had the unintended effect of encouraging wider financial transformation in Mexico. The original bank nationalization decree had brought with it an unexpected range of bank-affiliated non-bank financial holdings, which included insurance, bond and guarantee, leasing, and brokerage institutions (Tello 1984, 17; Stallings 2006, 186). It is important to recall that at the time of nationalization, in both practical and political terms, the immediate re-sale of the banks was impossible. However, this was not the case with the unexpectedly acquired non-bank financial holdings. Mexican capitalists wanted to regain access to the financial sector and the de la Madrid government wanted to rid itself of whatever holdings it could. This led de la Madrid to support a parallel, more market-based financial system that could compete with the nationalized banks. The interests of Mexican capital and de la Madrid coincided in 1984 when new legislation authorized the sell-off of the non-bank financial holdings, sparking the drive for a parallel private financial system. The PRI then set the nationalized banks and private market finance into direct competition in an increasingly open financial system. Large Mexican firms resisted financing through the banks and turned towards the private financial sector. As a result brokerage house capitalization increased from 6 to 30 billion pesos from 1982 to 1989 while that of the banks fell from 94 to 70 billion (OECD 1992, 172). While bank credit to the private sector had reached 19.5 per cent of GDP in 1972, by 1988 it had fallen to 7.2 per cent (Unal and Navarro 1999, 63). The stock market also expanded from 2.83 per cent of GDP in 1982 to 10.66 per cent in 1987 (Guillén Romo 2005, 235). Stock market capitalization would reach its highest level ever in 1993 at 50 per cent of GDP (Stallings 2006, 191). Nonetheless, the profitability of the nationalized banks improved despite government policy maintaining more restrictions over the activities of the nationalized banks than the newly emerging non-bank financial institutions.

To support the rise of financial capital in Mexico the de la Madrid administration began redirecting some official borrowing from the nationalized banks to the capital markets via short-term state debt bonds, the Certificados de la Tesorería (CETES; Treasury Certificates), which encouraged disintermediation and parallel financial market growth. This transformation had been in play since the 1976 crisis when the Portillo government began issuing petrobonds and CETES to help manage mounting state debts. The CETES became increasingly important because they formed a tradable debt instrument and soon became the most important reference rate in the financial system (OECD 1992, 171). This new form of fictitious capital, which as CETES involved a flow of money capital advanced against state revenues, helped state managers conduct monetary policy through open market operations. Yet the recycling of Mexican public debt obligations also provided a very profitable and secure investment for embryonic private financial capital entailing significant transfers of value. The growing payment of interest on state bonds thus contributed to the process of class reformation around privileging financial imperatives in society. Financial capital increasingly profits from the interest on state bonds, which involves the peasantry, popular, and working classes transferring more of their tax payments through the state apparatus to financial capital.

By the end of the 1980s and with the liberalization of capital accounts in 1989, all signs pointed to the end of the nationalized banks. A state-owned banking sector had simply become inconsistent with the prevailing market-oriented strategy of development, even though nationalization had facilitated neoliberal restructuring thus far. The stage was set for a structural shift back to private bank ownership in Mexico.

4.2   THE PRIVATIZATION OF MEXICO'S NATIONALIZED BANKS

As far as President Salinas was concerned there were no developmental options besides neoliberal ones, to which he was politically committed. The Salinas administration was of course not alone in this commitment. Following the Volcker shock the IFIs, foreign capital, the US government, and domestic capital had all lined up in favor of promoting private ownership and the liberalization of finance. State-owned banks simply did not cohere with this social logic and because, moreover, practically all the banks in Mexico were owned and controlled by the Mexican state this made for intense privatization advocacy at home and abroad. Unlike in other emerging capitalisms, such as Turkey, where bank ownership had been historically more mixed, capitalists in Mexico could not own a bank even if they wanted to. To rectify this contradiction Salinas unilaterally initiated and followed through with bank privatization via a series of presidential decrees in May, July, and September of 1990.

The first of Salinas's presidential decrees came in May 1990 and it officially announced bank privatization. This involved amending Articles 28 and 123 of the Mexican Constitution to permit the full private ownership of commercial banks. Salinas's ruling PRI government together with SHCP managers had made this decision behind closed doors while garnering political support from the Partido Acción Nacional (PAN; National Action Party). Following the announcement, members of the more leftist Partido de la Revolución Democrática (PRD; Party of the Democratic Revolution) put up some opposition in congress but without effect. Helping to legitimize the privatization decree the BdeM adopted a strictly neoliberal logic, arguing that bank privatization was necessary to reorganize the state apparatus around basic needs provisioning, that privatization would stimulate access to banking services, and that the context had changed since 1982 (1991 (1990–2006), 47). Nonetheless, Salinas had contradicted the very reasons given by Portillo in favor of bank nationalization. As such, the case for 'why' privatize still had to be legitimized publicly, especially since the decision itself had never been opened to democratic debate.

In the public discourse five recurrent themes emerged that framed the seeming benefits of bank privatization for Mexican society.[4] The first theme, and the most forceful, emphasized the need for economic stabilization. President Salinas set the tone by claiming that Mexico's prosperity and move towards democracy depended on market deregulation, foreign investment, liberalization, and privatization. SHCP Minister Pedro Aspe followed up by arguing that bank privatization would consolidate the market-oriented changes taken since 1982 and provide the linchpin to Mexican economic stability. Jaime Corredor Esnaola, President of the Asociación de Bancos de México (ABM; Banks' Association of Mexico), also supported privatization as an economic stabilization measure capable of ending 'statist' processes. In this line of thinking bank privatization had to occur so as to ensure the long-term health of the public and private sector. A second theme targeted questions of public debt management, and followed closely from the first. SHCP managers repeatedly underscored that bank privatization receipts would help reduce internal public debt and improve Mexico's debt to GDP ratio, which the PRI linked to the 1989 to 1991 PECE process. The argument rested on an anticipated $4 billion in one-time revenue from bank privatization. Without bank privatization helping to reduce internal debt reduction, the PRI argued that the PECE would be stillborn since public debt would absorb domestic resources and squeeze out economic growth to the detriment of all Mexicans. The ABM added that bank privatization would lower domestic interest rates and, as a result, save the state budget about 9 billion pesos/year. For advocates, the idea of bank privatization translated into a societal windfall of available state resources. A third legitimizing theme involved ideas of financial modernization. The SHCP presented this in unambiguous terms as removing the state's presence from the economy. Private bank ownership would encourage domestic savings, expand public access to financial services, more effectively channel financial resources, help internationalize Mexican banks, and spark financial competition, creating a true financial culture from micro-saver to large investor. Privatization would also lead to a more universal financial system with fewer divisions between banking groups and other market-based financial services. Without privatization Mexican finances would become archaic. A fourth theme focused on the so-called 'democratization' of bank capital. In this discourse privatization heralded the rise of financial liberty in contrast to the postwar period of financial repression. According to the SHCP democratization meant the breaking up of bank ownership widely enough to avoid any single controlling group. It also meant crafting new institutional barriers against any possible future political interference, that is, so-called de-politicization. Finally, a fifth legitimizing theme surfaced around the perceived popular threat of foreign control given Salinas's free trade negotiations. With no hint of irony state authorities argued that the nationalized banks had to be privatized or else the Mexican banking sector risked falling under complete foreign bank control because of international competition. Mexican capitalists argued in turn that the financial system had to be liberalized to enable the new Mexican bank owners to compete against the onslaught of foreign banks. Building on economic nationalist sympathies, advocates thus legitimized bank privatization as a defense of 'Mexican' banks. Discussed at the time of the May decree, these five themes – stabilization, debt management, modernization, democratization, and fear of foreign control – helped both to bolster the political legitimacy of the Salinas bank privatization by decree and to mitigate social resistance.

The second of Salinas's presidential decrees came in July 1990. This July decree established the institutional framework for bank privatization and for a more finance-led neoliberal strategy of development via the new 1990 Credit Institutions and 1990 Financial Groups Laws. In the first case, the Credit Institutions Law established a new series of shares that assured majority Mexican and minority foreign bank control (BdeM 1991 (1990–2006), 48–9). No single individual or group could control more than 5 per cent of a bank's total shares. With SHCP consent, however, the limit could be extended to 10 per cent. The law also increased the institutional powers of Mexico's bank insurance agency, the Fondo de Apoyo Preventivo a las

Instituciones de Banca Múltiple (Fonapre; Fund for Preventative Aid for Multiple Bank Institutions), which was first established in 1986. The law renamed it as the Fondo Bancario de Protección al Ahorro (Fobaproa; Banking Fund for the Protection of Saving), which continued to operate under the BdeM. While the change in name suggests the agency is meant to protect individuals' savings as opposed to individual banks, the changes in fact enhanced the state's capacity to keep Mexican banks solvent under an accumulation strategy that entailed higher debt loads and financial risks. In Mexico as in all emerging capitalisms, for financial capital to prosper state and government elites have had systematically to enhance their institutional capacity to support finance and to ensure investor confidence in financial markets, often by officially and/or unofficially guaranteeing the banks' deposits and financial profit risks. At the same time the 1990 Financial Groups Law removed restrictions on the breadth of banks' financial activities that had lingered since the 1970s. A Mexican holding company could now form a financial group around a commercial bank, insurance firm, or brokerage house acting as the primary financial institution (BdeM 1991 (1990–2006), 52–4). Alongside a commercial bank, financial groups can include general deposit warehouses, leasing, financial factoring, exchange houses, bonding companies, and investment companies. In other words, the 1990 law restructured the financial sector in such a way that bank and market-based financial institutions could be controlled within one holding company. This formally opened the door to a system of universal banking along with bank privatization.

The third and last of Salinas's presidential decrees came in September 1990. Keeping in mind Salinas's need to bolster the legitimacy of bank privatization, the September decree outlined the details of how privatization should proceed by establishing three conditions for each bank sale (Ortiz Martínez 1993, 260–1). First, the sale had to contribute to a more competitive and efficient financial system. Second, the sale had to guarantee diversified participation and guard against ownership concentration. Third, the sale had to promote transparent and sound banking practices. To ensure that these conditions were met, the decree created the Comité de Disincorporación Bancaria (CDB; Bank Privatization Committee) managed under the SHCP (BdeM 1991 (1990–2006), 51), which outlined a two-stage sale procedure: first, the pre-appraisal of the banks and, second, the early registration and approval of potential buyers (SHCP 1994, 27). The procedure allowed state managers and PRI officials to keep a hand on both the sale process and the bidders accepted, while appearing to allow free market processes. The prior assessment of the nationalized bank values was important to ensuring government legitimacy. Indeed, Salinas could not politically risk seeming to sell the banks at bargain prices. The

CDB used these assessments to set a reference price below which the PRI would not have to sell. In terms of managing the bidders, the buyer pre-registration brought together a small group of identified shareholders with a much larger number of small investors. The actual effect of the two-stage process would be quite contrary to the themes popularized by the PRI and neoliberal advocates of bank privatization. The dubious practices undertaken before and after the sell-off have led at least one commentator to label the bank privatization process as 'kleptocratic' (Cypher 2001, 12). By legal means, such as privatization by decree, and illegal means, such as fraud, criminality, and predatory practices, the sphere of the market and the power of capital to accumulate wealth were augmented by the sell-off of the nationalized banks in processes akin to David Harvey's idea of accumulation by dispossession.

4.2.1   The Mexican Bank Sell-Off

The bank sell-off process led to near complete private domestic control of the banking sector. Yet far from the idealized picture crafted by advocates above, bank privatization was far from transparent, free market-based, competitive, democratic, and stability enhancing. From the first sale to the last, the process spanned a mere 13 months: between June 1991 and July 1992 the PRI converted the remaining 18 nationalized banks into 18 private Mexican-owned banks.[5] The sell-off could proceed so remarkably quickly because Mexican state authorities had already restructured and rationalized the banks in a fashion consistent with market-oriented development. In a sense, state managers used public resources to prepare the banks for some sort of neoliberal 'take-off'. The point of sale also marked the quantitative end to the qualitative process of bank privatization initiated under the de la Madrid administration as it restructured the just-nationalized banks to operate as if they were private, profit-seeking banks (Marois 2008).

The CDB managed the sell-off by arranging the 18 banks into six packages of between two and four institutions each, which were then auctioned off in successive stages. If a Mexican financial group wanted access to the banking sector, it had to try and purchase a bank in this short window of opportunity. By selling the banks in this way a cascade effect was created and interested bidders could try for different banks at different stages of the process at increasingly competitive bids (Unal and Navarro 1999, 70). At the same time the speed of the sell-off served as a political strategy to mitigate possible social resistance – should any problems appear, there was simply no time to organize against further bank privatizations.

Contrary to official discourse around bank privatization and certain policy stipulations within the presidential decrees, the bank sell-off failed to democratize the sector. Mexican authorities nevertheless attempted to present the process as having done so. For example, SHCP manager Ortiz Martínez singled out the Mexican banking giant Banamex to laud its new ownership matrix, which, he argued, boasted almost 35000 individuals, many of whom were bank employees (Ortiz Martínez 1993, 261–2). Table 4.1 shows that Banamex was sold for $3.2 billion in 1991 to Grupo Regional, which included the Accival (Acciones y Valores de Mexico) corporation, Mexico's largest brokerage house. While the CDB had initially decided to sell the Banamex shares in three packages of 31 per cent, 21 per cent, and 19.72 per cent authorities deemed the Accival offer so competitive that the PRI decided to forgo additional bidding, based on the CDB recommendation, and to simply award Accival all the shares at once (Unal and Navarro 1999, 72–3). The Accival bidding group included some of the richest and most powerful men in Mexico, headed by Alfredo Harp Helú (former president of the Mexican Stock Exchange and close friend of President Salinas), Roberto Hernández Ramírez, and Jose Aguilera Medrano. Through their holding groups Ramírez took control of 39 per cent of Accival's equity capital and Harp Helú 36.23 per cent, forming a controlling partnership of the now Accival-controlled Banamex. Through other shareholdings Accival also held shares in Mexico's second largest bank, Bancomer (Ramírez 2001, 662–3).

Yet neoliberal advocates resist looking at anything but the aggregate number of shareholders. By doing so they can assert a very thin empiricist argument that the bringing in of perhaps 130000 individuals to the bank ownership structure has democratized the banks (Ortiz Martínez 1993, 262; compare Rogozinski 1998, 98). On the one hand, this ignores that fact that the nationalized banks were already in the public domain and therefore legally owned by millions of Mexicans (even though the banks were not subject to democratic oversight and planning, which was problematic). On the other hand, such empiricist claims obscure the fact that while many thousands of individuals owned a few pithy shares after privatization only a few wealthy Mexican individuals and families, via controlling sets of shares, in fact exercised effective control over the banks' operations. Large shareholders by no means need to own all or even anywhere near 50 per cent of a firm's shares to dominate all the other small shareholders and to take effective operational control of a firm (Hilferding 2006 [1910], 118–19). Moreover, only by selling the banks in shareholdings and not in block sales could Mexico's most powerful family groups mobilize the additional, often related, investors needed to raise the required capital and ensure effective control over the privatized banks (Motamen-Samadian 2000, 9). In this sense, shareholding eliminates many of the barriers to

Table 4.1 Mexican bank privatizations, 1991–92

State bank privatization packages	Official date of sale	Purchaser (financial group or individual)	Name after privatization	Nominal price ($ millions)
First package				
Multibanco Mercantil de México, S.A.	14 June 1991	Probursa Financial Group, represented by José Madariaga.	Probursa	201.9
Banpaís, S.A.	21 June 1991	Mexival Financial Group represented by Ángel Rodríguez and group of individuals represented by Julio César Villareal Guajardo, Policarpo Elizondo Gutiérrez, and Fernando P. del Real Ibáñez.	Banpaís	179.9
Banca Cremi	28 June 1991	Group of individuals represented by Hugo Salvador Villa Manzo, Juan Antonio Covarrubias Valenzuela, and Omar Raymundo Gómez Flores.	Cremi	246.8
Second package				
Banca Confía	9 Aug 1991	ABANCO, group of individuals represented by Jorge Lankenau Rocha.	Confía	292.6
Banco de Oriente	16 Aug 1991	Group of individuals represented by Marcelo Margáin Berlanga.	Oriente	73.1
Banco de Crédito y Servicio	23 Aug 1991	Group of individuals represented by Roberto Alcántara Rojas, Librado Padilla Padilla and Carlos Mendoza Guadarrama.	Bancrecer	139.2
Banco Nacional de México	30 Aug 1991	Accival Financial Group, represented by Roberto Hernández Ramírez, Alfredo Harp Helú, and José G. Aguilera Medrano. 'Regional Group'.	Banamex	3187.3

Third package				
Bancomer	8 Nov 1991	VAMSA, Group of individuals represented by Eugenio Garza Lagüera, Eduardo A. Elizonda Lozano, and Ricardo Guajardo Touche. 'Regional Group'.	Bancomer	2775.7
Banco BCH	18 Nov 1991	Group of individuals represented by Carlos Cabal Peniche and Manuel Cantarel Méndez.	Unión	284.5
Fourth package				
Banca Serfin	3 Feb 1992	OBSA Financial Group, represented by Gastón Luken Aguilar and Octavio Igartúa Araiza; as well as Sada family.	Serfin	911.2
Multibanco Comermex	17 Feb 1992	Inverlat Financial Group, represented by Agustín F. Legorreta Chauvet.	Inverlat	871.2
Banco Mexicano Somex	11 March 1992	Inverméxico Financial Group, represented by Carlos Gómez and Somoza.	Mexicano	603.3
Fifth package				
Banco del Atlántico	6 April 1992	GBM-Atlántico Financial Group, and individuals represented by Alonso de Garay Gutiérrez and Jorge Rojas Mota Velasco.	Atlántico	471.5
Banca Promex	13 April 1992	Finamex Financial Group, and group of individuals represented by Eduardo A. Carillo Díaz, Mauricio López Velasco, José Méndez Fabre, and José Guarneros Tovar.	Promex	344.7
Banoro	28 April 1992	Group of individuals represented by Rodolfo Esquer Lugo, Fernando Obregón González, and Juan Antonio Beltrán López.	Banoro	364.7

Table 4.1 (continued)

State bank privatization packages	Official date of sale	Purchaser (financial group or individual)	Name after privatization	Nominal price ($ millions)
Sixth package				
Banco Mercantil del Norte	22 June 1992	MASECA, represented by Roberto González Barrera, Rodolfo Barrera Villareal, and Alberto Santos de Hoyos.	Banorte	567.1
Banco Internacional	6 July 1992	Prime Financial Group, represented by Antonio del Valle Ruiz, Eduardo Berrondo Ávalos and Blanca del Valle Perochena.	Bital	474.5
Banco del Centro	13 July 1992	Multiva Financial Group, represented by Hugo S. Villa Manzo and Luis Felipe Cervantes Coste.	Bancen	277.2
Total		The state retained control of 8.8 per cent of the banking sector (composed of 20.4 per cent share in Bancomer, 15.98 per cent in Serfín, and 21 per cent in Banco Internacional).		$12.27 billion (at bid price)

Sources: SHCP (1994, 48–50); ABM (2006b); BdeM (1992 (1990–2006), 179; 1993 (1990–2006), 207).

owning large enterprises while allowing, moreover, for the share owners to engage in more speculative activities around price changes in shares (Hilferding 2006 [1910], 137–9).

According to Gregorio Vidal, the turn to private shareholders or joint stock ownership thus resulted in the concentration of bank control among Mexico's wealthiest individuals (2002, 22–5). All at once a new and concentrated pattern of private domestic bank control emerged dominated by a few Mexican ex-bankers and the new heads of powerful financial groups (Morera 1998, 52–6). The capacity for Mexican capital to be able to do this had been institutionalized in the July 1990 Financial Groups Law, which enabled financial intermediaries to merge into financial holding groups. Only in this way could Mexican capitalists overcome the legal ownership barriers that set a 5 per cent maximum participation limit for any single individual or investor. Having assumed control, the new bankers then put their new banks at the heart of their Mexican family holding groups to feed the groups' productive enterprises with cheap credits. The 1991–92 bank privatizations led not only to the restructuring of the Mexican banking system but also to that of Mexico's most powerful financial groups (Álvarez Béjar and Mendoza Pichardo 1993, 42). It follows that the structural transformation equated with an extraordinary expansion in the capacity of the private sector in Mexico to take on financial risk and engage in financial accumulation. Throughout the 1980s the PRI government and state elites had institutionalized greater liberties to the benefit of financial capital, and now a new collective of profit-eager bank owners was unleashed in Mexican society. Far from any liberal market utopia, however, bank privatization created new contradictions and economic volatilities.

I would like to pause on the issue of the prices paid for the banks for a moment because it is important to different interpretations of the subsequent 1995 crisis. According to past ABM president Esnaola, the 1982 bank nationalization cost the government about $637 million at book value at the time (Weiser 1990). By late 1989 the book value of the banks had risen to nearly $3.9 billion, or about six times the price paid in 1982. The final tally for bank privatization came in at $12.27 billion at bid value (Table 4.1). As reported on the World Bank's Privatization Database, between 1991 and 1992 the whole of the Latin American and Caribbean region earned just over $34 billion in privatization receipts. It follows that Mexico's bank privatization project, alone, constituted over a third of the entire region's total. This substantial figure, moreover, far exceeded the anticipated $4 billion expected by state authorities in one-time revenues (and would seemingly be cause for celebration). Drawing on official figures, the bank auction earned on average about 3.5 times the immediate pre-sale book value (Motamen-Samadian 2000, 7). Others, however, point out that the auction bids averaged higher in later packages, which were in and about 4.2 times the banks' book value (Unal and Navarro 1999, 78). Still others have taken the issue further to calculate the weighted 'bid to book' ratio – that is, a bid ratio that accounts for the size of bank – and arrived at a slightly lower ratio of 3.04 over book value (Haber 2005a, 2330). The accuracy of one's data is important, but too narrow a focus on the details sometimes leads one to miss the bigger picture. For example, many economists draw a thin empirical line from the perceived 'high' or 'too high' prices paid for the banks in 1991–92 to the subsequent 1995 banking crisis (for example, Haber 2005a). The problem is that other commentators on Mexico have come to accept and reproduce the 'high' or 'too high' discourse not as a matter for debate but as the basis of the 1995 crisis (for example, Williams 2001, 33; Avalos and Trillo 2006, 17; Stallings 2006, 187). In what seems a search for empirical parsimony in explaining the 1995 crisis, the 'price paid' debate has made the tail (the price paid) wag the dog (an increasingly finance-led neoliberal strategy of capital accumulation).

There is a range of complex, contingent, and structural factors that affect the logic behind the prices paid and the later unfolding of crisis that can get lost by focusing too much on the way in which the price paid is assessed. For one, the PRI announced more flexible payment terms late in the sale process and this enabled the new owners to search out new partnerships and to make higher offers. The owners could raise capital in international and domestic markets, through small investors, commercial securities, foreign banks, and other Mexican banks. In a particularly corrupt instance, the Mackey Report on the banking crisis shows how some purchasers were able to use funds borrowed from their newly purchased banks to pay for the bank itself – in one case nearly 75 per cent of the sale price. What was suggested as acceptable bidder's criteria by the PRI government, in fact, turned out to be quite unacceptable in retrospect. Furthermore, the PRI made it known that the new owners would enjoy protection from foreign bank competition under the new NAFTA for up to four years. Plus, the buyers were aware of the foregoing institutional reforms undertaken by the government meant to safeguard financial capital in Mexico (for example, bank insurance funds, international reserves, and so on) should problems arise. This, together with the reorienting of development in Mexico around NAFTA promised a future world market of potential buyers wanting access to the Mexican banking sector. Rather than just assessing a bank at this or that amount of book value (which of course they did), the new owners also anticipated their purchase to offer initially quasi-monopolistic domestic market access within a banking sector ripe for expansion after a decade of state-led banking. Moreover, having direct control over a bank provided a powerful competitive advantage for the controlling holding group in terms of favorable access to credits through their banks. The new bankers were not just buying banks but also buying into a new strategy of accumulation in which state authorities had practically ensured high returns. The prices paid are more of a morbid symptom of neoliberal competitive imperatives than a parsimonious causal explanation of the subsequent crisis.

4.3   THE TROUBLE WITH APPROXIMATING NEOLIBERAL BANKING IN MEXICO

At the time of bank privatization SHCP manager Ortiz Martínez spoke of the enormous potential for banking sector growth (1993, 263). He pointed out that in 1991 Mexico's ratio of financial savings (M4) to GDP was only 45 per cent compared to 75 per cent in the US and 80 per cent in Europe. However relevant or not such emerging to advanced capitalist comparisons are, it points to the desire of Mexican state and government officials to approximate the practices, processes, and levels of development seen in the advanced capitalisms. Since de la Madrid all PRI administrations have argued that this level of development was achievable by approximating neoliberal ideals and, by the late 1980s, an increasingly finance-led form at that. Achieving this ideal, nonetheless, entailed restructuring the state financial apparatus.

The turn to a more finance-led form of neoliberalism took an important step forward with capital account liberalization in 1989 and with the abolishment of foreign exchange rate controls and limits on US denominated deposits in 1991–92 (BdeM 1992 (1990–2006), 171–4). While enabling financial markets in these ways the SHCP still needed to develop capacity to supervise the entry and exit of financial capital. Likewise, the BdeM had to manage new liquidity requirements and any remaining foreign exchange regulations. The reconstituted semi-autonomous National Banking Commission (CNB) under the SHCP was given responsibility for establishing a new system of loan classification, provisioning, and capital adequacy guidelines along with new loan concentration limits and other banking rules compatible with Bank for International Settlements (BIS) guidelines (OECD 1992, 178; BdeM 1994 (1991–2006), 189–203). The new regulatory changes required Mexican banks to maintain a minimum capital/risk-weighted asset ratio of 8 per cent by the end of 1993. The CNB, at this time, took on greater powers to sign international banking agreements. In preparation for NAFTA (discussed shortly) the PRI

Table 4.2   Private domestic Mexican banks, 1992–95

	1992	1993	1994	1995
Number of banks	18	18	26	42
Number of branches	3 535	3 763	4 338	4 806
Number of employees	138 900	131 200	126 900	121 000
Profit before tax (%)	2.32	2.28	0.76	0.47

Source: OECD (1998a, 187–90).

passed a new Foreign Investors Law in 1993 that marginally increased foreign ownership limits and further reduced restrictions on financial group formation. Finally, as tied to Mexico's OECD membership in 1994, the PRI mandated the BdeM to promote price stability, granted the BdeM formal independence, and then adopted a free floating exchange rate policy (OECD 1998b, 37). The important point is that as the PRI opened up financial markets within Mexico and internationally, the PRI also led a process of state restructuring to bolster Mexico's financial apparatus. However, the state restructuring was premised around a more ideal form of neoliberalism and market-based coordination, and this created the conditions for heightened financial instability following bank privatization.

In the period between the 1991–92 bank privatizations and the 1994–95 crisis, what changes occurred in banking in Mexico? As Table 4.2 illustrates, there is intensified competition as a result of the proliferation of new banks, the opening of new branches, the shedding of bank employees, and temporarily high profits. Let us look in more detail. First, from 1992 to 1995 the number of commercial banks operating in Mexico more than doubled from 18 to 42. Earlier state-authored liberalization measures had enabled this and domestic capitalists took the opportunity to open banks – a prospect sweetened by the anticipation of NAFTA. Moreover, the new bankers recognized that state managers had held back on expanding the sector while the banks were nationalized. According to Ortiz Martínez, the spatial penetration of banks was thin prior to privatization and averaged 18 000 people per branch (versus 4000 people per branch in the US and 2000 per branch in Europe) (1993, 263). There was therefore a perceived opportunity for banking sector expansion by new bankers. This competitive drive was intensified by the need of all banks to capture more Mexican savings to bolster their capital base. Consequently, branch numbers grew from 3535 to 4806 (or by over a third) in only a few years. Bank workers, however, faced layoffs as the bankers cut back on labor costs to boost profits. OECD (1998a) data reveal that whereas the nationalized banks averaged 37.90 employees per branch in 1990 the privatized banks averaged 34.9 in 1993 and just 25.20 by 1995. The bankers benefited from reduced staff costs, which fell from 5.25 to 4.65 to 3.77 per cent of the banks' balance sheet. The new bankers reasonably expected little resistance from the bank workers to the intensification of labor given Mexico's corporatist union structure and since ratcheting down on the cost of labor had formed the core of Salinas's NDP strategy. More precisely, though, the leadership of the bank workers' union, Fenasib, had hitherto refused to militate either against austerity conditions under nationalization or to privatization. From 1982 to 1992 bank workers' real wages fell as state bank managers restricted growth in bank branches and staff numbers, and the new bankers had no reason to reverse this favorable trend. At the same time, the PRI government, as part of the privatization deal, also committed to protecting bank profitability: the new bankers would receive lower official interest rates in 1992 and 1993 than in 1991 while, at the same time, the bankers could increase the cost of borrowing to their customers (Ramírez 2001, 666). This helped drive up profits to help the bankers pay off their new banks: before-tax profits were well over 2 per cent in 1994, prior to the crisis. At the time Mexican authorities celebrated the banks' high profit levels, which averaged over double those in the US and Europe, as a sign of neoliberalism's success (Ortiz Martínez 1993, 263). However, the intensification of market competition, which led to a proliferation of branches and reduction in labor costs aimed solely at generating profit, created a liberal utopia that benefited only a few bankers. This would prove to be unrealistic, very short lived, and to have costly consequences.

4.3.1　Banking on the 1994 NAFTA

The 1994 NAFTA between Canada, the US, and Mexico aimed to renew profit levels and aggregate growth, which required a process of class reformation based upon Mexico's re-integration into the world market and commitments to open domestic commercial, investment, and financial movements. For Mexico, NAFTA ensured access to US markets, its largest trading partner, and assurances against future US protectionism. For the US, NAFTA was a response to unpredictable multilateral free trade negotiations and ensured a zone of influence against European and East Asian trading blocs. For the ruling elites, NAFTA helped to institutionally sanitize popular resistance via the environmental and labor side agreements (Marois 2009). The control that Salinas, as president, exercised over the NAFTA negotiations – to the exclusion of almost all social sectors in Mexico – is historically rooted in the fusion of the PRI within the state apparatus following the 1917 Revolution, the historic power of the presidency over the legislature and judiciary, decades of PRI control over the presidency and congress, and a corporatist structure that enabled the state to lead business negotiations (Otero 2004). In the final analysis NAFTA was very much about Salinas institutionally tying the hands of future Mexican governments to a neoliberal vision of state–market–labor relations (Guillén Romo 2005, 89). Marked by the armed Zapatista uprising in Chiapas and widespread popular dissent, NAFTA nonetheless came into force on 1 January 1994.

The specific regulatory initiatives of NAFTA aimed in general to ensure a predictable commercial framework and to enhance competitiveness by restructuring state and markets around reduced or eliminated trade and investment tariffs; open service provision across borders; intellectual property rights protections; a pro-trade dispute mechanism; and the easier movement of business and professional people across borders (NAFTA 1994, iii, 1). For our present purposes the key NAFTA section is Chapter Fourteen, which deals with domestic financial services and calls for financial liberalization and most-favored nation treatment of all investors as well as for new regulatory requirements, greater transparency, and a dispute settlement mechanism for financial services (NAFTA 1994, 297–307). In its text, NAFTA set 1 January 2000 as the latest date for further consultations on additional financial liberalization. Annex VII to Chapter Fourteen clarified each country's specific reservations. Notably, Salinas negotiated a list of reservations that exceeded the actual length of Chapter Fourteen itself (NAFTA 1994, 723–35). In stark contrast to how many normally think of NAFTA, Salinas stipulated that foreign capital could not exceed 30 per cent ownership of any Mexican holding company or commercial bank, thereby limiting American and Canadian entry. Foreign government-like organizations were banned from any type of ownership. Foreign bank affiliates could be authorized, but the maximum size of the bank could not exceed 1.5 per cent of the aggregate capital of all commercial banks. Moreover, the aggregate control of all foreign banks could not initially exceed 8 per cent of total bank capital. This limit was supposed to increase annually in equal increments until it reached the final limit of 15 per cent of total bank capital (NAFTA 1994, 730). The new NAFTA provisions also applied to the foreign banks already operating in Mexico and no phase-out commitments were stipulated. While it is true that Salinas established the institutional framework for liberalizing Mexico's banking sector in NAFTA, he did so in a way that left substantial control in the hands of Mexican authorities and that protected the new Mexican bank entrants. Through NAFTA Salinas committed Mexico to internalizing new financial imperatives but in ways differentiated by

Mexico's own national accumulation patterns and established relations of power. In practice, however, finance-led neoliberalism would come much faster than anticipated in NAFTA and as the government's response to the 1994 crisis (discussed in detail in Chapter 6).

4.3.2   The 1994 Crisis

Since the 1980s Mexican state officials and government elites have played an active role in restructuring the banks and state around new financial imperatives in ways that approximated neoliberal ideals. The signing of the 1994 NAFTA signaled a conjunctural moment in this history. Annual growth had averaged around 4 per cent during Salinas's six years in office. Foreign investors and governments, as well as domestic elites, had high expectations for future prosperity. The IMF applauded the PRI as model neoliberal reformers while President Salinas was being considered to head the World Trade Organization. Internally, SHCP manager Ortiz Martínez extolled the virtues of Mexican financial legislation as

> . . . one of the most advanced in the world, because it allows the offer of universal financial services while fostering openness, competitiveness, and efficiency. It also enables the authorities with the necessary capacity to ensure appropriate regulation and supervision of the whole financial system. (1993, 260)

Mexico's approximation of neoliberal development, however, began to show signs of trouble as the 1994 peso crisis materialized and the logic of liberalizing finances began to unravel before the eyes of Mexico's state officials (Cypher 2001; Soederberg 2004; Guillén Romo 2005).

The year 1994 was also a presidential election year and Mexican society was already mired in instability as a result of the Zapatista uprising and high-level political assassinations. While optimistic beforehand, foreign capital turned increasingly skittish over holding Mexican debt, which had continued to accumulate since the 1980s. To stem instability, state and government elites found themselves in the uneasy position of having to siphon off investors' financial risks by drawing some of their exchange risks into the state apparatus. State managers did this by converting the CETES peso denominated debt into short-term US dollar-indexed but peso-payable Mexican state securities – the now infamous Tesobonos, worth about $29 billion by late 1994. For a short time this slowed capital outflows but capital flight returned as Ernesto Zedillo was about to take the seat of the presidency in late 1994. Insider information of an impending peso devaluation, followed by devaluation itself on 20 December 1994, led to renewed capital flight, a foreign currency liquidity crunch, a jump in interest rates, and a sharp contraction in economic activity (OECD 2002b,

88; Sidaoui 2005). Mexico's foreign reserves fell from $2.3 billion in 1994 to –$1.5 billion in 1995. State financial authorities pushed domestic interest rates to near 25 per cent to lure in foreign capital. Yet because of the perceived financial risk of default (and because of the relatively high interest rates offered in the US at the time) the recycling of Mexico's high-risk Tesobonos became near impossible for the government and the possibility of sovereign default appeared. The new Zedillo government responded to the crisis by floating the value of the peso, which collapsed from about 4 to about 7 pesos to the US dollar within a week. Mexico was suffering its worst crisis since the 1930s (BdeM 1996 (1991–2006)).

The interconnectedness of financial markets developed over the preceding decade also meant that Mexico's troubles quickly impacted the financial stability of other Latin American countries (Saad-Filho and Mollo 2002, 125). The then managing director of the IMF, Michel Camdessus, famously labeled Mexico's 'Tequila' crisis as the first financial crisis of the twenty-first century. Moreover, the exposure of primarily American foreign debts in Mexico put great pressure on the US government to bail out its own banks, and by extension Mexico. The US took control of the situation by organizing an IMF, Bank for International Settlements, and Canadian government $50 billion bailout in early 1995 (OECD 1995, 160). The first $29 billion went to settling the Tesobonos directly in US dollars (Sidaoui 2005, 217). That is, the most important political priority was not to safeguard Mexican jobs but to honor financial capital's debts in Mexico. The balance of power between labor and financial capital had clearly fallen in favor of the latter.

Nevertheless, the 1994 Mexican peso crisis had openly exposed the inconsistencies of Mexico's idealized neoliberal or Washington consensus approach to development. The crisis revealed the problems of a privatized banking sector within a liberalized yet internationally subordinate emerging capitalist society that is dependent on far from guaranteed flows of financial capital. The 1994 devaluation, for example, caused the peso value of the privatized domestic banks' foreign denominated debts to rise abruptly. This exposed vast quantities of large and intertwined Mexican family and business groups' debt to default risk, which put the entire banking system at risk (BdeM 1996 (1991–2006), 1). Yet liberal theories advocating the end of so-called financial repression had supported the financial liberalization measures enacted since the late 1980s, which in turn had enabled the expansion of domestic credit – arguably intended to be disciplined by the market itself (see Levy 2003, 168). In contrast to any liberal developmental take-off, only more high interest rate consumer loans appeared to be fed by Mexican banks borrowing more short-term foreign credits (SHCP 1998, 10–1). This created problematic imbalances and increased financial risk in Mexican society as internal to neoliberal restructuring.

Other imbalances and social risks, not tied to consumer credit, also derived from the new competitive strategies of bankers. For example, changed financial regulations since 1990 had seemed to set more stringent lending rules for holding groups and their banks (Motamen-Samadian 2000, 10). In theory, the credits given to related bank owners, principal shareholders, members of the board, and/or firms owned by the bank could not exceed 20 per cent of a bank's total credits granted. The regulatory change created a contradictory situation in practice, however: the more credit each individual bank gave overall, the more the 20 per cent ratio meant in the actual quantity accessible to the bank owners and shareholders. This invited more decadent lending in the private banking sector because the bank shareholders themselves wanted more access to credit, which they were able to access at below market rates. As state financial authorities recognized after the fact, large holding group managers guided their own bank credits into other areas of the group experiencing financial difficulties – often at the expense of the holding group bank (see SHCP 1998, 48). Read within the context of neoliberal transition, this strategy formed one response of holding groups to the intensification of competitive and profit pressures within Mexico. It also formed the conditions for the subsequent 1995 banking crisis and state-led bank rescue explored in Chapter 6. While the crisis and rescue entailed hitherto unheard-of social costs to Mexican society, crisis and rescue also constituted the opening of a new phase of finance-led restructuring of state, bank, and labor relations in ways that would better support the stability of financial capital in Mexico.

4.4 CONCLUSION

Mexico's transition to neoliberalism has not been characterized by the weakening of the state financial apparatus, per se, but by state and government elites restructuring state, bank, and labor relationships of power and re-institutionalizing these in ways beneficial to capital accumulation in general and to financial capital in particular. In this, Mexico conforms to the universalizing tendencies of neoliberal strategies of development to subordinate workers, state, and society to competitive accumulation imperatives. Yet Mexico is equally unique in its transition to neoliberalism. As we have seen, and quite contrary to static interpretations, private bank ownership was neither a condition for the banks to be market- and profit-oriented nor was it necessary for the extension of market discipline in Mexican society. The nationalized banks achieved both. Bank privatization then led rapidly to crisis and, as we will see, a state-led rescue premised on Mexican society absorbing the costs of private financial risks. Crisis and rescue would not overturn the past fifteen years of institutionalizing neoliberalism, but would instead lead to the consolidation of its finance-led form.

NOTES

1. Aspects of this chapter follow a similar line of argumentation presented in Marois 2008.
2. This point is also made by the far-right Cato Institute, their solution being even greater exposure to market discipline (see Vásquez 1996).
3. The finer details of the mergers can be found on the Banks' Association of Mexico website, http://www.abm.org.mx/banca_mexico/historia.htm.
4. The following derives from archival research undertaken at the Hemeroteca Nacional de México, Universidad Nacional Autónoma de México, in 2007, where I examined *La Jornada, El Financiero*, and *Reforma* newspapers from late 1989 to 1991.
5. In most cases, the state's shares were sold off entirely. However, the government retained minority shares in Serfín, Bancomer, and Banco Internacional (SHCP 1994, 27). These were valued at about $1.5 billion and at the time held as an optional purchase for the acquiring group (Ortiz Martínez 1993, 263). In practice, the state held onto these until 2000 and the entry of foreign bank capital.

5. Crisis and the neoliberal idealism of state and bank restructuring in Turkey, 1980–2000

For years Turkish society had been suffering from economic uncertainty, social unrest, and political polarization. The 1979–82 US-based Volcker shock worsened matters as the resulting debt crisis reverberated throughout the global periphery. In Turkey instability culminated in the 1980 military coup and the unrolling of an authoritarian market-oriented restructuring program. The international financial institutions (IFIs) facilitated and pushed these changes, but the IFIs did not simply impose them. In the two decades following the 1980 crisis, I argue that domestic advocates actively brought about the neoliberal restructuring of the Turkish state and society in ways that increasingly favored financial capital. The Turkish banking and finance sector was at the heart of this restructuring, although not always in ways consistent with neoliberalism. Consecutive governments promoted financial liberalization and exposed domestic banking to world market competitive imperatives while state authorities manipulated the state banks' developmental missions and crafted a stronger state financial apparatus to support neoliberal restructuring. Two decades of economic sluggishness and recurrent crisis followed as a more finance-led form of neoliberalism took root.

I develop this argument in three sections. Section 5.1 looks at the 15 years following the 1980 military coup and how advocates sought as far as possible to approximate the ideals of neoliberalism within national constraints. Section 5.2 then analyzes the structural changes in Turkish banking over the first two decades of neoliberal transformation. Special attention is given to the importance of mounting state debts and the role of the state banks in ensuring neoliberal continuity. Section 5.3 links the volatility of the late 1990s to ongoing state restructuring by discussing how the changes exposed new contradictions that led to the 2000 banking crisis in Turkey. This is followed by a brief conclusion.

5.1 APPROXIMATING NEOLIBERALISM IN TURKEY, 1980–94

The opening turn towards a long period of neoliberal restructuring in Turkey came via the 1978 default, which led to the subsequent 1979 IMF bailout package, political instability, and the 1980 military takeover. The military's new draconian constitution enabled sweeping changes legitimated by the discourse of restoring stability. At this time Turkey was one of the first developing countries since the brutal Chilean experience to pursue market-oriented restructuring, and Turkey's political and state elites similarly did so through authoritarian and anti-democratic political measures (on Chile, see Taylor 2006). As a result, the social relations of power between state, capital, and labor market relations tipped decisively in favor of capital.

The breaking point came in January 1980 when the Adelat Partisi (AP; Justice Party) minority government led by Süleyman Demirel appointed a committed neoliberal technocrat, Turgut Özal, to implement the IMF-crafted structural adjustment reforms. Özal had made, however, little progress by the end of summer 1980. Political life remained paralyzed and social unrest was widespread. It is said that Özal then asked the Turkish military for 'a five-year respite from party politics for the success of his recipe' (Ahmad 2003, 147). What direct impact this had is hard to know but on 12 September 1980 the military started what became Turkey's longest military intervention. On taking power the military junta pledged support for Özal's neoliberal reforms, largely to assuage the fears of foreign and domestic capital in Turkey. At the same time the military aligned itself with the powerful Turkish Industrialist Businessmen's Association (TÜSİAD), a representative body of İstanbul and largely Kemalist domestic capitalists. To facilitate the neoliberal transformation envisioned by Özal military leaders suspended the more socially progressive 1961 Constitution, dissolved the Turkish parliament, closed political parties, arrested leaders, banned strikes, and shut down militant labor organizations. Not until 1983 did the military allow a limited return to parliamentary democracy with a fuller return having to wait until 1987. As with Turkey's 1960 and 1971 military interventions, the 1980 coup was at base an expression of class conflict and struggle over who would institutionally dominate state, capital, and labor relations in Turkey (Savran 2002).

Özal emerged as the key political figure behind Turkey's authoritarian transition to neoliberalism. Özal served first as the Minister of Economy from 1980 to 1982, then as Prime Minister (PM) and leader of the Anavatan Partisi (ANAP; Motherland Party) from 1983 to 1989, and finally as the President of Turkey from 1989 until his death in 1993. According to a close associate of his, Tezcan Yaramancı, Özal was always convinced of the need for market-led reform and moved forward as a pragmatist opting to solve problems as they arose (Interview, Investa Consulting, İstanbul, 21 August 2007).[1] Military rule enabled Özal to 'pragmatically' concentrate state and government power in the Turkish executive, to handpick a few state officials to work on the IMF structural reforms, and to neutralize any social or political resistance to neoliberalism (Yalman 2002, 38–9; Öncu and Gokce 1991). However, this also meant that in his drive to approximate the ideals of neoliberalism Özal did not dedicate the institutional resources necessary for establishing the rule of law and legal infrastructure needed fully to support a market-oriented capitalist economy (Öniş 2004, 114). This would lead to instability, if not the reversal of elements of the form of neoliberalism in Turkey.

At the time Turkish capitalists reasoned that market liberalization would allow them to restore profitability and power through greater integration into the world market and the suppression of organized labor (Ercan and Oguz 2007, 175). But their support for liberalization policies was not without complications. The TÜSİAD-based holding groups typically represented postwar Kemalist developmental capital, and they were mostly located around İstanbul and the more secular areas of the country. This fraction of domestic capital accepted the need for market-oriented reforms but they also did not want to relinquish their privileged access to the Turkish state apparatus with neoliberal restructuring (Atasoy 2007, 124). Other factions of Turkish capital also supported the reforms but for different reasons. For example, the Müstakil Sanayicileri ve İşadamları Derneği (MÜSİAD; Independent Industrialist Businessmen's Association) and the Union of Chambers and Commodity Exchanges of Turkey (TOBB) had historically taken issue with the close relationship between İstanbul capital and the state apparatus. In different ways, MÜSİAD and TOBB represented the interests of more Anatolia-based medium and smaller-sized capitalist enterprises, which often organized around Muslim business principles and political Islam (see also Kosebalaban 2007). Neither fraction traditionally had strong ties to the postwar state-led development strategy and both reasoned that liberalization, in addition to weakening the power of organized labor, would present new and previously unavailable opportunities for expansion.

Successful integration into the competitive world market demanded that Turkey have a disciplined and cheap labor force capable of producing competitively priced export-oriented goods. The military junta had already devalued the Turkish lira (TL) to make imports more expensive and Turkish exports cheaper, thus smoothing the reorientation of domestic production to the exterior. The greater challenge involved re-establishing the social primacy and logic of capital, which entailed suppressing the rise of labor power that had taken place since the 1960s and putting an end to class-based politics (Bedirhanoğlu and Yalman 2010). To help legitimize this Özal framed the neoliberal structural adjustment plans around a new myth of the self-regulating market while vilifying the past legacy of state-led development as an outdated form of economic and financial repression. The IFI officials argued that the free market was the only possible cure for Turkey's growing foreign debt, foreign exchange shortages, trade deficits, high inflation, and unemployment problems. These neoclassical and neoliberal ideas found their way into the military regime's penning of the new 1982 Constitution in ways that institutionalized measures intended to de-politicize, de-mobilize, de-radicalize, and de-unionize society (Cizre Sakallığlu 1991). The military regime forcibly shut down the more radical labor unions and supported corporatist relations with the remaining unions, which were more state and business friendly. Having lost many of the tools of workers' resistance wages fell during the 1980s to levels not seen since before 1963 (Duman et al. 2005, 127). The top-down restructuring of domestic production relations around cheap labor formed the core of Turkey's international competitive advantage in the neoliberal era (Onaran 2002).

5.1.1 Privatization in Turkey

The privatization of state-owned enterprises (SOEs) has been a vanguard strategy behind the transition to neoliberalism in Turkey as in other developing countries (Yeldan 2006b; Yalman 2009; compare Fine and Bayliss 2008; Marois 2005). Privatization, beneath its formal appearance as an economic policy, entails the restructuring of social relationships of power between the state, capital, and labor in ways that aim to intensify competitiveness by exposing individuals and collectives to profit imperatives. The agency of Turkish government and state elites have not been sidestepped in this restructuring process but have instead played an important coordinating role in privatization and served as a modifying force (for example, by refusing to relinquish control over the state banks).

In its attempt to approximate neoliberal development the Özal ANAP administration initiated plans for SOE privatization beginning in 1984. By 1986 this had found ideological and policy expression in a report written by the American investment bank, Morgan Guaranty. Unsurprisingly, the Morgan Guaranty Report suggested that Turkey should relinquish economic decision-making to the market, promote efficiencies, encourage wider private ownership, decrease the productive size of the state, sell off

SOEs to pay off state debts, and so on. In practical discourse, little has fundamentally changed since. Gazı Erçel (1997), Governor of the Central Bank of Turkey, wrote a decade later that privatization is simply about removing the public sector from the business sector to reduce the burden of inefficient public management and by so doing to increase the efficiency of the privatized enterprises. In both cases privatization is falsely presented as a technical matter independent of social relations of power and class.

The ANAP government initiated some minor SOE sell-offs in 1985 while, at the same time, beginning to internally restructure other larger SOEs to enhance their performance in preparation for later sale. The first major SOE sell-off came in 1988, and included the sale of Teletas (a telephone and communications firm) and a few dozen industrial SOEs. The proceeds from this first wave of privatizations were relatively negligible, earning less than $30 million from 1985 to 1988. This modest amount reflects the practical learning curve of state agencies and the slow rates of economic expansion in the late 1980s globally. Privatization receipts then jumped over the next few years, earning over $2 billion prior to the onset of the 1994 financial crisis in Turkey (discussed below) and the unveiling of the 1994 Privatization Law.

In late 1993 the first woman Prime Minister of Turkey, Tansu Çiller of the Doğru Yol Partisi (DYP; True Path Party), asked Yaramancı (see above) to take administrative control of the state's privatization administration and authority, the Özelleştirme İdaresi Başkanlığı (ÖİB), and to 'sell immediately whatever you can'.[2] Within a week of accepting the post, however, Yaramancı had reached the conclusion that neither the legal framework nor public sentiment supported the continued privatization of large Turkish SOEs, and that it was this that had slowed privatization to date. Yaramancı informed Çiller of this and then halted all further sell-offs. Within a year he had designed and written the 1994 Privatization Law, which the government passed on 27 November and which remains in force today with certain amendments. In addition to better institutionalizing the legal basis of privatization in the state apparatus, the 1994 law enabled state managers to restructure the internal operations of SOEs in preparation for privatization (OECD 1999, 113). So-called 'non-economic' incentives were to be replaced by market-based cost, price, and profit structures. Dovetailing this measure, the 1994 law made provisions to pay special compensation to Turkish state workers for job losses, relocations, retraining, and so forth in addition to maintaining already existing laws and collective bargaining agreements. In practice, state workers have not benefited (Yeldan 2006b). The so-called employment alternatives have often resulted in public employees forfeiting higher levels of pay, years of seniority, and benefits for lower level and worse paying jobs. The 1994 law has thus weakened the bargaining power and benefits of workers in Turkey. In the words of Yaramancı, having introduced 'private logic' into the state apparatus he then resigned from the ÖİB.

Since 1994, as a result of continuing economic instability and social resistance, privatization in Turkey has been a stop and go process. For example, privatization receipts peaked at just over $1 billion in 1998 before collapsing to $38 million in 1999. It has also been the case that privatizing larger SOEs by public offer or share flotation has proven difficult because of the limited size and depth of the Istanbul Stock Exchange (İSE; İstanbul Menkul Kıymetler Borsası) and domestic market. Selling off large SOEs by block sales (as a complete whole) is complicated because of the large amounts of capital required by individuals (which is not the case with share ownership where minority shareholders can nonetheless gain control over corporations, see Chapter 4). While various administrations had sold off over 130 SOEs by the end of the 1990s, the Turkish state nonetheless retained a substantial presence in many economic sectors. Regardless of international pressures to privatize 'as rapidly as possible', there were still 44 SOEs within the top 500 major Turkish firms by 1997, including the four largest overall (OECD 1999, 119–20). Moreover, the authorities had made very little progress towards altering the state's presence in the banking sector.

The seemingly slow pace of privatization in Turkey is of less analytical significance than the political achievements of neoliberal advocates (Atasoy 2007). The goal of substantively altering social relations of power between state, labor, and capital to the benefit of capital had been largely achieved through the opening up of the state apparatus to the private sector and by subjecting Turkish workers more directly to competitive imperatives. Organized labor now had fewer avenues and resources through which to pressure state and government authorities for higher wages, greater workplace rights, job security, and so on. In line with neoliberal theory, the so-called 'de-politicization' of economic processes was well under way in Turkey (insofar as the power of labor was reined in). As the pro-market reformer Yaramancı acknowledges, bringing the SOEs out of political influence was the real philosophical basis of Turkish privatization (Interview, Investa Consulting, 21 August 2007). In this sense, SOE privatization has meant the downsizing of the state's direct productive role in many sectors of the economy and the severing of many political links to workers through the state. However, this does not necessarily equate with the 'minimal state' ideas so dear to neoliberal mythology. Indeed, neoliberal strategies of development have demanded a larger and more expansive role for the state financial apparatus.

5.1.2   Restructuring the Turkish State in a Finance-Led Image

'Underdeveloped' and 'repressed' are the stock adjectives describing Turkey's financial sector prior to the 1980s, and these are reproduced with remarkable consistency (for example, Ozkan-Gunay and Tektas 2006, 419; ERF 2005, 38; Bakır 2006, 181). However, this more ideologically descriptive than substantive characterization brackets off many historical reasons why state authorities managed financial flows in ways demanded of an earlier phase of capitalist development. Such 'repression' accounts reproduce questionable neoclassical assumptions about the voluntary nature of individual exchanges as well as the neutrality, freedom, and benefits of open markets. History is more complex, and insofar as specific financial controls limited certain forms of financial accumulation prior to the 1980s these same controls facilitated capital formation and steady profitability for a range of far from repressed domestic capitalist classes with close and interrelated ties to financial capital. The significance of financial restructuring since the 1980s rests not in the analytical wastelands of ending repression but in coming to terms with the ways in which state-authored financial liberalization and restructuring processes have unleashed new financial imperatives to the benefit of financial capital.

Özal's approximation of an ideally open finance and banking sector in the post-1980 military coup period proved immediately destabilizing. The end of interest rate controls and other initially rapid financial liberalization measures in security markets encouraged a wave of new brokerage firms and smaller bank openings. Each new firm was betting on continued high financial profits and their ability to seamlessly attract new money. This resulted in a volatile, competitive, corrupt, and highly speculative situation that quickly turned into crisis and the collapse of the brokerage system in 1982 – the so-called Kastelli crisis. As would become the pattern for all neoliberal financial crises, the government followed up by acting on behalf of the collective interests of financial capital. A state bailout avoided any permanent fracture in Turkey's still fragile market-oriented development strategy. In practice this involved state authorities socializing the risks and liabilities gone sour of financial capital. Compared to later financial crises, the state-led rescue came with a relatively modest bill at an estimated cost of about 2.5 per cent of Turkey's 1982 GDP (ERF 2005, 38).

The 1982 crisis was indicative of neoliberal things to come as the crisis compelled state authorities not to emasculate state financial powers as per neoliberal idealism but to bolster them. As a first order of business Özal created the Saving Deposit Insurance Fund (SDIF; Tasarruf Mevduatı Sigorta Fonu) in 1983 – a state institution designed to guarantee Turkish bank deposits and, in so doing, to prop up the faith of financial capital in Turkey's financial sector. The Özal administration then moved to further strengthen the state's institutional footings vis-à-vis the banking system by drafting the new 1985 Banking Law. The 1985 law brought the Turkish financial apparatus more in line with the Bank for International Settlements (BIS) requirements by instituting stronger capital adequacy requirements and non-performing loan (NPL) provisions, by enhancing accounting, auditing, and reporting requirements, and by re-imposing minimum start-up capital requirements to reduce the number of new private bank entries. Each provision in its own way contradicted neoclassical and neoliberal tenets which hold that self-interested competition alone is the finest regulator of markets.

Following this initial financial setback and state-led rescue, the early phase of Turkish neoliberal restructuring, which relied on currency depreciation, export subsidies, and wage suppression, led to an economic rebound through the mid-1980s. However, by the late 1980s the recovery had reached its limits. Much as in Mexico, Turkish neoliberal advocates saw a renewed commitment to financial liberalization as the best means of continuing with market-oriented restructuring. This led to the 1989 Law of Protection of the Value of the Turkish lira – or the institutionalization of capital account liberalization (Ercan and Oguz 2007, 175). Contrary to more top-down accounts, this financial opening was not imposed by foreign actors but was driven as much by domestic pressures as by the global internationalization of capital since the late 1970s. State and government elites needed to ensure recurrent access to short-term financing so as to maintain Turkey's turn to neoliberalism (Öniş 2006, 249). Despite the Kastelli setback Özal was always committed to the financial restructuring of the state apparatus, albeit in ways modified by Turkey's own circumstances. In addition to removing loan and deposit interest rate limits following the 1980 coup Özal eased commercial bank liquidity and reserve requirements and allowed the entry of foreign bank capital. Authorities then wrote the 1982 Capital Markets Law, which opened opportunities for new market-based financial instruments. Even at this early stage foreign capital was permitted to buy TL securities and to freely repatriate profits. Further reforms in 1984 permitted Turkish residents to open foreign currency deposit accounts in domestic banks and domestic banks to hold foreign currency abroad, to grant foreign currency loans, and to borrow in international markets. To facilitate trade in Turkish state bonds the ANAP government established the TL interbank market in 1986. In this same year the İSE reopened, which expanded the availability of funding sources for Turkish firms. Within a short period state authorities established a secondary market for fixed income securities. To regulate growing financial market operations state authorities established the Capital

Market Board in 1987. Then in 1988 the Turkey Fund became operational with the goal of attracting greater sums of foreign capital investment to Turkey. State financial apparatus building and restructuring through the 1980s meant that by 1989 the Turkish financial sector was poised to handle the greater and more rapid flows of short-term financial capital presupposed by capital account liberalization. Henceforth foreign exchange rates were lifted, limits on foreign borrowing by Turkish banks removed, and limits on foreign control of domestic assets repealed. Foreign capital could now openly trade in company stocks and government securities in the İSE. International creditors responded in the early 1990s by rewarding Turkey with an investment grade rating and improved access to foreign capital.

The 1989 financial liberalization measure triggered an initial upturn in economic activity by drawing in international flows of capital, but this too proved to be short-lived. In early 1994 Turkey became one of the first emerging capitalisms to face a major neoliberal financial crisis (Mexico's Tequila crisis a few months later is most often cited as the first such crisis). Financial restructuring had accelerated the internalization of foreign currency and encouraged TL substitution, and this was within an already unstable and inflation-prone peripheral economy. Whereas in 1986 foreign denominated deposits measured 12.8 per cent of all deposits in Turkey by 1990 this had doubled to 25.5 per cent and it continued to climb through the 1990s to over 45 per cent (Bahmani-Oskooee and Domaç 2003, 307–10). This caused the shrinking of money resources in TL terms, which pushed up domestic interest rates and shortened the maturity structure of credit. A series of credit downgrades and the erosion of financial market access exacerbated the situation. In 1993 capital flight reached 2.15 per cent of Turkish GDP and a financial crisis seemed imminent (Duman et al. 2005, 128). The federal budget deficit reached nearly 7 per cent of GDP and by early 1994 the Turkish state agencies were only able to rollover public debt at extremely high costs. To make matters worse, imports had doubled relative to exports and this too put great pressure on the capital account deficit. In the words of the World Bank, the 'long-predicted financial crisis finally struck' (2005, 1).

The Çiller DYP administration responded with the April 1994 IMF-crafted stabilization program to help regain control of the Turkish economy without sacrificing its neoliberal orientation. This involved a 14-month IMF stand-by arrangement that totaled nearly $1 billion, sharp fiscal adjustment, 70 to 100 per cent price increases in Turkish SOE products, and further pressure to privatize SOEs. The DYP also rolled out a blanket bank deposit guarantee to stop bank runs (Akyüz and Boratav 2003, 1552). The result was a contraction in domestic demand, a rise in inflation, and skyrocketing interest rates amidst increasingly volatile exchange rates. Turkey's popular and working classes felt the direct impact of neoliberal adjustment through a public wage freeze, cuts to public spending, and tax increases. Neoliberal and financial liberalization measures had led to the 1994 crisis, which in turn induced working-class austerity in order to secure the conditions necessary for financial capital to prevail in Turkish society. Nevertheless, the 1994 stabilization package could not immediately solve Turkey's problems with approximating a finance-led form of neoliberal development. By late 1994 inflation was still over 120 per cent on average, the TL had depreciated by 170 per cent against the US dollar, state bond interest rates had climbed to 190 per cent, GDP had shrunk by 5 per cent, and capital outflows amounted to $4 billion (BAT 2000). Bank loans fell dramatically as the cost of credit nearly doubled. Working-class austerity measures had, however, helped to improve the current account and fiscal balance. By early 1995 the Çiller administration adopted a crawling peg exchange rate and soon after this growth began to rebound from crisis, interest rates fell, and the İSE recovered by almost 100 per cent by late April. The March 1995 European Union (EU) Customs Union Agreement with Turkey was read as positive news for foreign capital and Turkey's economic future. As the 1994 crisis settled out, advocates of a better coordinated neoliberalism have suggested that Turkey emerged 'without major dislocations' (Öniş 2006, 249). However, there is no avoiding the fact that the bulk of adjustment fell onto labor and the popular classes as the result of actions by state and government elites intent on bolstering the Turkish state's financial image.

It is important to recall that while Turkish state and government elites were attempting to internalize and approximate neoliberal competitive imperatives, this is a process always modified and contested domestically. For example, while it was argued that the Turkish state banks were involved in creating the 1994 crisis, subsequent Turkish governments did not surrender the state banks to privatization despite IFI conditionalities. This reflects the reality that the IMF did not simply 'impose' conditionality at the height of crisis and Turkey respond in kind (Evrensel 2004). According to one senior IMF official in Ankara, the process of market reform is 'never black and white'; the 'Fund plays the role of shifting responsibility to a foreign actor. The common reader gets the idea of "imposition". But no self-respecting government does anything just because the IMF says. If there are no common objectives, there is no program' (Interview, 27 August 2007). In other words, the universalizing thrust of neoliberal transformation is always modified by and grafted onto domestic circumstances in ways that distinguish and differentiate neoliberalism according to national patterns of accumulation and pre-existing institutionalizations of power (compare Judson 1993). This is evident in the changes undertaken within the Turkish banking sector leading up to the 2000–01 banking crises.

5.2   TWO DECADES OF BANKING ON NEOLIBERAL DEVELOPMENT IN TURKEY

The approximation of neoliberal strategies of development in Turkey has tended to increase financial instability, provide more opportunity for financial crises, and in many ways short-circuit national developmental options in favor of financial imperatives. The restructuring of the banking sector has been part and parcel of this process. In fact, successive Turkish governments looked more and more to the banking sector, and especially to the state-owned banks, as integral to the political goal of neoliberal transformation. This has entailed the restructuring of social relationships of power between the state, the banks, and financial capital, along with changes in the operations of the banks themselves.

The basic structure of the Turkish financial system, while increasingly market-oriented since the 1980s, remained bank-based insofar as banking institutions continued to dominate control over financial assets in Turkey. Separate non-bank or market-based financial institutions have not become serious competitors of the Turkish commercial banks (Isık and Akçaoğlu 2006, 5). This has to do with Turkey's peripheral location within the world market, its historically less developed stock market, and with the banks being legally formed as universal banks. As regards the latter, universal banks engage not only in traditional depository functions but also in investment banking activities such as debt and equity financing. Financial reforms in the 1980s allowed Turkish banks to issue their own securities, to act as intermediaries in primary and secondary markets, and to establish mutual funds. By the mid-1990s the banks handled over 90 per cent of all securities traded in the İSE. During this period commercial bank assets, as a percentage of GNP, grew from 31 in 1980, to 43 in 1990, to 80 per cent by 1999 (BAT 2000). In terms of the range of financial services provided and money resources managed, the banks assumed a much larger and more powerful position within Turkish society and the economy. What have been the dynamics of this change?

During the first two decades of neoliberal restructuring Turkish state and government elites promoted bank liberalization alongside increased private and foreign bank ownership, ostensibly to increase competition and efficiency. This encouraged an increase in the number of banks by 23 since 1980, reaching a relatively significant total of 62 commercial banks by 1999 (Table 5.1). This suggests a process of relative de-concentration

Table 5.1   Number of commercial banks by ownership group, 1980–99

	1980	1990	1999
State banks	11	8	4
Private domestic banks	24	25	31
Foreign banks*	4	–	–
Operations founded in Turkey	–	8	5
Representative branch	–	15	14
Savings Deposit Insurance Fund (TMSF)	–	–	8
Total	39	56	62

Note: * By 1990, the BAT began distinguishing these categories within foreign ownership.

Sources: BAT (1981 (1963–2010); 1991 (1963–2010); 2000).

in bank numbers (if not necessarily asset control). Foreign banks registered the most dramatic increase, growing from four in 1980 to 19 by 1999 (although this did not translate immediately into more asset control, which lingered around 3.5 per cent throughout the 1980s and 1990s, see Table 5.2 below). While initially facing stiffer restrictions, including being prohibited from retail banking, financial authorities relaxed foreign bank regulations in the 1990s. The lucrative Turkish state securities market then drew in additional foreign bank capital. Some private Turkish banks also sought out joint ventures with foreign banks to augment profitability.

The total number of new private domestic banks, by contrast, grew by only seven from 1980 to 1999. However, this number obscures two important features, namely banking sector volatility and holding group ownership and control. Regarding volatility, many private domestic banks closed, were taken over by the state, and/or merged into the state banks as financial authorities granted new private banks operating licenses in their place. In 1999 alone, for example, eight private banks collapsed and were taken over by the SDIF as a result of the guarantees given in 1994 (Akyüz and Boratav 2003, 1552). The number of banks controlled by large Turkish holding groups also rose. It is important to recognize that in Turkey, much as in Mexico, the private banks are often tied to other forms of productive and commercial capital through larger holding groups. Since the 1980s a small number of powerful Turkish holding groups have taken control of more and more of the private domestic banks. Taking control of the banks conferred important competitive advantages on the holding groups (Gültekin-Karakaş 2008). According to the OECD, since the 1980s Turkish holding group executives have increasingly directed banks under their control to lend primarily to customers with 'known' credit credentials; that is, to people with whom the groups are acquainted or with whom they share 'related' activities (OECD 1999, 42, 126–7). Holding group activities that might not otherwise have had access to credit thus found easy access to cheap credit. To complicate matters, the holding group's productive branches often appropriated the profits of their associated banks. This resulted in a cartel-like situation where the most powerful groups came to control the bulk of society's money resources, which they directed towards their own best interests. In the words of Güngör Yener, Chair of the Ankara branch of TOBB, 'The economy is in the hands of 200 families. These families are part of a trend toward monopolist behavior, and can easily adjust financial balances via their banks' (quoted in Cokgezen 2000, 534). Contrary to Hilferding's understanding of finance capital in Germany – as banks controlling industry – in Turkey it was more about industrial and commercial-based groups increasingly taking control of the banks to further the accumulation strategies of their holding groups.

Aside from lending to their group affiliates, the private banks lent to the Turkish state as part of a very lucrative, stable, and growing trade in state debt. The post-1980s turn to debt-led growth strategies in Turkey saw state credit demands grow systematically from 11 per cent to 46 per cent of GDP from 1980 to 1995. This took place alongside the reluctance of governing authorities to tax increasingly mobile capital for fear of its choosing to transfer to cheaper productive locations (compare Karataş 1995). The state's borrowing requirements paradoxically pushed up domestic interest rates and pushed down maturity periods, which had a punishing impact on state finances because the state received 85 per cent of its public borrowing requirements from the private sector. Financing official debt became a socially costly and destabilizing burden on Turkish society. For example, whatever credits the holding group banks made available to the remaining private sector often proved to be too expensive to be of any use – especially to small and medium-sized enterprises (SMEs), which had to self-finance their investments (OECD 1999, 42). At the same time, dealing in state debt was very profitable for financial capital, which also enjoyed exercising more and more structural power over society given its capacity to offer or withhold loanable money from the government.

Table 5.1 also reveals some changes to the Turkish state banks that facilitated finance-led development. One of the first items on the restructuring agenda was the rationalization of the state banks along more market-oriented lines. State authorities began by centralizing the capital and operations of eleven state banks in 1980 into four by 1999. The process included the minor privatizations of four smaller banks

Table 5.2   Percentage of banking sector asset control by ownership,
            1981–97

	State banks	Private banks	Foreign banks
1981–85	45.3	44.4	3.5
1986–90	44.1	43.9	3.4
1991–97	38.9	50.5	3.5

Note: Investment and development banks not shown.

Source: BAT (1999a).

(Sümerbank, Etibank, Denizbank, and Anadolu Bank) and the merger
or closure of others. The state also sold off its minority stakes in private
banks, including a 10 per cent share of Şekerbank in 1993. The sell-off of
the state banks and insurance companies from 1988 to 1997 totaled only
$275 million (Karataş 2001, 100). The largest transaction prior to the 2001
crisis occurred in 1998 with the sale of the state's 12.3 per cent share in İş
Bank for $651 million. So while it is true that by 1999 only Ziraat Bank,
Halk Bank, Emlak Bank, and Vakiflar Bank remained, these four state
banks were now very large by Turkish standards and the state retained
full control and ownership of them. After nearly two decades of neoliberal
restructuring state bank control was just under 40 per cent of all banking
assets, having contracted only by about 6 per cent since 1980 (Table 5.2).
The evolution of the Turkish state banks under neoliberalism has not been
about shedding state capacity but about crafting larger, more powerful,
and more concentrated state banks. For their part, the Turkish private
domestic banks expanded their asset control by just over 6 per cent, basically absorbing the asset space shed by the state banks.

Nonetheless, in line with neoliberal assumptions, financial liberalization spurred a mild process of bank asset de-concentration (albeit of an
already rather concentrated sector). In 1990 the five largest public and
private banks controlled 54 per cent of all banking assets and the top ten
controlled 75 per cent (BAT 2000). By 1999 the assets controlled by the top
five banks had fallen to 46 per cent of assets and the top ten banks to 68
per cent. This mild reversal of asset concentration should not be confused
with the ongoing centralization of Turkish banking capital and power. As
Isık and Akçaoğlu report, the large Turkish holding groups gained control
over most of the private banks and their assets during this period (2006,
5). In terms of the state banks, assets became relatively more concentrated:
whereas in 1980 the eleven state banks had controlled about 45 per cent of
all bank assets, in the late 1990s the remaining four state banks controlled

Table 5.3   Profitability indicators by ownership, 1976–97

Average return on equity (%)

	State banks	Private banks	Foreign banks
1976–80	–13.0	34.7	58.0
1981–85	26.4	30.8	108.5
1986–90	35.0	47.8	61.2
1991–97	23.2	60.5	94.3

Average return on assets (%)

	State banks	Private banks	Foreign banks
1976–80	–0.5	0.9	1.6
1981–85	1.8	1.4	4.8
1986–90	2.0	3.1	4.4
1991–97	1.1	4.4	7.5

Source: BAT (1999a).

about 40 per cent. In comparison to Mexico, then, the concentration of assets within the largest five to ten banks was not as high, but was nonetheless significant. Turkey has differed, however, in its bank ownership and control structure insofar as not all bank ownership is concentrated in the private sector or in foreign hands but is balanced out by the significant holdings of the state banks, which operated under different operational imperatives (discussed later as 'duty losses').

The evolution of bank profitability – shown in Table 5.3 in terms of the average return on equity (ROE) and return on assets (ROA) for Turkish banks from 1976 to 1997 – offers some important insights into Turkey's transition to finance-led neoliberalism. Since the 1980 military coup and Özal's turn to market-oriented development private and foreign bank profitability has improved considerably, even dramatically so. From an ROA of 0.9 per cent by the 1980s the private banks' profits more than quadrupled by the late 1990s (with the smaller foreign banks making even more dramatic gains). On average the private domestic banks earned an astounding 2.97 per cent ROA from 1981 on (and the foreign banks 5.57 per cent). By way of comparison, the ROA of Spanish banks averaged 1.38 per cent, Italian 1.14 per cent, and German 0.5 per cent from 1981 to 1989 (Akçaoğlu 1998, 92). Insofar as in neoliberal terms profitability is a harbinger of competitiveness and efficiency, Özal's reforms in the financial sector seemed to be yielding results. Even the 1994 financial crisis did not slow the aggregate growth in ROA and ROE profits of the private domestic and foreign banks. By contrast, following a period of losses prior to 1980 the state banks were revenue generating from 1981 to 1997 with an average ROA of 1.63 per cent (which was also higher than banks in other OECD countries). Recall that the state banks since their inception had been mandated to support national developmental goals rather than respond to profit imperatives. The lower profit levels at times of crisis also suggests that, contrary to the activities of the private and foreign banks, the state banks' lending practices did not seek to gain from crisis.

The very high and fluctuating levels of ROE for the private domestic and foreign banks are a reflection of the expansion of state debt along-side a growing share of bank profits derived from dealing in government securities. For some, the channeling of bank capital into state debt means the banks were not acting as 'real' banks. Yet the very logic of capital-ist development is first and foremost to maximize the accumulation of money capital, and this is precisely what the private banks did. The banks increased their leveraged debt, evidenced by their high ROE, which was facilitated by the government institutionalizing more open access to international financial markets. The debt-laden governments likewise provided the banks with a lucrative and stable outlet for their leveraged debt. More and more the Turkish banks as well as foreign and domestic capital in Turkey redirected money resources towards the financial sector where high profits were being earned. Some domestic holding groups began to shed industrial affiliates to redirect their resources towards lucrative interest-based profits. The high interest demanded by financial capital in Turkey also opened arbitrage opportunities and encouraged short-term capital flows, thereby augmenting financial instability. High-leveraged debt accumulation strategies are difficult to sustain at the best and most certain of times, let alone in emerging capitalisms like Turkey where both economic and political uncertainties prevail. Lastly, in terms of Turkey's finance-led transition, it needs to be signaled that the payment of interest on public debt involves a transfer of wealth from the majority of working-class taxpaying citizens to a minority of financial capitalists who own and control money resources. The payment of interest on state debts, as opposed to increasing corporate taxation to cover annual fiscal costs, at the same time represents the institutionalized privileging of the needs of capital, particularly financial capital, over those of the working population.

Turkey's increasingly finance-led development strategy led to further changes in the banks' accumulation strategies. Whereas during the 1960s and under stricter capital controls one strategy had been to increase the number of bank branches across Turkey to capture more domestic deposits, financial liberalization opened up new sources of foreign capital resources. For the larger banks with foreign access this eclipsed the need to expand geographically. Consequently, the Turkish banks could seek labor productivity gains by maintaining the same number of branches relative to an expanding pool of capital resources managed. For example, the number of bank branches remained effectively flat from 1980 to 1997 for all owner-ship groups. About 85 per cent of all branches that were open in 1999 were in fact opened prior to 1980 (BAT 2000). Whatever branch openings have occurred since the 1980s originated with the new smaller banks trying to capture some market share. The bankers also sought productivity gains by targeting bank employee growth rates. Through the 1980s and 1990s private domestic bank employee numbers grew by less than 5 per cent (BAT 1999a). In the largest private banks, like İş Bank, Akbank, and Yapı ve Kredi Bank, employee numbers hardly grew at all (Isık and Akçaoğlu 2006, 11). Yet this relative stagnation in employee growth occurred while the ratio of bank assets to GNP grew from 30 per cent in the early 1980s to 80 per cent in the late 1990s. Perhaps the more revealing point is that while the asset share of Turkish private domestic banks grew by 6 per cent to over 50 per cent, the percentage of private domestic employees fell to just 45 per cent of the sector's total. This means that private bank asset base growth outpaced employee growth, which is partly linked to introducing new technologies. More critically, we can see that, first, fewer workers are dealing with more financial resources in ways that intensify their produc-tivity (in Marxian terms, an increase in fixed over variable capital) and, second, as a result the bargaining power of bank workers is weakened (vis-à-vis the threat to withdraw their labor power).

How did the Turkish state banks react? As we know, during the 1980s and 1990s the asset share of the state banks fell from 45 to 39 per cent and profitability improved from a position of loss in the late 1970s to positive gains by the late 1990s. In contrast to the private sector where assets and profits grew while employee levels fell, the shrinking state bank sector con-tinued to employ about 50 per cent of the entire banking sector's employ-ees. The state banks did this by increasing employee numbers by over 10 per cent, or from about 67 000 in the early 1980s to about 74 000 by the late 1990s (BAT 1999a). Contrary to neoliberal mythology the growth in state bank employee numbers need not be attributed to any innate characteristic of corrupt state bank management. To be sure, the largely authoritarian and undemocratic transition to neoliberalism itself can be seen as corrupt at heart, but I suspect advocates do not want to go down that road. A more historically specific account can be found in Turkey's volatile transi-tion to neoliberalism and the political leadership's unwavering political commitment to sustaining neoliberalism. Rather than seeking any sub-stantive alternative, state and government officials protected neoliberalism by rolling several failed private banks (the supposed vanguard agents of the new economy) into the state banks (the supposed dregs of economic progress) during the 1980s and 1990s. For example, authorities forcibly merged the private domestic İstanbul Bank, Hısarbank, İstanbul Emniyet Sandigi Bank, and Ortadoğu Iktisat Bank into the state-owned Ziraat Bank in 1983 and 1984 and Anadolu Bank into Emlak Bank in 1988 (Isık and Akçaoğlu 2006, 10–12). In 1992 and 1993, authorities then folded the assets of Töbank (private) into Halk Bank (state). On the one hand, state authorities stabilized the potentially destabilizing collapse of a private bank by socializing its financial risks through the state banks. On the other hand, state authorities ensured that the state banks absorbed the private sector bank workers in order to quell possible social tensions due to job losses. This forced an increase in the number of state bank employees in the name of neoliberal stability. In other words, by absorbing failed private banks, socializing their financial risks, and accommodating redundant private bank employees the Turkish state banks helped to contain the social volatility of finance-led neoliberal restructuring. The state bank duty losses were also significant in this regard.

5.2.1   The Problem of State Bank Duty Losses

The problem of Turkish state bank duty losses is a controversial yet under-analyzed issue. This is in large part due to the reluctance of state authorities to release reliable information on the duty losses leading up to the 2000–01 crisis.[3] It is also due to the unwillingness of analysts to critically ask what duty losses are and what relations they imply between the state, banks, and development in Turkey.

Duty losses historically represented the institutionalized capacity of Turkish governments to politically direct financing via the state-owned banks to socially important sectors of the economy. For example, postwar governments assigned Ziraat Bank agricultural duty losses, Halk Bank small trades duty losses, and so on as part of state-led development strategies. The actual 'duty loss' is a state bank's claim on the Turkish Treasury (that is, on future state revenues) derived from state subsidized lending and the interest accrued on the subsidized loans (BAT 2001). For six decades or more until the mid-1990s the political intent of the state bank duty loss mechanism was to overcome structural barriers to financing national developmental projects. In other words, state authorities had institutionalized a stable way to socialize some of the costs and financial risks of postwar capitalist development.

The national and international turbulence of the 1990s changed matters. Under the Çiller administration state and government elites began systematically underestimating (read: hiding) government spending via state bank duty losses, mostly through Ziraat and Halk Bank (compare BAT 2009c, 34). Duty losses became, according to the BRSA, hidden budgetary deficits (2003, 10). In practice this meant the government's commitment to paying the duty loss difference back to the state banks evaporated. Herein lies the rub. Duty loss claims appeared as illiquid fixed assets in the state banks' balance sheet belonging to the Turkish Treasury, but these claims did not show as liabilities in the state Treasury's budget accounts (compare BAT 2009c, 90). As such, the state bank duty losses existed as off-budget spending left unrecorded in government expenditures (OECD 1999, 57). As a senior manager of Halk Bank commented, the mandate of providing subsidized and targeted credits had worked well – but only when the government was committed to paying the difference (Interview, 24 August 2007). During the 1990s rising state financing costs, mounting official debts, and a phobia against raising corporate tax made the lure of the state bank duty loss mechanism irresistible to a string of weak coalition governments. Consequently, the quantity of state bank duty losses exploded from 2.2 per cent of 1995 GNP to 13 per cent of 1999 GNP (or from about \$2.77 billion to about \$19.2 billion) (World Bank 2000, 96). Where did these billions go?

Neoliberal and mainstream end-of-financial-repression accounts have tended to frame the historically specific question of duty losses as universally problematic and as little more than a 'vote getting' tool for corrupt politicians via populist rent distribution – albeit without much or any actual evidence (see BAT 2000; ERF 2005, 106). Yet the interesting point is not about the presumed human nature of politicians (who, for liberal interpretations, are corrupt independent of time, place, or historical circumstances). Rather, what can we reasonably see as the social logic or political intent of the duty loss mechanism given the decision-makers' historical circumstances? Why do Turkish duty losses explode after its 1994 crisis and as the 1997 East Asian and 1998 Russian crises unfold? Why only under neoliberalism has the duty loss mechanism created problems unseen during the previous six decades? Answers to these questions require further research that is presently outside the scope of this book. Nonetheless, one can start piecing together a critical interpretation. To begin with, and according to the OECD, duty loss issuances by the Treasury helped governments meet some of their financial obligations to other parts of the state apparatus, including to the Central Bank of Turkey (CBT; Türkiye Cumhuriyet Merkez Bankası), Turkish SOEs, and even to other state-owned banks (1999, 56). According to the World Bank, Turkish governments channeled duty loss resources into everything from disaster relief operations to small business support to the rescue of insolvent Turkish banks. Most duty losses, however, relate to agricultural support and loan write-offs for struggling Turkish farmers (World Bank 2000, 96). As one financial commentator noted after the 2001 Turkish banking crisis, 'the state banks that have led to Turkey's demise were, after all, only trying to help the local farming community' (Rhode 2001, 40). In this case, the intention goes beyond mere 'help' insofar as the duty losses directed at agriculture were politically motivated to help to mitigate the social conflicts arising from neoliberal restructuring in Turkey. Given the centrality of agriculture to the Turkish economy neoliberal advocates could not risk the sector falling into sustained crisis without risking the overall neoliberal project (Oyan 2002). The agricultural duty losses helped to mitigate this tension. Moreover, this could be done outside of demo-cratic political struggles over access to limited state funds. The same can be said for duty loss resources directed elsewhere in the economy. The larger point is that hiding these dedicated state resources in the state banks via duty losses simultaneously freed up money for Turkish governments to ensure debt repayments to foreign and domestic financial capital, thus helping to maintain Turkey's creditworthiness in the eyes of the interna-tional community. One might explain this as typical of universally corrupt politicians, and this may well be, but such an a priori hypothetical deduc-tive approach obscures more than it reveals, such as the constitutive role of duty losses in neoliberal transformation. Unwilling to tax internation-ally mobile capital, state authorities looked to the once developmentally oriented duty loss mechanism to help resolve the contradictions and costs created by neoliberal transformation. Ironically, the amassing of duty losses led to unintended new contradictions and costs as Turkey approached its second major neoliberal financial crisis at the end of the 1990s.

5.3   PRELUDE TO THE 2000 BANKING CRISIS

Since the 1994 crisis the Turkish economy had been as volatile as the Turkish political situation, even though the settling out of the crisis had brought some initial aggregate recovery and growth. From 1995 to 1997 Turkish GDP growth rebounded and averaged over 7 per cent. The expansion derived from the ratcheting down on the wages of labor, renewed export growth, foreign worker remittances, black market trade with the former Soviet Union, tourism investment, and the unfolding of the EU Customs Union Agreement. However, the international impact of the 1997 Asian crisis caused capital inflows from advanced capitalist states into Turkey to slow dramatically, which in turn led to the collapse of growth to 3 per cent by 1998. This economic volatility constrained the range of options politically. Whereas one year earlier, in November 1997, the Yılmaz minority government had rejected an IMF and World Bank endorsed one-year shock therapy program, in early 1998 the coalition government (given its commitment to neoliberalism) had few options but to adopt an even more stringent three-year disinflation program while pledging itself to bringing about an immediate primary budget surplus via tight fiscal policy (OECD 1999). As had been the case during the crisis of 1994, instability once again entailed public sector austerity, which dispro-portionately impacted the working and popular classes. The 1998 Russian crisis only worsened matters. Capital flight accelerated and this put greater pressure on domestic capital resources, especially since the Turkish economy was already slowing. To retain inflows of financial capital the government brought the interest rates of Turkish state bonds upwards of 130 per cent. To take advantage of these high-yield state bonds and the spectacular speculative profits they yielded the domestic Turkish banks exposed themselves to larger open foreign exchange positions (Akyüz and Boratav 2003). The banks' ROE profit measures hit the 60 per cent range reflecting their increasingly leveraged accumulation strategies.

The OECD predictably blames the unstable economic situation and inflationary troubles of Turkey on profligate government spending and Turkish SOE subsidies. Yet the OECD also makes a rare admission of the disproportionate class-based benefits of financial capital in neoliberal debt-led growth in Turkey (1999, 12):

> some segments of the population actually gain from this situation: especially net lenders (corporations, banks and high-income households), who receive higher unearned income receipts in the short term (though tax reform has begun to bite into these gains). Inflation thus works to the benefit of an urban *rentier* economy vis-à-vis other social groups, resulting in an extremely skewed income distribution.

Those who owned and controlled money resources in Turkey were making the best of a bad situation, and indeed were taking full advantage of the opportunities Turkey's neoliberal turn had opened.

Since the 1994 crisis no political party had exercised hegemony and neoliberalism remained the default position for Turkey's main political parties, which offered no political alternative to further market-oriented reform. From 1994 to 1999 seven different coalition governments under four different leaders came into power. This volatile period also saw the rise in popularity of the Islamic influenced Refah Partisi (RP; Welfare Party) under Necmettin Erbakan from 1994 to 1996. At the time Erbakan seemed to pose a political challenge to the secular stance of Kemalist capitalists and their political force within Turkish society and the state. As a result the Turkish military, with the backing of TÜSİAD, effectively brought down the RP-led coalition government on 28 February 1997. By July a three-party minority coalition headed by Mesut Yılmaz and the ANAP had assumed control of the government. Yılmaz called for early elections for the following April, but the ANAP coalition government fell in November 1998 when the CHP pulled out amidst economic turbulence stemming from the 1998 Russian crisis. A caretaker government headed by Bülent Ecevit was formed in January 1999 in order to bring Turkey to the April 1999 elections. The elections, however, resulted in no clear majority and another three-party coalition was formed in June 1999, this time led by Ecevit's Demokratik Sol Parti (DSP; Democratic Left Party) alongside an uncomfortable bedfellow – the right-wing Milliyetçi Hareket Partisi (MHP; Nationalist Action Party) under Devlet Bahceli. Over the next couple of years this leftist-led coalition would become a major innovator of the form that finance-led neoliberalism would take in Turkey, notably with the 1999 disinflation program.

5.3.1 The 1999 Bank Law and 1999 Disinflation Program

By the late 1990s, after two decades of financial liberalization and high state debt requirements, the Turkish banks found themselves able to take very large open foreign exchange positions – which exploded from $3.6 billion to $12.6 billion between 1997 and 1999 – and to recycle high yielding flows of finance capital through the state. Insofar as Turkish financial capital was overexposed, the mounting financial risks began to cause concern for foreign investors and for state elites. The Yılmaz coalition had attempted to regulate foreign borrowing by limiting domestic banks' exposure ratios, but this had the unintended effect of pushing up domestic interest rates even more and further exacerbating the Turkish state's precarious financial position. It appeared that neither the Yılmaz coalition nor the 1998 IMF program could resolve Turkey's ongoing instability (Yeldan 2002). The incoming Ecevit coalition government seemed to bring a thaw in Turkey's deadlocked political and economic instability. The international community had sent a strong signal of confidence in Turkey by drawing the country into the Group of Twenty (G-20) – a forum of advanced industrialized and big emerging market finance ministers and central bank governors established in 1999. Late that same year the long awaited European Council's Helsinki verdict unanimously accepted Turkey's EU candidacy for full membership. Moreover, Ecevit's coalition seemed to be holding. Yet rather than attempt any break from market-oriented development the coalition passed the new 1999 Bank Law and replaced the 1998 IMF program with a new one, the December 1999 disinflation program.

The DSP coalition intended the June 1999 Bank Law to modernize banking regulation along EU market-oriented guidelines. In this regard government and state managers envisioned the Bank Law as the center-piece of state and bank restructuring by, first, responding to decades of high and chronic inflation and, second, serving as the cornerstone of building the state's financial regulatory capacity. The law aimed to do this by institutionalizing enhanced bank supervision, regulation, and opera-tions in line with Basel principles for bank supervision and EU directives. For example, all banks had to comply with the Bank of International Settlements (BIS) model of risk-weighted capital adequacy ratios, open foreign currency positions had to be kept at or below 20 per cent of capital, and large credits extended by holding groups were subject to new restric-tions (BAT 2000). Ideally this stronger institutional footing would help to stimulate finance-led development in Turkey that in turn would create more credits for all sectors of the economy. Stipulations required the banks in Turkey to meet the new requirements within five years.

To bolster state capacity the 1999 Bank Law simultaneously created a new state financial institution – the Banking Regulation and Supervisory Agency (BRSA; Bankacılık Düzenleme ve Denetleme Kurumu) – which began operations in late August 2000. The logic behind establishing the BRSA was to enable state authorities to respond to emerging financial imperatives by guarding against banking threats and volatility. The law mandated that the BRSA facilitate bank efficiency and competitiveness, minimize banking sector losses in the economy as a whole, fortify the sector in general, and protect savers' rights and interests. Facilitating both neoliberal de-politicization and the internationalization of the state apparatus, the law crafted the BRSA as an independent state agency. This entailed removing bank supervision from the Treasury and the CBT to place it in the hands of the BRSA. The powers handed to the BRSA included the right to audit banks, recommend the issuance or cancellation of bank licenses, transfer failing banks to the SDIF, or force the merger of two or more banks in trouble. With approval from the Turkish cabinet, the BRSA could close down a bank. While independent in law, in practi-cal terms the power of the BRSA is underwritten by the Turkish state and constitutive of the state form – a form that has increased its institutional capacity to manage financial capital within its borders while internalizing financial imperatives.

Along with the 1999 Bank Law the DSP coalition adopted the new IMF-crafted 1999 disinflation program, uniquely without being in the midst of an acute financial crisis (Öniş 2006, 249). The 1999 disinflation program represented continuity in the political leadership's commitment to neoliberal development strategies. IMF and Turkish authorities framed the 1999 program around three neoliberal pillars: tight fiscal and monetary policies; ambitious market-oriented structural reforms; and the use of a pre-announced exchange rate to reduce inflation (BAT 1999b). The program also named four neoliberal developmental goals: to reduce the inflation rate; to reduce real interest rates; to create economic growth; and to more effectively and fairly allocate economic resources. The core political intent was to send foreign financial capital a positive message about Turkey's dedication to inflation management and debt service capacity. To gold-seal this message the coalition adopted a new currency board-type arrangement which shaped monetary policy and tied liquidity expansion to foreign currency inflows (BRSA 2002). A crawling peg exchange rate restricted Turkish lira (TL) devaluation to 15 per cent per year. State financial authorities planned that by July 2001 – 18 months after the crawling peg was adopted – they could begin to widen the bands around central parity. The government hoped to gradually acclimatize Turkish banks to greater exchange rate flexibility. The government justified the measure as a way of combating high inflation, namely by solving Turkey's credibility and coordination problems in the eyes of financial capital.

In its first ten months the 1999 program seemed to be succeeding in its own terms. State authorities largely met the monetary, fiscal, and exchange rate goals set. Inflation fell from almost 100 per cent only a year earlier to around 35 per cent, giving some respite to the federal budget. Debt service aside, the DSP government's austerity measures created a budget surplus. The DSP coalition held firm to its commitments to deregulation and privatization, while promising to clean up the state banks' duty losses. Market advocates applauded the Ecevit coalition's political resolve behind continued neoliberal restructuring. Financial capital proffered its vote of confidence as Standard and Poor's adjusted Turkey's credit rating upwards to a single B category in August 1999, which was reconfirmed in December 1999 and then upgraded again to B+ in April 2000. A net $12.5 billion in foreign capital flowed into Turkish markets (Akyüz and Boratav 2003, 1554). The İSE rose by a spectacular 650 per cent by early 2000. The signs seemingly pointed to a new cycle of virtuous investment and growth. Was it possible that with this IMF program Turkey might break free of its perennial cycles of recurrent economic volatility?

It would not be so. Turkey remained anchored to the financial muddle of emerging capitalist development. Just as the Ecevit coalition was unveiling the 1999 program and capital was beginning to see renewed profits the government announced on 22 December 1999 that it was also rescuing five more failing small and medium-sized domestic banks by drawing them

under SDIF control. This made for a total of eight rescued banks representing about 8 per cent of the sector's assets. The cost of socializing the
banks' bad financial risks drained state resources and the DSP coalition
was unsure whether to fully nationalize the banks or to try to immediately
re-sell them. Earlier stock market gains began to recede as concerns grew
over the stability of the Turkish banking system.

Problems internally specific to the 1999 disinflation program also soon
appeared. For one, the decision to pre-announce exchange rates, ostensibly as a signal of Turkey's financial stability and credibility, paradoxically created more instability and greater financial risk. Pre-announced
exchange rates alongside the real appreciation of the TL entailed reduced
foreign currency liability costs for banks in Turkey. From the perspective
of individual banks, then, the logical thing was to borrow in short-term
foreign currency and lend in longer-term TL terms (the potentially profitable but risky carry trade). Collectively, this created problematic credit
maturity mismatches and greatly increased the foreign currency open
positions of domestic banks (BRSA 2002). Financial liquidity, interest
rate, and exchange rate risks accumulated in Turkish society to hitherto
unknown levels. In another paradoxical situation, the 1999 program led
to a decline in domestic interest rates, which was good for state finances.
Yet this meant that the banks in Turkey also had to reduce their deposit
and lending rates. Since the 1990s the banks had heavily increased their
exposure to state debt. As inflation fell so too did the interest rates
offered by the Treasury – from about 100 per cent to 35 per cent. Without
these practically guaranteed high profits from servicing state debt the
banks were compelled to source new profitability avenues and to draw
on foreign capital resources. The private domestic banks adopted new
competitive strategies which involved a shift to retail banking, investment
in automatic tellers, card payments, and so on. Consumer credit provision became increasingly important to the new strategy, which expanded
fourfold through 2000 – as did the risks tied to consumer debt (Duman et
al. 2005, 129). Given Turkey's subordinate position within the financial
world market the balance between the successes and paradoxes of the 1999
program could not hold indefinitely. At some point financial capital would
lose confidence and withdraw the recurrent flows of money on which
Turkey was dependent.

Nonetheless, the DSP coalition was more interested in deepening
finance-led reforms than in coming to terms with the mounting financial
instability. This is, for example, the case with its continuing to press for
state-owned bank privatization. In June 2000 the parliament approved
a law giving the DSP coalition the ability to enact 'decrees with the force
of law'. The DSP used this law to push through legal changes enabling

the privatization of the state-owned, but independent, Vakiflar Bank. A Constitutional Court challenge rescinded the rule-by-decree law in October 2000, by extension rescinding the Vakiflar privatization decree. Yet even as the sector looked increasingly shaky the DSP took the opportunity to legalize the privatization of three more state banks, Ziraat, Halk, and Emlak. Then in late November the government passed another law to enable the privatization of Vakiflar and to further provide for the commercialization and privatization of Ziraat, Halk, and Emlak. By this time, however, volatility had fully gripped the Turkish economy thereby foreclosing any immediate state bank sell-off.

By the fall of 2000 escalating banking sector instability had compelled the DSP coalition and BRSA to rescue *cum* socialize three more failing private Turkish banks, which were placed within the SDIF on 27 October. Ironically, Etibank – a state-owned bank that had been privatized only in 1998 – was among the private banks socialized. The coalition accompanied the rescue with a $6.1 billion transfer from the Treasury to the SDIF (that is, from the public to the private sector) to cover the private banks' losses (OECD 2001b, 206; World Bank 2003, 52). The IFIs, as such robust advocates of financial liberalization, now expressed their uneasiness over Turkey's dependence on foreign capital inflows. And rightly so. In November 2000 the first of two back to back banking crises struck. Foreign financial capital withdrew nearly $6 billion from Turkey causing a collapse in foreign reserves and an increase in domestic interest rates, bringing Turkey to near financial collapse. The situation forced the newly instituted BRSA to shift priorities from fulfilling its supervision duties to coordinating banking sector resurrection and restructuring. To support BRSA efforts the IMF delivered a $10 billion relief package in December 2000 to reassure financial capital by increasing liquidity and reserve levels. With IMF resources in hand, Prime Minister Ecevit boasted that the Turkish economy was still on track to grow.

The rapid IMF intervention and Ecevit's optimism, however, brought only temporary calm. Longstanding political tensions remained and the structural imbalances of neoliberal development had not been resolved. The November crisis had eroded the private banking sector's weak capital base and in so doing had exposed its fragility. In turn, this uncovered the Turkish state banks' problematic exposure of billions of dollars in neoliberal duty losses that would lead to the second, and more serious, banking crisis in February 2001 (which we pick up in Chapter 7). In somewhat understated terms the former World Bank Country Director for Turkey Ajay Chhibber (2004) argues that the IMF should have better considered 'country fit' in developing the 1999 disinflation program, which was now introducing Turkey to its largest ever neoliberal financial crisis.

5.4 CONCLUSION

Over the first two decades of neoliberal transformation in Turkey political leadership supported the interests of financial capital within Turkey's borders by crafting a more substantial state financial apparatus – one that is increasingly independent of democratic processes but institutionally subordinate to financial imperatives. This occurred hand in hand with the political opening of the financial and banking sector to world market competition and foreign capital flows. Because raising domestic taxes on capital is anathema to neoliberalism, Turkey's financial opening has been crucial to its debt-led strategy of development, which depends on government and state elites recycling state debts and on creditworthiness. The strategy also served to reinforce competitive, short-term, and speculative behavior among those who own and control money. Given Turkish society's still subordinate position within the hierarchy of states and world markets, this contributed to near continuous political and economic instability through the 1990s. To help manage instability Turkish authorities created forms of fictitious capital via the state bank duty loss mechanism to ease neoliberal restructuring – a tactic that would carry a heavy cost for the popular classes in Turkey with the 2001 crisis. Regardless of the apparent economic troubles and social inequalities government elites refused to articulate an alternative developmental strategy during the 1990s. Instead advocates institutionalized an increasingly finance-led form of neoliberalism premised, as it is, on reducing workers' wages, restraining labor organization, privatizing SOEs, and forcing austerity at times of crisis alongside the socialization of financial risks.

NOTES

1. Tezcan Yaramancı worked for Koç Holdings from 1968 to 1991. As a senior Koç executive, Yaramancı served as a chair of TÜSİAD. In 1992, Yaramancı became president and CEO of the state-owned Turkish Airlines on the request of Prime Minister Demirel. In 1994, Yaramancı became the head of the Privatization Administration and wrote the 1994 Privatization Law (see below). Yaramancı then returned to the private sector in late 1994 and first worked with Doğan Holdings. He then formed his own brokerage house in İstanbul in 1996, Investa Consulting.
2. The following is drawn from an interview with Tezcan Yaramancı (Investa Consulting, 21 August 2007).
3. According to a senior official at the CBT, government reports exist but they are confidential and not made public due to the possible political ramifications (Interview, 14 August 2007).

6. Another round of tequila? Interpreting the costs and benefits of emerging finance capitalism in Mexico

The decisive political turn to market-oriented strategies of development following the 1982 debt crisis in Mexico led to persistent economic instability and further financial crisis in 1994–95. The impact of Mexico's 'Tequila' crisis necessitated a massive internationally financed state-led rescue of the banks – if a finance-led neoliberal trajectory was not to be abandoned and if the growing centrality of financial capital to development was to be preserved. Subsequently, state and government elites further restructured state, bank, and labor relations to favor the needs of financial capital, particularly foreign capital. The benefits accrued to financial capital have not come without social costs and complications. Following a period of relative financial stability in Mexico in recent years, the US sub-prime crisis revealed new sources of financial instability from outside the banking sector. Much as in 1995, the form the resolution took, while differing in its specific content, was premised on Mexican society absorbing the costs of financial accumulation risk taking.

In this chapter I argue that the response to the current crisis signifies the consolidation of nearly three decades of neoliberal and finance-led restructuring of state, bank, and labor relations in Mexico as emerging finance capitalism. This current phase of capital accumulation represents the fusion of the interests of domestic and foreign financial capital in the Mexican state apparatus as the institutionalized priorities and overarching social logic guiding the actions of state and government elites, often to the detriment of labor. I develop this argument in five sections. Section 6.1 looks at the 1995 bank rescue as a case of saving neoliberalism from the overzealousness of its advocates. Section 6.2 looks at the subsequent internalization of foreign capital. The third section details the ways in which change continues to benefit the banks and financial capital in Mexico. Section 6.4 then assesses the current crisis vis-à-vis the culmination of emerging finance capitalism. This is followed by a brief conclusion.

6.1   SAVING NEOLIBERALISM FROM THE NEOLIBERALS: THE 1995 BANK BAILOUT

Contrary to popular mythology neoliberal capitalism in Mexico has not been about minimizing state institutional capacity but about restructuring the state apparatus so that state and government elites can better support market-oriented capital accumulation, much as is the case in other emerging capitalisms (compare Kiely 2007). While the beginnings of Mexico's market-oriented restructuring pre-dated Partido Revolucionario Institucional (PRI) President de la Madrid (1982–88), in many respects de la Madrid managed the first concerted wave of neoliberal restructuring following the 1982 bank nationalization decision and amidst the debt crisis of the 1980s. Yet it was PRI President Salinas (1988–94), who assumed power under fraudulent electoral conditions, who intensified market-oriented restructuring and Mexico's continental integration by unilaterally negotiating and institutionalizing the 1994 North American Free Trade Agreement (NAFTA). To facilitate the dismantling of Mexico's state-led legacy of capitalist development the PRI framed the desired changes around four policy objectives: to increase aggregate economic efficiency and productivity; to promote private investment and technological improvements; to minimize public budget pressures; and to free public resources for investment in infrastructure and social investment (Ortiz Martínez 1993, 259). The political legacy of the PRI has been one of trying to approximate these neoliberal ideals.

Approximating neoliberalism entails changing institutionalized relationships of power. As discussed in Chapter 4, neoliberal restructuring from the start involved the PRI enabling the interests of capital in Mexico over the interests of organized labor, the peasantry, and the poor, most notably by making Mexico a site of cheap, globally integrated productive labor. Then, as now, the PRI and Partido Acción Nacional (PAN; National Action Party) governments have facilitated this strategy by keeping wage increases below the rate of inflation (Rodríguez Araujo 2010, 40). From 1996 to 2002 this brought down the purchasing power of Mexican workers' wages by 50 per cent (Soederberg 2010a, 82). At the same time state authorities' efforts to increase market discipline have meant salaried labor has become more precarious and subject to workplace flexibilization, thereby reducing the collective power of workers (Guillén Romo 2005, 268). The policy tools used to achieve this shift in power relations have included systematic cuts to social spending and state-owned enterprise (SOEs) privatizations. The result is exacerbated social inequality and instability with the very rich getting richer and everyone else getting poorer (Teichman 2008; Nissanke and Thorbecke 2010). As but one notable example, whereas Mexico sported two billionaires in 1991 it boasted 24 by 1994 (Rodríguez 2010, 47). The liberal ideological basis of this transformation revolves around notions of competitive self-reliance – or the idea that win or lose, individuals make it on their own and alone. However, in practice competitive self-reliance in Mexico has mostly applied to working people and less to capital, which has benefited tremendously from state support. This is perhaps most striking in relation to the 1995 banking crisis and rescue, the point at which the PRI demanded that Mexican society and labor help mitigate financial instability by paying for a costly state-led banking rescue. Mexican society consequently found itself in the unenviable position of socializing the costs of the Mexican elites' experiment with approximating neoliberal ideals (the Washington consensus).

In Mexico the transition to neoliberalism, with the profit and competitive imperatives specific to this phase of capital accumulation, led to the 1994 peso crisis and the subsequent 1995 banking crisis. Mainstream academic and official accounts, however, restrict blame for the 1995 banking crisis to weak state regulation and political failures, which enabled market failure in the form of inexperienced Mexican bankers.[1] Indeed, the hindsight of market liberalization advocates has been 20/20: since the Mexican banking crisis, the East Asian, Russian, Argentinean, Turkish, and the current Great Recession have all been fundamentally due to state failure, which in one way or another allowed market failure (Haber 2005a; Demirgüç-Kunt and Servén 2009; Rogers 2010). As lucidly captured in a BIS working paper on diagnosing and predicting developing country banking failures, 'Weak enforcement due to political interference is the Achilles' heel of any regulatory system' (Honohan 1997, 27). Thus, liberalization advocates' foresight is also 20/20 since future bank failures are also due to state failure of one form or another. Because such a priori analytical frameworks admit practically no fault in the market that is not due to political interference, the problems can be rectified by recourse to better – if minimal regulatory – policy: what has become known in international financial institution (IFI) circles as the post-Washington consensus. Ironically, liberal skepticism over government interference – and this is rather important – does not extend to questioning governments' political commitments to the unequal social relations of power between capital and labor constitutive of neoliberal capitalism. Yet only by turning a blind eye to issues of power and class could state authorities pitch the 1995 bank rescue not as saving a few private bankers or financial capital collectively, but as necessary for the benefit of all Mexicans (compare SHCP 1998, 21, 26–7). To protect society's interests, moreover, the PRI argued that the government must protect Mexico's image as a model market reformer unwilling to revisit the bank nationalization option exercised in 1982, which would prove too costly in monetary and reputation terms. Ideologically unshaken by the 1994–95 crisis President Zedillo demonstrated a historic commitment to neoliberalism by rescuing the banks, which carried with it a mammoth social cost. In practice Zedillo's bank rescue occurred in two closely related phases. The first phase in 1995 entailed the immediate bank rescue and was intended to resolve the crisis, but in fact did not do so. This failure necessitated a second phase in 1998 to ensure the stability of the banking sector, which it did but not without introducing complications. Both phases entailed the PRI socializing the recently privatized banks' bad debts and financial risks (Cypher 1996; Ramírez 2001; Marois 2011b).

Socialization in this regard refers to market-oriented governments – under structural pressure from financial capital and from fear of economic collapse – accepting ownership of and responsibility for the banks' financial risks that have gone sour and instigated systemic crisis. In this critical understanding socialization is not primarily a technical problem but a political one tied to class power and capital accumulation dynamics. Governments socialize financial risks to rescue and re-invigorate financial capitalism, which is defined by the structural primacy of money and credit in the circuits of production and circulation alongside the structural inequality between financial capital and labor. While mainstream accounts recognize that the fiscal costs of financial crisis resolution effectively mean a transfer of wealth from taxpayers to financial capital (Furceri and Mourougane 2009; Detragiache and Ho 2010), they do not expand on how the process is fundamentally an expression of unequal social relations of power between finance (which benefits disproportionately) and the laboring classes (who must pay disproportionately through austerity measures and tax increases). This is not to suggest that Mexican popular classes passively accepted socialization. Despite the process being hidden within high-level negotiations many Mexicans organized collectively against the bailout that they saw as corrupt (Marchini 2004; Biles 2010, 262).

How has socialization as a strategy of bank rescue and recovery worked in practice in Mexico? When Mexico's first major neoliberal banking crises struck Mexican financial authorities had not demanded from the bankers sufficient money resources to fortify the capacity of the Banking Fund for the Protection of Savings (Fobaproa; Fondo Bancario de Protección al Ahorro), whose role was to stabilize the financial system. The Salinas administration had placed its faith in market discipline and an 'appropriate yet minimal' state regulation, which was intended to support financial markets. Much to their chagrin amidst the crisis of 1995, just two years earlier the new Secretary of the Secretaría de Hacienda y Crédito Público (SHCP; Ministry of Finance and Public Credit) Guillermo Ortiz Martínez (appointed by Zedillo in 1994) had boasted that Mexico's financial system was 'one of the most advanced in the world' and that Mexican financial managers had the necessary capacity to ensure the adequate regulation of Mexico's newly privatized banks (1993, 260). The ideals of neoliberalism had failed to translate into practice, and to confront the unfolding 1995 banking crisis the Zedillo PRI administration mobilized the full force of the state financial apparatus to restore immediate economic stability and foreign investor confidence in Mexico. This involved mobilizing the combined resources of the BdeM and Fobaproa. The PRI also moved to centralize financial supervision by merging the National Securities Commission (CNV) and the CNB into the Comisión Nacional Bancaria y de Valores (CNBV; National Banking and Securities Commission) (BdeM 1996, 133). However, containing the crisis demanded more than institutional tinkering. Unwilling to reverse or sacrifice Mexico's neoliberal experiment Zedillo's PRI resorted to drawing the costs of bank rescue into the state apparatus, that is, socialization. The PRI did this through the executive budget, and it did it without public consultation (SHCP 1998, 33). The financial authorities assured Mexicans that the state-led bank rescue would cost no more than 5.5 per cent of 1995 gross domestic product (GDP) (BdeM 1996 (1990–2006), 8). When all was said and done the state authorities would take over thirteen banks and the socialized costs would dwarf the initial estimate of 5.5 per cent.

The first phase of the 1995 rescue package included a mix of immediate and long-term government responses. In execution the programs were very uneven. Nevertheless the allocation of public resources broadcast an unambiguous message that the interests of financial capital are the sine qua non of government policy. The political intent was immediate crisis containment by restoring the confidence of financial capital in Mexico and in its banks. Five government programs facilitated banking sector recovery. One of the first programs quickly injected US dollar liquidity into the cash-strapped banks. A second program, the Temporary Capitalization Program (Procapte), provided short-term loans (five-year maximum terms) to help individual banks reach an 8 per cent capital to asset ratio. While at the time these programs drew public resources away from other fiscal and social priorities the state recovered all funds and bore no long-term social costs according to the SHCP (1998, 34–5). This full cost recovery proved more an aberration than a standard as the remaining measures became very costly in the long run. For example, a third Fobaproa initiative stretched out and restructured the individual debts of fisheries, families, small and medium-sized enterprises (SMEs), and so on while providing incentives for banks to renew lending (SHCP

1998, 35; OECD 2002b, 155). Note that consistent with neoliberal disciplinary aims the PRI did not dedicate public resources to debt write-offs among Mexico's poorest and most needy, but to ensuring individual debt discipline. Neoliberal state technocrats argued the measure was intended to combat what they saw as Mexico's so-called 'culture of non-payment'. In apparent contradiction to market disciplinary mechanisms (if not the actual existing class-based practices of neoliberal development), the measure also served to insulate Mexican bankers from their own profligate and even fraudulent lending. How widespread the non-payment problem was and who in the end would actually repay the debts remains open. Some suggest that nearly 80 per cent of the debts belonged to only 2000 wealthy Mexicans (Biles 2010, 263), many of whom have never been held accountable. At the other end of the wealth spectrum, the crisis had caused widespread loss of income for the poorest sectors amidst rising interest rates. In consequence, the individual debt restructuring program proved largely inadequate for the average debtor (Avalos and Trillo 2006, 25). This program cost about 3 per cent of Mexico's GDP (SHCP 1998, 35). And it carried a more working-class disciplinary than economic stabilizing effect.

With the fourth Fobaproa program the PRI channeled yet larger social resources to those financial capitalists who had caused the crisis. This program enabled state managers to intervene in and sanitize the bad debts of banks when existing shareholders or new investors refused to increase the bank's capital base (SHCP 1998, 36–9). In practice this meant state managers had to, again, take on a very active role in restructuring the banking industry to make it work within the confines of market discipline. Yet because market actors were unwilling or unable to respond, between 1995 and 1997 state managers had to take control of thirteen mostly smaller banks, then close, merge, sanitize their debts, and/or re-sell them to domestic or foreign banks. As an incredible indictment of Salinas's earlier neoliberal development strategy, only five of the eighteen banks privatized in 1992 survived under the control of the original purchasing group. The Mexican public, moreover, was incensed at the fact that the failed bank shareholders received twice what they had paid for the banks just a couple of years earlier (Biles 2010, 263). The combination of domestic crisis and the failure of private Mexican bank ownership as the road to financial prosperity prompted Zedillo to consider increasing foreign bank capital participation beyond existing NAFTA limits as the solution to the banking sector's immediate capitalization problems (discussed shortly). The PRI understood, in any event, that the new bank owners, Mexican or foreign, would benefit by acquiring the branch networks of the failed banks but that the deal had to be sweetened by the Mexican government to draw in buyers. As a consequence, many of the state-organized bank mergers and sales that occurred after 1995 left, by design, Fobaproa and the Mexican state with the bad financial liabilities and private capital with the sanitized banks (Stallings 2006, 189; Martinez-Diaz 2009, 60–7). The social cost of this initiative reached about 8.3 per cent of Mexico's GDP (SHCP 1998, 42).

A fifth Fobaproa measure involved a permanent recapitalization scheme and it has proven to be the most expensive program to date with the social costs continuing to accumulate (SHCP 1998, 38). Through Fobaproa Mexican state authorities purchased from the still-functioning commercial banks their non-performing loans (NPLs) at prices above their then current market value with 10-year state bonds. The deal was that for every peso a bank's individual shareholders injected into their troubled banks Fobaproa bought two pesos of bad debt. The bonds were non-negotiable and capitalizable every three months at an averaged CETES rate (that is, the PRI agreed to add interest to public injury). In theory, if a bank recuperated any of its bad debts the money went to liquidating the Fobaproa bonds. In practice, this has yet to occur with any regularity. Instead the Mexican bankers gladly accepted the virtually risk-free Fobaproa bonds that were, to all intents and political purposes, backed by the Mexican state. Within a few years the socialized costs of the bankers' bailout had nearly tripled the disingenuous estimate given by the SHCP in 1995, reaching about $60 billion in 1998 or around 15 per cent of GDP. At almost three times the initial bailout estimates this cost was five times the $12 billion received for bank privatization just a few years earlier. At this point the Zedillo administration acknowledged that the limited resources commanded by Fobaproa could not honor the recapitalization bonds as they came due. This would lead President Zedillo not to break with the pattern of privileging the needs of financial capital but, in March 1998, to propose that all Fobaproa debts be officially drawn into the state (SHCP 1998, 51–2). That is, he wanted the state to directly socialize the costs of rescue to better ensure the return of financial stability.

I will return to Zedillo's March 1998 proposals shortly, but it is necessary to remind readers of the institutional mechanisms by which Zedillo's PRI and subsequent Mexican governments have been able to socialize and service the bankers' debts gone bad. The primary tool involves the recurrent sale of state bond debt certificates. As Hilferding elaborates, state officials can create fictitious capital by selling state bonds. These bonds represent the price of a share in the state's annual tax yield or, put otherwise, a capitalized claim on future tax revenue (2006 [1910], 111). Because Mexican state officials are legally endowed with the institutional power to create fictitious capital in the form of state bonds, these state agents are also endowed with great financial flexibility and enormous allocative power. Selling state bonds enables the Mexican government to circumvent and displace in time the current limits of annual revenues. States and sovereigns had long had this capacity, but the financial innovations undertaken since the mid-1970s have augmented the Mexican state's capacity to create and circulate fictitious capital (for example through petrobonds and CETES). This institutional capacity has taken on ever-greater significance insofar as state elites can and do mortgage the costs of financial rescues onto future generations of Mexicans.

The seemingly necessary and official creation of fictitious capital to resolve financial crisis, however, obscures the dark social and class-based side of the rescue. Underlying the creation of state bonds by state officials is the Mexican people's capacity to work, create value, and pay taxes – the distribution and use of which is always a matter of political contestation. On the one hand, the OECD regularly reports that Mexico has among the lowest taxation levels among OECD countries. This has much to do with the public revenues historically generated from oil and the state-controlled PEMEX corporation, which allowed postwar governments to demand relatively little tax from capitalists in Mexico. It also has to do with Mexico's corporatist state–society structure wherein capital, labor, and the peasantry are drawn collectively but unevenly into the state apparatus in ways that have disproportionately privileged Mexican capitalists who have had the most direct access to and influence over state tax policy formation (Elizondo 1994, 161–3). As a result, wealthy Mexicans have been able to avoid much taxation through loopholes and weak enforcement whereas average wage earners cannot easily escape income tax and have therefore borne the brunt of income tax payments. In similar ways socially regressive forms of taxation have arisen in Mexico alongside neoliberalism, notably the consumption tax or the value added tax (VAT).[2] For example, the Portillo government announced a new 10 per cent VAT rate in 1980 as a means of increasing state revenues during the 1980s debt crisis. Mexican capital did not openly oppose the new tax because there were a range of loopholes available for use by firms and because the VAT targeted individual consumption more than business (Elizondo 1994, 175). By the mid-1990s the OECD reports income tax revenues contributing 5.1 per cent of public revenues followed by VAT at 2.7 per cent with excise taxes and import duties contributing 2 and 0.9 per cent respectively (OECD 1998a, 57). The IMF projects PEMEX to continue contributing 3 to 3.5 per cent of public revenue until at least 2015 with income tax revenue constituting 8 to 10 per cent (of which VAT is no longer disaggregated) (2010, 35). This post-1980s pattern of shifting the public revenue burden onto individuals has not changed under the PAN. In 2005 the Fox administration passed a reduction in the corporate tax rate to 28 per cent by 2007, while proposals to reduce VAT to 12 per cent were rejected (OECD 2005, 135). This is consistent with the neoliberal push of IFIs to ensure tax reforms are aimed at broadening the public basis of VAT (Sanchez 2006).

The dark social and class-based side of the bank rescue, as such, derives from the fact that the covering of Fobaproa debt depends on state elites creating and recycling state bonds to socialize the banks' financial losses, the public costs of which fall disproportionately on the majority of working taxpaying Mexicans without democratic consultation or consent.

6.1.1   Zedillo's March 1998 Proposal

From the first moment Zedillo rescued the banks in Mexico the accumulated Fobaproa debt was already 'socialized' in practical and political terms. In actual legal terms, however, the state bonds used to absorb the private sector's bad debts were *only* backed by the assets within Fobaproa alone and by Fobaproa's capacity to collect the bad debts in due course. That the bad debts had not yet been fully socialized by the state gave rise to uncertainty in the financial markets: theoretically Fobaproa could go belly up and the bankers' Fobaproa bonds along with it. Because Mexico's debt-led neoliberal strategy of development had become dependent on recurrent flows of finance capital PRI President Zedillo's 1998 reforms, therefore, attempted to legalize what had already been done in practice so as to appease the concerns of financial capital (compare Stallings 2006, 190). This involved both internally managing Fobaproa debt and further restructuring the state apparatus to support financial capital.[3]

The most contentious feature of Zedillo's 1998 proposals involved dealing with the banks' bad debts. Yet by 1998 the PRI and Zedillo's political capacity to push through reform had dwindled since Zedillo could no longer count on the immediate backing of Congress. The 1997 elections had ended the PRI majority in the Chamber of Deputies, and the PAN and Partido de la Revolución Democrática (PRD; Party of the Democratic Revolution) were eager to exercise their newfound political influence. Zedillo was also trying to push through these unpopular reforms in a society still inspired by the Zapatista uprising but shaken by the December 1997 Acteal peasant massacre – and these occurred alongside persistent and mounting levels of poverty and recurrent revelations of government corruption. The PRD had obtained the names of those who had benefited most from the 1995 bailout. Unsurprisingly, they were among Latin America's richest people, many whom were also openhanded PRI contributors. The content of Zedillo's 1998 proposals served only to provoke many Mexicans and unleash enduring fury over the initial 1995 bank bailout and the fact that a tiny minority of ultra-rich Mexicans would again benefit from a state-led bank rescue. It was as evident then as it is now that the costs of the bank rescue were not allocated justly but socialized by state elites to the cost of Mexican society in the name of financial stability. The remaining months of 1998 saw angry political debate and the eruption of public hostility. Recognizing the tenuous political situation but nevertheless wanting to secure continued stability around Mexico's increasingly finance-led neoliberal strategy of development, Zedillo brokered a deal with the up and coming PAN that resulted in a modified debt *cum* socialization plan that became institutionalized in the December 1998 Bank Savings Protection Law. Therein it was stated that the costs of *servicing* the bankers' debts gone bad held by Fobaproa would be included in Mexico's annual budget, but without being formally drawn into the state.

There should be no mistaking the clarity with which Mexican authorities acted. In 2008 while offering some advice to US regulators over the 2008 sub-prime crisis Guillermo Ortiz, serving as BdeM governor, reflected on Mexico's 1990s crisis experience. In a stark admission of their conviction at the time Ortiz urged US authorities to do 'whatever it takes to restore confidence . . . Once you lose it, it's very difficult to get it back.'[4] In Mexico's case 'it' meant socializing the bank losses in a way that ensured the debts became the enduring responsibility of Mexico's taxpayers (Ramírez 2001, 657–8; Soederberg 2010a, 85). Even the normally conservative OECD appreciates that Mexican state authorities succeeded in rescuing the banking sector only 'at a significant cost to the public treasury', a cost which has snowballed to a net fiscal total of almost 20 per cent of Mexico's GDP in 2000 terms (OECD 2002b, 89). In actual dollars the Mexican state has taken responsibility for servicing $100 billion in debt with little chance of full recovery (Correa 2004, 163). Even the IMF has expressed concern over this $100 billion in accrued debt fearing possible renewed uncertainty within financial capital circles (2006, 28). Negotiations with Mexican authorities forced some of the largest banks in Mexico to reassume $826 million in bad loans in 2004, but this had little substantive impact on the overall amount (Stallings 2006, 190). Searching for a market mechanism to reduce investor concerns the PAN allowed the banks in Mexico to exchange the old non-tradable Fobaproa bonds for new, tradable, financial instruments (Mannsberger and McBride 2007, 327). Yet neither of these measures have done much to alter the deeper social impacts. As the PAN President Fox administration's IPAB Special Commission revealed, it could take up to 70 years for Mexico to pay off the 1995 bailout with each year representing a direct transfer of wealth from Mexican society to financial capital in the form of interest paid on the rescue bonds.

In addition to socializing the bankers' bad debts Zedillo's reforms also aimed at restructuring and internationalizing the state financial apparatus in order to further bolster the confidence of financial capital in Mexico. As noted earlier, Ortiz and the SHCP had praised Mexico's advanced regulatory capacity before the crisis. Following the crisis, the SHCP expressed quite a different view suggesting that 'the *absence* of an adequate system of bank regulation and supervision' contributed to the banking crisis (1998, 12; author's translation and emphasis). Read critically this amounts to an admission of Mexico's failed attempt to approximate the ideals of neoliberalism and the Washington consensus. Yet rather than having to question the foundations of neoliberalism itself the SHCP self-critical about-face opened the door for Zedillo to focus solely on reforming state supervision and regulation protocols (SHCP 1998, 51–2). To be sure, many pointed to certain *bank market* failures. Yet the ethos and logos of change in Mexico targeted *state* failure almost exclusively and sought ways both to 'de-politicize' bank supervision and to enhance state regulatory capacity – the stuff of what would become post-Washington consensus reforms. For example, Zedillo's 1998 reforms, if falling short of full institutional autonomy, gave greater independence to the CNBV. Zedillo also made changes to the beleaguered Fobaproa (BdeM 1999 (1990–2006), 232). The December 1998 Bank Savings Protection Law replaced Fobaproa with the new Instituto para la Protección al Ahorro Bancario (IPAB; Bank Savings Protection Institute). As the BdeM argues, institutions like the IPAB are important to domestic financial stability because they constitute a 'safety net' for the banks, with an open door to 'the possibility of access to Banco de México's liquidity' (BdeM 2007 (2007–10, 49). These state-led changes have created the institutionalized foundations on which finance-led accumulation has been built in Mexico and through which Mexican state and government elites facilitate financial stability in their corner of the world market.

Yet the crisis considered to have been 'managed' by IFIs and Mexican state officials remains burdensome for the majority of Mexicans beyond the socialized bankers' debts. For example, the post-1995 contraction in available bank credits has left the Mexican middle class and SMEs without easy access to finance (Levy 2003, 168). Mexican farmers, workers, peasants, and the middle class alike have shared the burden of restrictive monetary policy, austerity, the collapse of Mexican peso purchasing power, and very high interest rates (Vadi 2001, 133). Lower real wages alongside weak investment into or the closure of social programs further suggests that the 1995 rescue was contrary to the interests of many Mexicans (Williams 2001, 31; Guillén Romo 2005, 248). Inevitable discontent was manifested in the cross-class El Barzón social movement, which challenged, ultimately unsuccessfully, both the government's bailout of corrupt bankers and then the new bankers' usurious policy of charging interest on the accumulated interest from a loan's principle (González 2004, 217).

The collective memory of the Mexican public is not short, however, and the PRI and PAN support of bankers above other social interests played an important part in the 2006 presidential elections. On the one hand, a collective of bank workers actively supported the PRD under the banner of 'Bancarios por López Obrador' (Bank Workers for López Obrador). On the other, the 1995 bailout and ongoing social costs formed a beacon around which anti-PRI and PAN corruption charges (the 'manios sucios' or 'dirty hands' campaign of the PRD) manifested throughout the election. The negative social side of the banking recovery, however, was systematically discounted by the PRI and PAN as well as by state elites who instead focused on how the banking industry had become internationally competitive, stable, and attractive to foreign investment. The PRD candidate López Obrador eventually lost the questionably run, likely fraudulent, 2006 federal elections to the PAN candidate, Felipe Calderón. Yet Obrador had garnered substantial support from the south and rural areas where long-established patterns of uneven development, high poverty, and poor banking access were more than evident. Some of the most dramatic expressions of this discontent took the form of direct attacks, protests, and even bombings against foreign banks, especially as seen during events at the Oaxaca commune in fall 2006.[5] These incidents bring us back to a final important measure within Zedillo's post-crisis banking reforms, namely the easing of restrictions on foreign bank capital entry into Mexico.

6.2 THE INTERNALIZATION OF FOREIGN BANK CAPITAL

As discussed in Chapter 4, in the lead up to bank privatization in 1990 the Salinas administration and advocates of bank privatization had done much to paint the sell-off of the nationalized banks as a defense of a 'Mexican controlled' banking industry. Salinas went even further within the NAFTA agreement to protect the new Mexican bankers from foreign bank competitive pressures as a means of ensuring the successful sell-off of the nationalized banks. With the unfurling of the 1995 crisis, however, Salinas's and earlier PRI efforts to protect Mexican bankers had become untenable. Consequently, the Zedillo administration looked beyond simply socializing the debts to seizing the opportunity to allow the internalization of foreign banking, ostensibly as a stabilizing force.

The turn to foreign bank capital was therefore rooted in the conditions of economic crisis but also facilitated by the fact that Zedillo was more concerned with neoliberal continuity than with PRI ruling hegemony (Rodríguez Araujo 2010; Martinez-Diaz 2009, 57). As the crisis first transpired Zedillo announced in early January 1995 and then quickly enacted on 15 February 1995 a modification to the 1990 Credit Institutions Law. The institutional change encouraged 'strategic alliances' between domestic and foreign capital by relaxing foreign participation limits. According to the BdeM, the foreign alliances would help improve Mexico's systemic efficiency, restore stability, and increase the banking sector's capital base (1996 (1990–2006), 133, 230–5). With the East Asian crisis following soon after Mexico's the orthodox mainstream quickly took up this line of defense in favor of foreign bank capital arguing that barriers to foreign bank entry should fall because this will increase competition and lead to better economic performance (Demirgüç-Kunt, Levine, and Min 1998, 103). To this end Mexican authorities reduced the 99 per cent foreign affiliate stake required under NAFTA to only 51 per cent and then increased the maximum limit of 10 per cent individual ownership with SHCP authorization to 20 per cent (OECD 2002b, 131). Foreign controlling shares could be acquired but still only in banks that controlled less than 6 per cent of the total net capital (BdeM 1996, 230–5). While Zedillo had at first hinted at the possibility of a complete opening to foreign banks, the 6 per cent marker responded to popular fears over foreign bank dominance and served to shield the biggest Mexican-owned banks from immediate takeover – banks which historically have had privileged access to bank policy formation (compare White 1992, 84). The change nonetheless represented a significant opening from the 1.5 per cent maximum stipulated under Salinas's NAFTA, wherein only two banks were eligible. At 6 per cent Zedillo opened up all but the three largest banks (Banamex, Bancomer, and Serfín) to foreign control. Moreover, these systemically important Mexican banks believed they would benefit from continued liberalization and would be capable of profitably competing with foreign banks. At the very least renewed domestic stability alongside the deepening of Mexico's post-NAFTA continental integration would likely yield increases in the market value of the largest banks. To bolster the legitimacy of foreign bank capital internalization, moreover, orthodox economists began to argue that the foreign bank restrictions retained at the time of the 1991–92 bank privatizations were the probable cause of the 1995 bank crisis (OECD 2002b, 88).

   Table 6.1 depicts the first and second waves of foreign bank entry into Mexico between 1995 and 2002. The first wave came from Spain, Canada, the UK, and the US. The BBVA purchase of Probursa represents the initial foreign take-over of a Mexican bank and was politically important for

Table 6.1   Internalization of foreign bank capital, 1995–2002

Foreign bank (country of origin)	Date of transaction	Acquired or merged Mexican bank	Transaction cost
Post-crisis internalization of foreign capital			
BBVA (Spain)	June 1995	Probursa	$136 million
Scotiabank (Canada)	Feb 1996	Grupo Financiero Inverlat (10%)	$31.2 million
Santander (Spain)	Nov 1996	Banco Mexicano (majority share)	$379 million
BBVA (Spain)	1997	Cremi and Oriente	n/a
HSBC (UK)	March 1997	Serfín (20%)	$290 million
Citibank (US)	Oct 1998	Banca Confia	$195 million
Total foreign bank transactions			$1.03 billion
Second wave of foreign capital internalization			
BBVA (Spain)	August 2000	Bancomer (60%)	$1.4 billion
Scotiabank (Canada)	November 2000	Grupo Financiero Inverlat (increased equity stake to 55%)	n/a
Citibank (US)	July 2001	Banamex	$12.5 billion
BBVA (Spain)	February 2004	Bancomer (remaining 40%)	$4.1 billion
HSBC (UK)	November 2002	Bital	$1.14 billion
Total foreign bank transactions			$20.68 billion

Sources: OECD (1995, 161); Steinfeld (2004, 12).

establishing the legitimacy of the process. State authorities in the CNBV actively promoted the sale to BBVA while Fobaproa injected capital resources into Probursa to sweeten the deal (Martinez-Diaz 2009, 65–6). More foreign bank capital began to trickle in, most of which involved the purchasing of minority shares often with government guarantees and future purchase options attached. For example, when Citibank took over Confia in 1998 Fobaproa took over three-quarters of Confía's $4 billion bad loan portfolio for which Citi refused to be responsible. At a level of just over $1 billion from 1995 to 1999 the actual dollar values of foreign capital entry were relatively small reflecting ongoing restrictions and global uncertainty that dampened foreign bank interest in Mexican banks.

By the time the newly triumphant PAN government of President Vicente Fox (2000–06) came to power Zedillo's PRI government had removed most ownership barriers – a task Fox would complete (OECD 2002b, 131). Fox's PAN opened the way for a new phase of financial accumulation premised on a more aggressive internalization of foreign bank capital, which would complement the renewed commitments of the PAN to market-oriented approaches to development (discussed shortly).[6] As seen in Table 6.1, from 2000 to 2002 over $20 billion in foreign bank capital entered, which is more than twenty times the amount from 1995 to 1999. The sale of Banamex to Citi represents the zenith (some say nadir) of the process. Sold for $12.5 billion the sale was tax-free and made without requiring the repayment of outstanding Fobaproa bonds. Fox had graciously offered to hold onto the bill for the 1995 crisis. The record-setting sale price was not the result of the entrepreneurial diligence of Banamex's controlling owners. While surviving the 1995 crisis without major state interventions Banamex (and Bancomer for that matter) still suffered large losses from NPLs. The size and importance of the bank granted Banamex owners privileged access to state managers, however. In consequence, the bankers were able to successfully negotiate alterations in banking regulations to make the bank's balance sheet appear healthier than it really was. For example, the bank could defer tax payments to state authorities and use the retained money to strengthen the bank's capital base (Martinez-Diaz 2009, 72). This official massaging of regulation constitutes another form of socialization only made available to Mexico's wealthiest people (such regulatory tinkering is not restricted to Mexico but is also seen in Turkey with the so-called Istanbul Approach, which allowed banks to redefine NPLs as performing to support their capital adequacy ratios).

The magnitude of Mexico's bank ownership changes over about a decade should not be underrated. Whereas in 1990 the Mexican state controlled 97 per cent of the banking system's assets by 2002 foreign banks controlled 82 per cent and private domestic banks 18 per cent of all banking assets in Mexico (BIS 2004, 9). Recall that the 1994 NAFTA had anticipated foreign bank capital would increase gradually from about 8 per cent in 1994 to a maximum of 15 per cent by 1999 (NAFTA 1994, 730). Mexico has since come to have one of the highest foreign bank control ratios of all the Latin American countries (Vidal et al. 2011). In official discourse this is a testament to Mexico's financial reforms, which have been successful because they have brought in significant foreign bank resources (Interview, high-ranking SHCP director, 13 February 2008). Yet contrary to neoliberal idealism the results have not been encouraging. A recent CEPAL study concluded, 'there is no evidence that the "foreignization" of banking has benefited the productivity or efficiency of the Mexican banking system' (Avalos and Trillo 2006, 79; author's translation). Foreign banks in Mexico have in particular shied away from productive lending in order to hold more lucrative Mexican state debt certificates (Stallings 2006, 197). Regardless, the IMF has by and large praised the

PAN for its financial restructuring efforts, at least prior to the 2008–09 crisis in Mexico (IMF 2006; 2007). Since then the IMF has become somewhat more attuned to the downsides of financial risk tied to systemically important foreign banks dominating Mexico's financial system (2010, 25). Even certain Mexican financial authorities question the utility of foreign bank control. As one high level director in the CNBV stated in an anonymous interview, 'there is no relation between the internalization of global banks and economic development, other than the picture it gives to developed countries that allows Mexico to participate in international markets' (Interview, CNBV, 12 February 2008). How, then, has neoliberal crisis, state-led recovery, and the internalization of foreign bank control affected the operational structures of banking in Mexico, and why is this important?

6.3 THE STRUCTURED BENEFITS OF MEXICO'S FINANCE-LED NEOLIBERAL BANKING STRATEGY

The importance of the change in political rule from the PRI under Salinas and Zedillo to the PAN under Fox and Calderón is not fundamentally about any change in party ideology, but rather how the shift in party rule ensured continuity in the neoliberal state form and economic trajectory (Álvarez Béjar and Ortega Breña 2006; Rodríguez Araujo 2010). And this is precisely what has occurred. Since 2000 pro-market PAN political forces have continued to facilitate the deepening of financial imperatives within Mexican society, and this has been to the benefit of foreign and domestic financial capital alike.

On coming to power in December 2000 the Fox administration prioritized the strengthening of the national financial system along neoliberal lines in its National Development Plan (2001–06) and National Development Finance Program (2002–06) (SHCP 2005, 105). For example, there was no attempt to break with an inflation targeting and price stability monetary regime. These policies form the hardcore orthodoxy of mainstream economics and IFI financial development recommendations, which institutionally subordinate many possible Mexican state developmental options to inflation and price stability objectives (see Epstein and Yeldan 2009; Galindo and Ros 2009). Fox did not promote the needs of finance in his plans merely because of ideology but also because of wider material constraints, such as the growing presence of foreign bank capital. According to one high-ranking SHCP director, before foreign banks flooded into Mexico there was much less need for the degree of regulation within Mexico that is now required (Interview, Bank and Saving Unit, 13 February 2008). Change in Mexico is matched by change in the world market. According to the current president of the CNBV, Guillermo Babatz, Mexico's financial system is internationally connected, which makes it necessary to 'focus on macro-prudential regulation and supervision of the banking institutions' and to communicate 'between local and international financial authorities'.[7] In other words, the emergence of financial capitalism in Mexico is neither natural nor simply about voluntary choices but about material and institutional imperatives specific to the current phase of capital accumulation. These do not simply unfold but are enacted and institutionalized by state authorities within Mexico in ways that have facilitated the internationalization of the state financial apparatus and the internationalization of capital in the world market.

Fox went beyond affirming Mexico's commitment to inflation targeting. For one, the Fox administration amended the Banking Law, Securities Market Law, Mutual Fund Act, Insurance Law, Popular Savings and Loan Law, and the Law for Credit Information Institutions so as to enhance state regulatory capacity while facilitating the development of domestic financial markets (OECD 2002b, 163–4). For another, the Fox administration aimed to bring Mexico closer to international best practices and in so doing to promote foreign investor confidence in Mexico's open financial system. To this end state financial managers pursued compliance with the Basel 25 core banking principles (IMF 2006). The CNBV also took on the responsibility of setting up formal communications with other national bank regulators and for undertaking joint bank examinations of the global banks operating in Mexico. The CNBV did this by penning new joint cooperative Memorandums of Understanding (MoUs) with foreign banking authorities. By the end of Fox's six-year term CNBV authorities had internationalized the financial apparatus via twelve new bilateral bank supervisory MoUs while negotiating six more with Central American bank agencies (IMF 2007, 15). The MoUs enabled all banks operating in Mexico to penetrate the borders of Mexico's southern neighbors.

Such changes are neither neutral nor without difficulties. Recently the IMF recognized the potential complications of making Mexico a platform for southern bank expansion: 'Given the strong international links of financial systems in Mexico and much of Latin America, existing MoUs with home regulators of global banks may require steps to further clarify the responsibilities of each party in case of failure of subsidiaries or parent bank' (IMF 2010a, 26). In other words, Mexican society faces identifiable risks vis-à-vis the global banks it hosts and promotes from within its borders. More is said on this later, with the immediate point being that as state managers create an enabling environment for financial capital to flourish at home and abroad, Mexican society becomes more beholden *to* financial imperatives and increasingly responsible *for* the activities of financial capital undertaken from within its borders. This is one of the many ways in which financial capital internationalizes but does not transnationalize in the sense of escaping or transcending nation states.[8]

The PAN President Felipe Calderón's National Development Plan (2007–12) continues to facilitate financial imperatives within Mexican society and by extension to support the financial world market. For example, Calderón's NDP signals the need to minimize the risks investors face so as to encourage new financial entrants into Mexico. This means enhancing the disciplinary rights, hence power, of financial capital to recover loan defaults more swiftly. It also means dedicating public resources to institutionalizing more prudential regulation (in line with IFI best practices) and building up sufficient foreign reserves (elaborated below) to manage new financial crises as they emerge. At the same time Calderón's PAN prioritizes increasing individual access to financial services. Coherent with all World Bank, IMF, and OECD banking and financing for development initiatives, including microfinance, this PAN initiative is not about the state providing financial resources but enabling markets (Weber 2004). By supporting financial capital's rights, by promoting competition, and by 'democratizing' finances through such things as the stock market the PAN sees this neoliberal strategy as resulting in a diversity of new private market-based financial sources. In neoclassical and liberal discourse and theory this ought to give more people more access to finance, which will spur competitive development, which will lead to more efficient investment and growth. The theoretical growth then ought to trickle down not only to the resource-starved SMEs but even to the poorest segments of Mexican society. As we will see, however, there are good reasons to be skeptical of the supposed universal benefits of intensified financial imperatives.

6.3.1 The Forms of Bank Concentration in Mexico

Given its history of nationalization, rationalization, privatization, and foreign bank internalization the structure of neoliberal banking in Mexico, perhaps more than in most emerging capitalisms, has varied considerably. Yet contrary to the idealized burgeoning of a diffused competitive sector tied to liberalization banking in Mexico continues to be highly concentrated and centralized (compare White 1992; Martinez-Diaz 2009; Marois 2011a). Recall that after the 1982 bank nationalization decree state managers merged 58 banks into 18, which authorities then sold in 1991–92 to Mexican capitalists. While Salinas's approach to liberalization at this time resisted new foreign bank capital entry, relaxed regulations allowed the number of private Mexican banks to explode. By the time of the 1995 crisis and state-led rescue there were 41 banks, which suggested some movement towards bank asset de-centralization and de-concentration. Yet the biggest banks remained and new entrants made little impact on asset concentration. As a result of the 1995 crisis, subsequent banking failures, mergers, and the reluctance of Mexican financial authorities to grant new banking licenses for fear of the speculative excesses that had led to the crisis bank numbers then fell to 30 by 2004.

In line with the financial strategies laid out in Fox's NDPs the SHCP reversed its policy and authorized nine new multiple banks in late 2006, including the retail-based Walmart and Azteca banks. The BdeM suggests that allowing retail players into banking was needed to encourage competition and to help bring formal banking access to more people (2007 (2007–10), 50). In practice, the banks focus on usurious high-interest consumer debt and comprise a mere 1.3 per cent of the sector (BdeM 2009 (2007–10), 100). Once again, while this particular opening suggests some form of de-centralization it has not brought competitive de-concentration. Today there are 41 commercial banks in Mexico. Yet the same few banks that monopolized the sector prior to 1995 continue to do so (albeit with some changes in shareholders). For example, the historically dominant Bancomer (now controlled by the Spanish banking giant BBVA) and Banamex (now controlled by the US banking giant Citibank) continue to be the two largest banks in Mexico and together control a phenomenal 44 per cent of all private sector loans and 60 per cent of all mortgages (BdeM 2007 (2007–10), 79, 83). If you tack on the Spanish Santander-Serfín and the UK HSBC-Bital, then these four banks control 69 per cent of private sector loans and 79 per cent of mortgages. As of April 2009 six banks controlled 82 per cent of all banking assets in Mexico (BdeM 2009 (2007–10), 100). After decades of finance-led neoliberal reforms the control over Mexicans' money savings is highly concentrated in the hands of private, profit-oriented banks.

Another way that bank and financial capital concentration and centralization have manifested in Mexico is through large cartel-like financial group formations. In general, financial capital has an interest in eliminating competition between different financial services by drawing all services into a single holding group so as to maximize profit, financial control, and power in the sector and society (compare Hilferding 2006 [1910], 199). In the 1960s and 1970s state and government elites – under the rationale of expanding financial resources in Mexico – began encouraging the informal cartelization of financial services within universal banks (see Chapter 3; White 1992). With the transition to neoliberalism state and government advocates have further facilitated financial group formation. As the BdeM concludes, the Mexican financial system is going through 'an important evolutionary process driven by the reform of its legal framework, growing links between commercial banks and non-financial companies, as well as the latter's incursion in traditional banking business' (2007 (2007–10), 9). This evolution of financial groups has been shaped by the historic dominance of universal banks in Mexico.

It is worth noting that in many emerging capitalisms more market-based financial services characteristic of advanced capitalisms like the US and UK exist but have not historically predominated, even though financial authorities intend to encourage this (Mihaljek 2010, 40). In Mexico, however, more market-based financial institutions, such as brokerage houses, insurance, mutual funds, and so on now account for 33 per cent of all financial assets (which is higher than in Turkey, for example). This represents a waning of the commercial banks' postwar dominance, even though the banks continue to be the dominant type of financial interme-diary controlling 57 per cent of financial assets (the development banks control about 10 per cent) (BdeM 2009 (2007–10), 49). Yet the impor-tance of this lies less in the relative control of market- versus bank-based institutions in Mexico than in the almost complete control of all financial services within financial groups (and the financial power this confers on these groups). For example, financial groups now control 93.5 per cent of all commercial bank assets as well as 84 per cent of all mutual fund assets (BdeM 2007, 49; 2010, 32 (2007–10)). In other words, less than 7 per cent of bank assets exist independently of other integrated financial services. Indeed, by law financial groups must integrate both bank and market-based intermediaries to exist. This concentration of assets in financial groups, moreover, overlaps with the internalization of foreign bank capital. The BdeM reports that nearly three-quarters of all bank assets are controlled by an affiliated foreign financial entity. Overall, the seven largest financial groups – BBVA-Bancomer, Citibank-Banamex, Santander-Serfín, Banorte, HSBC, Inbursa, and Scotiabank-Inverlat – control 93.2 per cent of all financial group assets (CNBV 2005 (2001–10), 19).

In early twentieth-century Germany Hilferding (2006 [1910]) saw bank and industrial cartels defining the form of finance capital concentration. In Mexico today concentration is instead defined by many forms of foreign and domestic money capital concentrated in massive cartel-like financial groups. Contrary to liberal theory, there is little evidence of more freedom to choose. Should the average Mexican wish to be 'banked' he or she must opt for a private bank, of which a handful monopolize the sector, wherein most are foreign-owned giants.

6.3.1.1   Focus on Banamex, Serfín, and Banorte

Looking in more detail at the cases of Banamex, Serfín, and Banorte can help to illustrate the concentration and centralization of financial capital since privatization. In the first case, Mexico's second largest bank, Banamex, surfaced relatively well after 1995. Banamex remained in Mexican hands and owned by the original initial purchasing group headed by financiers Hernandez and Harp Helú. Even though Fobaproa injected some capital into Banamex foreign capital was not needed to stabilize its operations (Ramírez 2001, 667–8). By 2001 the shareholders of Banamex wanted to cash in on escalating market values and sold Banamex to the US-based Citibank Mexico for $12.5 billion. PAN President Fox sweetened the deal by making the sale tax-free for Citibank. Unlike other foreign banks, Citibank had long been established in Mexico but first began to expand in 1997 by acquiring Banca Confía. The 2001 Banamex acquisition then allowed Citibank to merge Banca Confía and Citibank of Mexico operations into Banamex and to assume a dominant position in the sector. On 12 March 2002 the SHCP authorized Banamex to operate as the Banamex Financial Group, thus removing all barriers to centralized financial operations (SHCP 2008). As of September 2010, the Banamex Financial Group was Mexico's second largest such body controlling 20.08 per cent of all assets (BBVA Bancomer is first at 21.6 per cent) (CNBV 2010 (2001–10), 11).

Banco Serfín was the third largest bank in Mexico at the time of privatization, but its sell-off was followed by severe operational problems and rampant corruption (Núñez Estrada 2005). In 1995 the Mexican authorities stepped in to rescue Serfín with an injection of almost $6.9 billion of fresh capital through Procapte and Fobaproa. The government encouraged HSBC to acquire a 20 per cent stake in Serfín in 1997, but Serfín's problems continued and it was taken over again by IPAB in 1999, its debts socialized, and its balance sheet recapitalized with public funds. In late 1999 Spanish banking giant Santander beat out HSBC for the remaining shares of Serfín in a state auction at a heavily discounted price (Tschoegl 2004, 59). Serfín and Santander banking operations then merged in December 2004 creating Santander Serfín (CNBV 2005, 29). On 29 May 2006 the SHCP authorized the merger of all Serfín and Santander financial operations under the Santander Financial Group (SHCP 2008). As of September 2010 Santander was the third largest financial group in Mexico controlling 14.4 per cent of assets (CNBV 2010 (2001–10), 11).

Since privatization and the 1995 crisis Banorte remains the only major bank that is Mexican owned and controlled, from which it draws marketing strength. From being a relatively small regional bank in 1982, Banorte aggressively expanded operations after the 1995 crisis by absorbing smaller banks that were in trouble. For example, in 1997 Banorte acquired Banco de Centro and then BanPaís through negotiations with Fobaproa (BdeM 1998 (1990–2006), 158). In February 1999 Banorte became one of the first banks to be authorized as a financial group by the SHCP, which enabled it to grow further (SHCP 2008). Much as Citibank and Santander internationalized by acquiring Banamex and Serfín in Mexico, so too has Banorte internationalized by acquiring smaller US banks to capture the lucrative US-Mexico remittance market. As of September 2010 the Banorte Financial Group was the fourth largest in the country controlling 11.4 per cent of assets (CNBV 2010 (2001–10), 11). However, a merger with the IXE financial group in February 2011 allowed Banorte to overtake Serfín and to become the third largest financial group in Mexico.

6.3.2 New Strategies of Profitability

How has bank profitability responded to processes of concentration and centralization since the 1995 crisis and state-led rescue? Quite positively. The OECD reports the banks turning a return on assets (ROA) profit of 0.71 per cent of the balance sheet total in 1996, 0.57 per cent in 1998, and 0.94 per cent in 2000 (2004, 306–7). This is well within the average of OECD countries: for example, UK, US, and Spanish banks averaged between 0.60 and 1.15 per cent during the late 1990s and early 2000s (OECD 2004). That the Mexican banks profited at all prior to 2000 is extraordinary given the severity of the 1995 crisis and the subsequent 1997 East Asian and 1998 Russian crises, which hit most emerging capitalisms hard. In this period the profitability of banks in Mexico was dependent on Zedillo socializing their financial risks and on a number of other favorable state policies that facilitated new profitability strategies (discussed shortly; compare Martinez-Diaz 2009). Since 2000 and up until the US sub-prime crisis gripped Mexico in 2008, the evolution of bank profitability takes on a different magnitude (CNBV, various years). The banks' ROA exploded by more than two and a half times, or from 0.94 per cent in 2000 to 2.75 per cent in 2007. Banamex and Santander, for example, basically doubled their profits while Banorte nearly tripled its. Official sources like the BdeM suggest the rise in profitability for the six largest banks is the result of changes in their financial structure that significantly improved income from interest and growth in revenue from fees and commissions from the increased usage of banking services (2007, 51–5). Underlying this empirical observation is a normative assessment that the profits accrued to the banks because of their strategic entrepreneurship, which ignores underlying institutionalized power relations. Individual banks are carving out higher profits, but this is by no means simply their 'just reward' for entrepreneurial prowess conceived of without unequal class-based foundations.

To begin critically unpacking the nature of bank profits it is useful to understand the sources of revenue for the six largest banks. Just over 70 per cent of income comes from interest while fees and commissions amount to under 23 per cent and trading just under 7 per cent (BdeM 2009, 104–9). The importance of interest income to a bank's bottom line can also be understood relative to its total assets. In Mexico, interest income averages around 5 per cent for the biggest banks whereas banks in Canada and Spain average between 1 and 2 per cent and in the US the figure is just under 3 per cent. The variation suggests that banks in Mexico enjoy a large difference between what they need to pay for people's deposits and foreign sources of finance capital and what they can charge in interest to lend money out to people in Mexico.

The Mexican state debt market is a vital, safe, and profitable source of the banks' interest income. Drawing on CNBV data, Babatz Torres (2010) shows that in 2000 the state required financing equal to about 25 per cent of GDP, of which 17 per cent was in securities. By mid-2010 the state required financing equal to over 41 per cent of GDP, of which nearly 31 per cent was in securities. During this time Mexican authorities increasingly privileged domestic sources of financing, which has proven lucrative for the banks. In terms of the banks' private loan portfolio, the BdeM reports that in mid-2010 corporate financing comprised 57 per cent of all bank credits given to the non-financial private sector. Over 85 per cent of this was provided by the seven largest banks, of which over 60 per cent went to large firms in Mexico (2010 (2001–10), 48–9). According to Babatz Torres (2010), the Mexican private sector acquired financing in the range of just over 13 per cent of GDP in 2000 (1.2 per cent in securities), which rose to just over 21 per cent in 2010 (2 per cent in securities). Given these requirements, the largest banks have been able to successfully skim the cream off of the Mexican market (that is, service the largest and safest firms). The cartel-like financial groups in Mexico have strategically targeted the most lucrative state securities and private sector clients within the non-financial sector across the commercial, consumer, and housing sectors (compare BdeM 2010, 33–4; Guillén Romo 2005, 248). The remaining three dozen or so largely Mexican owned medium-sized and smaller banks have to craft competitive strategies around other non-premium clients, either commercial or consumer, in which to concentrate their lending risks. This has entailed uncertainty and meant lower levels of profit for these smaller banks (BdeM 2009 (2001–10), 107–09; 2010, 34). Yet this is not an unintended consequence or perversion of market processes or the result of failed neoliberal policies, but the logical consequence of privileging financial capital given Mexico's historical patterns of accumulation.

All banks' profitability strategies entail historically specific social relations of power. For one, day-to-day Mexican state operations depend on recurrent flows of finance capital from the banks and the banks' profitability depends on recurrent interest payments from servicing state debt. This suggests a structural fusion of interests between state and government elites and financial capital in Mexico. Underlying this debt-led interrelationship, it needs emphasizing that the interest paid out on state debt and the profits gained come out of state revenues, which in Mexico are largely based on income-based taxation. State debt interest payments thus represent a transfer of worker's taxable income via state revenue generation to financial capital. More fundamentally, as discussed in Chapter 3, the interest paid to banks by firms in Marxian terms represents a deduction from the average social profit and a claim on the surplus-value created by workers in the production process, and as such also represents an exploitative transfer of wealth from labor to financial capital (Hilferding 2006 [1910], 172).

This also points towards financialization (Lapavitsas 2009). In advanced capitalisms financialization has appeared historically and alongside the emergence of neoliberalism as larger enterprises turn away from traditional banks as a source of credit and towards more open market operations or retained earnings for self-financing. There is evidence of this occurring in ways specific to Mexico (Lapavitsas and dos Santos 2008). The 1982 bank nationalization and de la Madrid's crafting of a parallel financial sector pushed this process along. More recently many large Mexican corporations have turned to open market operations for financing as well as to profit from speculative derivative operations (Vidal et al. 2011). This has impacted back on banks insofar as they too must acquire new sources of profit, one of which includes offering new financial services to individual workers (which dovetails nicely into the neoliberal argument for improved access to financial resources). Banks now lend increasing amounts directly to individuals, for which there is a demand due to neoliberal austerity, downsizing, pension privatization, closing of public housing, and so on. Lapavitsas and dos Santos (2008) see this as a process of financial expropriation, which they define as the extraction of financial profits directly out of individual personal income. Finally, the strategies of financial capital in Mexico are also indicative of financial imperialism: 'the massive repatriation of earnings of foreign banks operating in the country has converted Mexico into one of the principal profit centers for these banks' (Marshall 2010, 93). Time and again, and in many forms, financial capital exercises increasing disciplinary power over workers, state officials, and those in need of financial resources – all legitimized by the neoliberal idea that it will lead to a developmental renaissance in Mexico.

Yet even critical mainstream analysts contest what has become a very tenuous assertion by neoliberal advocates on the developmental benefits of broad financial liberalization (notably, Ocampo et al. 2008). In neoclassical and liberal terms, high profits are a valid measure of efficiency and productivity, a harbinger of innovative development, and a testament to private ownership. Yet high banking profits have done little to launch Mexico into the ranks of the world's wealthiest countries like its American neighbor to the north. The OECD reluctantly acknowledges that the 'slow pattern of Mexico's convergence towards higher-income levels is at odds with what is suggested by conventional economic theory' (2009, 105). Indeed, Mexican society has become worse off compared to the US since the late 1980s. Even to look at the years between 1997 and 2007 – a decade of relative prosperity threading Mexico's 1995 and 2008 crises – you can see that Mexico switches from economic divergence to limited convergence, which as the OECD concedes 'would still take a very long time'. At some *1848 years* to convergence with US levels of prosperity, 'a very long time' for the OECD is nothing less than a gargantuan understatement (2009, 107). How does bank labor fit into the overall profitability picture?

6.3.3   The Intensification of Bank Labor in Mexico

Critical accounts of Mexico's transition to neoliberalism recognize the importance of restructured capital–labor relationships. Yet the restructuring of the bank capital–bank labor relationship has been left relatively unanalyzed (compare Bouzas Ortíz 2003). Alongside official strategies to craft Mexico's competitiveness around cheap labor (a constant theme of all national development plans since Salinas), the bank owners in Mexico have systematically driven the costs of bank labor down since privatization in strategic response to crisis and as a long-term competitive strategy.

Figure 6.1 illustrates the changing relationship between bank employee numbers and staff costs since the late 1980s (which are considered alongside increases in the number of bank branches, which are not illustrated). Using these indicators, a telling story unfolds regarding the bankers' post-privatization neoliberal strategies. After privatization, for example, the new private bankers sought to capture more domestic savings to help feed the lucrative business of supplying state debt, individual consumer credits, and cheap related lending: as a result, between 1991 and 1995 the number of bank branches exploded by nearly 33 per cent, or from 3621 to 4806 branches. The new bankers, however, simultaneously cut the number of bank workers employed by 12 per cent, or from 137 500 to

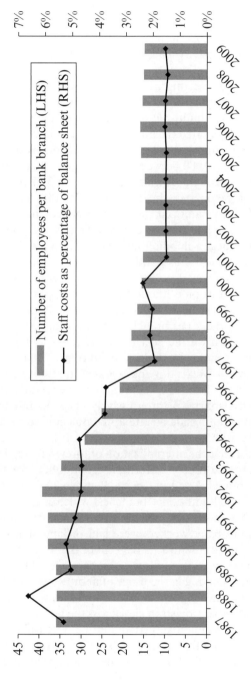

Notes: Mexico submitted data to the 2004 OECD Bank Profitability report cited in the sources below, but not to the 2007 report. Mexico did submit to the recently published June 2011 report. There are discrepancies between some of the 2011 figures and the 2004 figures for years 2001–03. For the 2000–09 period, I use the 2011 report figures.

Sources: OECD, *Bank Profitability: Financial Statements of Banks* (various years); CNBV, *Boletín Estadístico Banca Múltiple Diciembre* (various years).

Figure 6.1 Bank employees and staff costs, Mexico 1987–2009

121 000. Figure 6.1 also shows that staff costs responded in kind by falling from 4.89 to 3.77 per cent of the banks' overall balance sheets.[9] This suggests the new owners saw labor costs as a first line of cost reductions and began to demand greater productivity from the bank workers but without redistributing the gains.

It would be a mistake to see this as a one-off post-privatization response rather than a general finance-led neoliberal strategy. Following the 1995 crisis and the state-led multi-billion dollar rescue the surviving and new bank owners again increased the number of bank branches by an additional 12 per cent while reducing bank employee numbers by over 16 per cent – or from 130 600 to 110 000 between 1996 and 2000. In doing so bank managers aggressively brought down staff costs from 3.77 per cent in 1995 to 2.38 per cent of the balance sheet by 2000. The PRI and state authorities had also effectively sanitized the banks' bad balance sheets and removed barriers to complete foreign control. This is the point at which foreign bank capital began flooding into Mexico, and with good reason. The PRI had shown enormous political goodwill towards financial capital, not least of which was demonstrated by the banking rescue and subsequent internationalization of the state financial apparatus. But also since privatization the Mexican bankers had more than halved the average number of bank workers per branch – from around 38 to just over 15 – and ratcheted down on the cost of labor, intensifying bank worker productivity without major workplace disruptions. Fenasib, the organizing collective body for Mexican bank workers, had not actively contested labor restructuring. This is, of course, good news for potential bank buyers – Mexico sported a progressively cheaper and well-disciplined bank labor force alongside a state apparatus crafted around enabling financial accumulation.

We also see in Figure 6.1 that the internalization of foreign banks since 2000 has not much altered the post-privatization profitability strategies from the vantage point of branches and staff costs. Between 2002 and 2009 the banks opened nearly 4000 additional branches, which is an expansion of over 50 per cent. Yet at the key moment of foreign entry between 2000 and 2002, 10 000 more bank workers were laid off and staff costs were driven further down, from 2.38 to 1.53 per cent of the balance sheet. Since 2002, however, growth in bank employee numbers overall has kept pace with branch expansion, staying in the range of about 15 workers per branch. This suggests some leveling off of bank worker intensification demands relative to branch expansion strategies across the board and with the introduction of any new technologies. It should be noted that 2007 marked the first time in 15 years that aggregate bank employee numbers surpassed 1992 levels, which was the last year of the nationalized banks.

There is also little to differentiate between the strategies of large Mexican and large foreign banks in these terms. Overall, for example, the number of branches grew by over 25 per cent from 2000 to 2007. In the Mexican Banorte's case, management expanded branches most aggressively by more than doubling its numbers from 452 in 2000 to 1052 by 2007. The Spanish Santander also exceeded the 25 per cent average by increasing branches by just over 42 per cent. Yet the American Banamex fell below the average at 16.4 per cent. Likewise the overall number of bank employees grew by just over 25 per cent from 2000 to 2007 (keeping pace with branch expansion). Again it is hard to differentiate based on ownership category. Banamex's employee base growth was below the average at 13 per cent (but still below its branch growth rate). Santander's employee base grew by 43 per cent (marginally over its branch growth). By contrast, Banorte expanded branches by over 50 per cent but held down employee growth to only 27.5 per cent. If ratcheting down on labor costs is a measure of neoliberalism (as I and others argue), then the large Mexican-owned Banorte is the most neoliberal of all. This is without even highlighting the fact that Mexican bank owners intensified bank labor far more aggressively during their tenure from 1991–92 to 2000 while bringing about Mexico's most socially costly financial crisis. At least from the vantage point of bank labor, the evidence belies any recourse to the Mexicanization of banking as a viable alternative to the dominance of foreign banks and neoliberalism (compare Vidal et al. 2011).

The analysis above is not an attempt to reduce the complexities of bank profitability changes to labor intensification alone. As already illustrated, interest rate differentials, fees and commissions, and trading income, alongside competitive imperatives, state restructuring, and so on are all fundamental determinants. Yet neither should bank profitability be thought of independently of bank labor, which has been the norm for practically all banking analyses – be they mainstream or critical. This was a point raised in Hilferding's analysis of German banking (2006 [1910], 172), and it is also a point raised by the BdeM Deputy Governor, José Sidaoui (2006, 288, 292). In more celebratory than critical terms Sidaoui suggests that the rise in banking profits has been closely tied to a contraction in operating expenses since the late 1990s, itself mostly due to reductions in staff numbers. Moreover, one critical observer has found that bank workers' jobs are now being outsourced in Mexico. The benefits of which accrue to bank owners, foreign or domestic, who need not negotiate with labor unions, pay standard benefits, or offer profit-sharing payments established in law.[10]

On the surface Mexico went through an important political watershed with the rise to power of the PAN in 2000. In essence there has been a remarkable consistency in the market-oriented and pro-financial reforms of the PRI and PAN, which have further institutionalized structural benefits for financial capital. In the current phase of financial accumulation in Mexico it seems politically reasonable, ideologically consistent, and economically rational from the perspective of neoliberal state authorities to restructure the state, promote financial imperatives in society, and to ratchet down on bank labor costs as a national competitive strategy supportive of financial capital, especially at times of crisis.

6.4 THE LATEST CRISIS AND THE CONSOLIDATION OF EMERGING FINANCE CAPITALISM

The financial crisis that hit Mexico most acutely in late 2008 and early 2009 is unique in two ways. First, because the trigger originated not from within Mexico or other emerging capitalisms. Rather, the problems started in the advanced capitalist states as the result of new patterns of financial accumulation that culminated in the US-based 2007–08 sub-prime crisis that then morphed into a world financial crisis impacting emerging capitalisms (Hanieh 2009; Radice 2010). The resulting continued instability, or Great Recession, persists into late 2011 particularly in peripheral Europe (Albo et al. 2010; Lapavitsas et al. 2011). Second, the crisis in Mexico was also unique because the banking sector was not at the epicenter of financial distress. This time Mexican popular classes found themselves covering the costs of Mexico's largest non-financial corporations' speculative financial ventures through the response of the state financial apparatus.

Just days before the now infamous collapse of the US investment banking giant Lehman Brothers in late September 2008 IMF, Mexican government and state elites, and even the Mexican bank workers' union (Fenasib) protested that the US sub-prime crisis would have little impact on Mexico's banks and economy. However, the façade of Mexican economic autonomy and stability collapsed alongside Lehman and the impact on Mexican society became unavoidable and undeniable. Trade with the US (about 80 per cent of Mexico's total) fell dramatically, domestic industrial output plummeted, and remittances into Mexico slowed. Authorities from the BdeM state that from May 2008 to May 2009 non-oil exports dropped 28 per cent (Sidaoui et al. 2010, 284). Contradicting all their earlier optimism the BdeM authorities go on to argue that Mexico's dependence on US exports, a result of the post-NAFTA reallocation of labor-intensive production, both enabled and intensified the US sub-prime shock in Mexico. As a result Mexico's GDP growth slowed to 1.3 per cent in 2008 then nosedived to –6.8 per cent in 2009 and over the course of 2009 as the peso depreciated 15 per cent in real terms (although this helped Mexican industry by making its manufactures destined for the US cheaper vis-à-vis China) (IMF 2010a, 19). More than was the case in many other emerging Latin American capitalisms, such as Brazil and Argentina, the fate of Mexican growth and development was still very much dependent on US fortunes (Vidal et al. 2011).

The knock-on effect of the global financial crisis was that capitalists began hoarding their money, and this sudden deleveraging meant flows of finance into emerging capitalisms like Mexico suddenly evaporated. In retrospect, Mexican financial authorities thought domestic finances more solid than they were because few assets were tied to the risky US mortgage market (BdeM 2009 (2007–10), 39). Yet large Mexican corporations, holding groups, and the state were highly dependent on recurrent flows of finance that were far from guaranteed. When the climate of 'extreme risk aversion' materialized global deleveraging meant Mexican finance lost access to international markets. The collapse of Lehman thus sparked volatility in Mexico's financial sector, if not necessarily in the banks, to which Mexican financial authorities responded aggressively. The BdeM and SHCP, at the time headed by governor Guillermo Ortiz and finance minister Agustin Carstens, fed billions of dollars into the domestic market to help defend the finances of businesses in Mexico. In October 2008 the BdeM sold, in less than 72 hours, a record 11 per cent of its foreign reserves (nearly $9 billion). The amount climbed to $11 billion over 10 days and then to a total of $31.4 billion by mid-2009 when the liquidity injections halted (IMF 2010a, 9). The PAN government quickly negotiated an $80 billion lifeline of precautionary financing with the US Federal Reserve and the IMF to help maintain calm over Mexico's finances.

To further restore the confidence of financial capital in Mexico Mexican authorities publicly released details over how the SHCP had hedged oil prices at $70 per barrel for 2009 (earning $10 billion over the current lower oil prices) and how the federal government had increased IFI borrowing to cover revenue shortfalls. The PAN government committed to using these external public sector revenues to offset the private sector's deficit, which was understood as 'essential in restoring investors' confidence' (Sidaoui et al. 2010, 289–90). And what a signal! By December 2009 Mexican state authorities had amassed nearly $170 billion in available state-backed financial resources composed of foreign reserves, an IMF credit line, and the US Federal Reserve swap line. Moreover, the Mexican state development banks, Nafin and Bancomext, began offering up to 50 per cent guarantees to refinance domestic private corporations' and non-bank securities. This new role assumed by the development banks represents another example of state restructuring in support of financial imperatives. In January 2009 President Calderón appointed Héctor Rangel Domene to head Nafin and Bancomext. Rangel is a past executive of Citibank, a past president of the powerful Business Coordinating Council and the Bankers' Association of Mexico, and chaired the boards of many large corporations in Mexico, including for the BBVA Bancomer financial group. Calderón's handing Rangel power over the Mexican development banks 'was like delivering the Church to Luther' (Rodríguez 2010, 56). Financial capital in Mexico had received another strong signal of support from state and government authorities.

But who in Mexico needed this explicit state-backed support, if not the banks? It is generally acknowledged that the banks in Mexico were not the immediate source of financial instability. According to official accounts the banks remained well capitalized (at around the 15 per cent mark) and enjoyed a low reliance on external funding (BdeM 2009 (2007–10), 9; IMF 2010a, 3). These same accounts, and most commentators, likewise stress that the banking sector has benefited from enhanced state supervision since the 1995 crisis. That the banks were not the immediate source of crisis, however, is different from saying they did not need to adjust their operations to crisis. The banks in Mexico, much like in other emerging capitalisms, increased interest rates, drew on BdeM resources, cut back on new lending to business and households, shifted money resources into safer places like government bonds, and even expanded branch networks to draw in deposits and improve liquidity (Mihaljek 2010). While not the source of instability, neither were the banks necessarily a stabilizing force (more is said on this below).

The immediate source of domestic financial instability instead came from Mexico's largest corporations, which had been using very risky foreign exchange and interest rate derivatives – created in the process of Mexico's finance-led restructuring processes – to feed higher rate investments in Mexico (BdeM 2009 (2007–10), 39). The US crisis caused massive losses in these corporate derivatives that also unleashed sharp demand for US dollars and put unexpected pressures on Mexican state finances. In the preceding years, neoliberal policymakers had privileged exchange rate stability. This had allowed Mexican capital to profit handsomely from the difference in rates of return (the carry trade, again). However, the late 2008 peso devaluation turned speculative corporate windfalls into spectacular losses. Major companies like *Cementos Mexicanos* and *Controladora Commercial Mexicana* lost millions of dollars in foreign currency operations. Financial capitalists' uncertainty as to the extent and breadth of these losses worsened already manifest instability that in turn exacerbated the drying up of US markets for credit in Mexico and instigated a domestic credit crunch. The corporations' lucrative carry trade came to an end but their speculative financial operations directly impacted Mexican society. The resulting credit crunch drove up the cost of borrowing for the Mexican government and for IPAB, which is still servicing debt commitments from the 1995 bailout; in consequence, more tax revenues flowed into interest payments and to financial capital (Munoz-Martinez 2008, 19; BdeM 2009 (2007–10), 42; IMF 2010a, 11). The 2008–09 corporate derivative losses had revealed new vulnerabilities linked to financial capitalism in Mexico.[11] However, state financial managers revealed their unwavering support by mobilizing an institutional arsenal of state resources capable of managing and socializing these vulnerabilities on behalf of financial capital.

6.4.1 A Sign of the Times: Foreign Reserve Accumulation

The years since the financial crises in Mexico and Turkey in 1994–95 have seen a marked increase in financial volatility among emerging capitalisms like Brazil, Russia, South Korea, and so on. Perhaps the most significant response by these countries' state financial managers and government elites has been the accumulation of massive foreign reserves. On the magnitude of this build-up the World Bank's new *Global Development Horizons* report is worth quoting at length (2011, 142–3):

> The expansion of financial holdings and wealth in emerging markets is most prominently reflected on the official side, in the accumulation of foreign exchange reserves by monetary authorities. . . . In 1999, developed countries' foreign exchange reserves represented approximately $1.1 trillion (62 percent) of the $1.8 trillion of global foreign exchange reserves and developing countries' reserves the remaining 38 percent. One decade later, these proportions had reversed: developing and emerging economies held approximately $5.4 trillion (66 percent) of the total global reserve stock of $8.1 trillion as of end-2010.

No one, however, is really sure how large foreign reserves should be – despite the popularized Guidotti-Greenspan rule of a 1-1 ratio of reserves to short-term external debt. In Mexico during so-called normal times the international community and financial capital had seemed satisfied with Mexico's level of foreign reserves. Once crisis appeared, however, Mexico's reserve levels suddenly seemed more 'modest' relative to holdings in other emerging capitalisms like Turkey and Korea (IMF 2010a, 9, 29).[12] The IMF concedes that the shift in the sentiments of financial capital stems not from a break in Mexico's 'fundamentals' but rather from 'relative risk perceptions' tied to Mexico's US dependence and foreign reserve levels (IMF 2010a, 9).

In practice the growth of Mexican foreign reserves from their nadir of

–$1.5 billion in 1995 has been nothing short of fantastic. After the 1995 crisis and the adoption of a market-determined exchange rate (floating peso) state financial managers strategically pursued more liquid financial markets. State authorities perceived foreign reserve accumulation as a necessary policy objective to facilitate this liquidity (Sidaoui 2005, 218–19). The logic behind the policy decision involved crafting a state financial apparatus able to respond to the demands of financial capital. Reserve accumulation achieved this by (1) signaling Mexico's capacity to service foreign debt payments; (2) offering positive signals to foreign investors and international rating agencies so as to earn lower country risk assessments (that is, large reserve stocks can mean lower external financing rates); (3) enhancing the state's capacity to respond as a lender of last resort in foreign currency to Mexican banks; and (4) demonstrating capacity to intervene in financial markets in such a way as to end speculative pressures on the peso (Sidaoui 2005, 219, 226). By 2001 state authorities had socked away $38 billion; by 2002, it was $48 billion. Sidaoui notes that research conducted by the BdeM at this time suggested Mexico's foreign reserve levels were more than adequate. Yet officials continued to build reserves, which neared $69 billion by 2005. At this time, again, state authorities made motions towards slowing reserve accumulation because they deemed that 'the financial and opportunity costs induced by the rapid inflow of reserves had exceeded the benefits' (Sidaoui 2005, 229). Nonetheless, authorities brought reserves to over $85 billion by 2008. Following the record sell-offs to defend the peso and with the fading of the foreign exchange crisis by mid-2009, the BdeM restored reserves to well above pre-crisis levels at nearly $95 billion (IMF 2010a, 17). In July 2010 reserves reached a record level of over $100 billion with official projections for this to surpass $120 billion by 2011 – nearly triple what the BdeM believed adequate eight years earlier in 2002. This pattern, wherein Mexico is no exception, has led the IMF to acknowledge 'the need to take due account of the costs and externalities of reserve accumulation' (2010b, 3). Regardless, the new BdeM governor, Agustin Carstens, stated in an early 2011 speech that Mexico has 'accumulated a lot of reserves and we're going to continue with that process'.[13] This at a time when gross public sector debt, which is serviced by incoming public revenue that supports reserve accumulation, increased from 38.3 per cent of 2006 GDP to 44.6 per cent of 2009 GDP, where it is projected to remain until 2015 (IMF 2010a, 34, 40).

Unlike the more exposed socialized costs of bank rescues and bailouts, the social costs of foreign reserve accumulation are more hidden from the public's eye. Economist Dani Rodrik (2006) has attempted to quantify these social costs (compare Akyüz 2008). Rodrik (2006, 254) writes:

Each dollar of reserves that a country invests in these assets comes at an opportunity cost that equals the cost of external borrowing for that economy (or alternatively, the social rate of return to investment in that economy). The spread between the yield on liquid reserve assets and the external cost of funding – a difference of several percentage points in normal times – represents the social cost of self-insurance.

In other words, the Mexican state must offer higher rates of interest for its peso state bonds because Mexico sits much lower within the international hierarchy of states (that is, it supposedly means greater risks for financial capitalists who therefore demand higher returns). The US offers much lower rates of return because it sits at the top of the international hierarchy and US Treasury bonds carry effectively no risk (even, it should be added, when they suffer a downgrading from their AAA status).[14] The difference absorbed by the Mexican state is the 'social cost of self-insurance'. As Rodrik qualifies, the measurable costs of this difference are technical and difficult to calculate due to uncertainty over the exact rates of interest, definitions over what should be included, and so on. Nonetheless Rodrik calculates that the social costs of the rise in reserves since the 1990s is about 1 per cent of annual GDP for developing countries on average (2006, 254). This is a conservative estimate since the 1 per cent only applies to the *increase* in reserves since the 1990s, not to the entire social cost of international reserves today.[15] According to one BdeM estimate, the measurable costs of reserves held from 1997 to 2002 neared 78 billion pesos (about $7.8 billion) (Sidaoui 2005, 225). The Mexican financial media typically estimate current costs in the range of $4 billion per year. The point being that Mexican political leadership is willing to dedicate enormous public revenues to amass foreign reserves to sustain financial confidence in Mexico. This tool within Mexico's arsenal bears significant social costs, and this is without even accounting for the annual fiscal costs of running the ever-growing state financial apparatus (for example, the BdeM, CNBV, IPAB, SHCP, and other state financial institutions, for which there is a need for further empirical and historical research).

What needs to be remembered (but is routinely omitted from economistic and technical analyses) is that these social costs are particular to the current phase of financial capitalism, arise in response to the increasing prevalence of financial crises since the 1990s, and represent an institutionalized imbalance of power between capital and labor in the state. The complexities of these relationships are simply whitewashed by neoclassical terms like 'revealed preferences' (that is, the idea that Mexico simply prefers to participate in global finances because, apparently, it is) or lost in institutionalist terms that see financialization as a series of failed policies. As even Rodrik acknowledges, emerging markets are compelled to increase the liquidity of foreign reserves to ward off financial panic and stem sudden reversals in capital flows (2006, 254). Yet Rodrik remains unsure whether or not the 'insurance premium pays for itself' and generally sees reserves as a reasonable response of governments who attempt to maintain competitiveness without restricting capital inflows, but he does accept that '[d]eveloping nations are paying a very high price to play by the rules of financial globalization' (2006, 254–5, 261). In more critical terms, the benefits of reserve accumulation accrue disproportionately to financial capital while the costs fall disproportionately onto Mexican popular classes.

6.4.2   On Foreign Banks, Crisis, and Alternatives in Mexico

Another unintended consequence of Mexico's neoliberal finance and development strategy has emerged from the current crisis, namely the troublesome place of foreign banks. In the wake of the 1995 crisis government elites, state managers, mainstream analysts, and IFI officials presented foreign bank ownership as a stabilizing and modernizing force for Mexico. While neoclassical economists recognize that foreign bank dominance entails certain problems with national outreach or skimming the best clients in Mexico (which problems are, as always, rectifiable by more competition) they qualify this, as Thorsten Beck and Maria Soledad Martinez Peria observe, because of the belief that 'few would dispute the potential benefits that foreign banks can bring in terms of innovation in technologies, products, and risk management, greater access to capital, and improvements in human capital' (2010, 53). Yet when the US-based Citibank suffered severe losses due to their involvement in the US subprime debacle, its troubles generated instability in Mexico. In the words of the BdeM, 'No one stopped to think that troubled foreign institutions could have a contagion effect on the Mexican financial system despite some of them being the parent companies of Mexican-based banks' (BdeM 2009 (2007–10), 39). This is, to say the least, a bit disingenuous since foreign bank dominance in emerging capitalisms like Mexico have long been the targets of substantial criticism. Only a couple of years earlier even the IMF had expressed concern about Mexico's capacity to enforce an 'efficient resolution process in the case of failure of a foreign-owned financial group' given its level of financial opening (2006, 23). Much of the IMF's concern linked back to IPAB (the deposit insurance fund), which remained resource-weak because it still had to service the $100 billion in debt from the 1995 bank bailout and was therefore having difficulty building a sufficient deposit fund to insure later foreign bank operations. The

IMF thus recommended transferring the IPAB debt to the federal government (IMF 2006, 28) – a plan that reflects Zedillo's original 1998 program, but which was still too politically sensitive. Instead, the PAN has more covertly offset the weakness of IPAB by building up Mexico's foreign reserves as a signal of creditworthiness.

While the Mexican government seeks to stabilize the world market by amassing public resources in the service of financial capital the world's global banking giants have been actively destabilizing the world market through their speculative financial practices (leading to the sub-prime crisis). This would negatively impact Mexico. As Dubravko Mihaljek, a senior economist at the BIS, points out, because of the relative strength and profitability of foreign bank affiliates in Mexico the foreign parent banks could attempt to displace the crisis in the core to the periphery either by transferring loans to their Mexican affiliates to reduce leverage or by borrowing from them (Mihaljek 2010, 44). At the same time foreign banks repatriated billions in affiliates' profits to support faltering operations in the core (that is, a transfer of wealth from the poorer countries to the wealthier).

Foreign bank dominance in Mexico has also created other conundrums, for example, the US state-led rescue and partial nationalization of the American Citibank (about 36 per cent by early 2009). According to Mexican banking law foreign states are prohibited from owning banks in Mexico. The US government nationalization of Citi thus meant the American state illegally owned a piece Citi-Banamex. The Calderón administration refused to act against Citi-Banamex by compelling Banamex to be sold. Instead, it became tangled up in court proceedings with the PAN offering Banamex a three-year window of opportunity to rid its operations of US state ownership. The political conundrum this caused was resolved as the US government sold off its remaining shares in December 2010. Nevertheless, for nearly two years Banamex enjoyed the privilege of openly flouting the law.

The range of troubles caused by the magnitude of foreign bank control in Mexico has been singled out as one of the most egregious policy errors made by the PRI and PAN administrations (Girón and Levy 2005; Stallings 2006; Avalos and Trillo 2006; Martinez-Diaz 2009; Vidal et al. 2011). The alternative, many argue, is to return the banking sector to Mexican ownership. For reasons alluded to earlier and discussed more in the book's conclusion, a return to private Mexican banks is no alternative. If stretched to the extreme, perhaps an argument can be made that domestic banks are less likely to spirit capital abroad at times of financial crisis, but this is optimistic within a financially liberalized world market and in light of Mexico's past experiences (namely, the 1982 and

1995 banking crises). Without downplaying the importance of foreign bank agency and power, the domestic versus foreign dichotomy has become a classic case of failing to see the wood for the trees. Why would domestic banks even want to challenge the benefits they derive from financial capitalism? As we have seen, the Mexican owned banks have at times been the most 'neoliberal' of all the banks – driving up worker productivity, absorbing state financial support, advocating on behalf of austerity measures, and pressing for greater benefits from the state. The same can be said in the Turkish case. As even the BIS admits, at times of crisis domestic and foreign banks tend to react in similar ways (Mihaljek 2010, 31). I am not suggesting that political forces and state authorities do not have to come to terms with the power of foreign banks in Mexico, for indeed they must if there is to be any break with neoliberalism. But posing private domestic bank ownership as a substantive alternative in and of itself – outside of the structural constraints and social relations of power specific to emerging finance capitalism – is a theoretical, political, and practical dead-end.

6.5   CONCLUSION

Why does Mexican society find itself in an era of emerging finance capitalism? Based on the last 30 years of neoliberal restructuring, emerging finance capitalism has consolidated because – in the context of a hierarchical interstate system, a capitalist world market defined by mounting competitive and profit imperatives, and a system of social reproduction that is more and more articulated through financial means – Mexican state and government elites have led the restructuring of the state financial apparatus in ways that have institutionalized the interests of financial capital over and above other social interests. Bankers and financial capital have supported and helped to shape this process. The converging social logic of financial imperatives in society is especially notable in the way state managers and financial capital resolve crises. On the one hand, this has involved state-led rescues, the socialization of various forms of financial risks, the rationalization of the banks (even when this involves acting against the interests of any single bank or financier), and the restructuring of the financial apparatus. On the other hand, it has involved banks and financial capital adjusting their operations to first and foremost maximize profits, to militate against any extra-market coordination of their accumulation strategies, centralize and concentrate capital, intensify labor processes, and enhance their power over society. Finally, emerging finance capitalism has consolidated because organized labor and popular classes have been unable to collectively resist the deepening of financial imperatives in society. The result is an ever-greater institutionalized imbalance of financial capital–labor relations in the Mexican state form. We see today in Mexico a general populace that is subordinate *to* but ultimately responsible *for* the risks of financial capital within their borders, from which they derive few if any benefits. The search for substantive alternatives must therefore begin not by glorifying national capitalists of a time gone by but by questioning and overcoming the institutionalized social relations of power defining capitalist state, bank, and labor relations which privilege the needs of financial capital over those of the working and wealth-creating majority of Mexicans.

NOTES

1. A high level SHCP director in the Banking and Saving Unit affirmed this official interpretation (Interview, 13 February 2008, Mexico City).
2. According to OECD figures, VAT as a percentage of total revenue in OECD countries has risen from 12 per cent in the 1960s to 20 per cent in 2007, making this a feature of neoliberalism (see 'Tax revenues fall in OECD countries', 15 Dec 2010, www.oecd.org).
3. Martinez-Diaz 2009 goes into further specifics on the 1998 reform process.
4. David Luhnow, 'Mexican Crisis Holds Lessons for US', 13 October 2008, *Wall Street Journal*, available online at http://online.wsj.com.
5. For more on the Oaxaca Commune, see Roman and Arregui 2007.
6. President Zedillo's National Development Plan 1995–2000 had also encouraged market-oriented restructuring, but its implementation reflected the urgency of the financial crisis management (OECD 1998b, 79).
7. Author's translation, 'Presente de la Banca en México', Presentación en la Facultad de Economía de la Universidad Autónoma de México, 27 May 2010. Available online at http://www.cnbv.gob.mx.
8. On transnationalism, see Robinson 2003 and Morton 2003. On internationalization, see Marois 2005 and Hanieh 2011.
9. Information on investment in new information technologies, which can affect employee numbers, is not readily available. Nonetheless, the most dramatic decline in labor costs occurs during times of crisis precisely when there is no money to invest in new technologies – a pattern repeated during Turkey's 2001 crisis.
10. Kent Paterson, 'Mexico's other Crisis: Foreign Banks', 15 May 2009, www.corpwatchorg. The benefits that bankers realize from 'flexible' bank labor are not restricted to Mexico. As reported in a *McKinsey Quarterly* piece on Latin American banks and the Great Recession, to 'offset declining revenue growth, banks have tried to cut operating costs' (Andrade et al. 2009, 7). Increasing bank labor productivity is also the core argument of a 2003 McKinsey report on Turkish banking.
11. The BdeM notes that other emerging capitalisms, such as South Korea, Brazil, Indonesia, China, and so on also suffered from derivative speculation (2009, 39).
12. Ironically, Turkish state ministers have gone on record as saying their reserves are also too modest and must be increased as a sign of stability.
13. 'UPDATE: Mexico To Continue Accumulating Foreign Reserves', *Wall Street Journal*, 7 Jan 2011, available online at http://online.wsj.com.
14. On the benefits of peripheral reserves held in US bonds for the US economy, see Duménil and Lévy 2004 and Ocampo et al. 2008.

15. To put these figures into a political context of struggles over social resources, Mexico's federal government flagship anti-poverty program, PROGRESA/Oportunidades, received about 0.3 per cent of GDP in 2004 (OECD 2005, 142). Rodrik also refers to PROGRESA (2006, 261). The program targets the poorest households with direct cash payments for education, health services, and even basic food consumption and also helps to fund infrastructure such as water drainage and sewerage, electricity, rural roads, housing improvements, and so on. For Soederberg, the program represents the minimal cost required to manage social dissent in Mexico (2010a, 90; see also Teichman 2008 for a critique). Anti-poverty thus receives less than a third of the annual resources dedicated to foreign reserves.

7. Richer than Croesus?
Understanding the subordination of state and banks to emerging finance capitalism in Turkey

The approximation of neoliberal social rule in Turkey since the 1980s had proven unrealistic by the late 1990s. To better institutionalize neoliberalism the coalition government embraced the 1999 disinflation program that, rather than resolving neoliberal financial instability, ushered in two new and more severe banking crises (Cizre and Yeldan 2005; Erbaş and Turan 2009). The impact of the crises did not lead state and government elites to reject neoliberalism. Rather, the crisis served as an opportunity to consolidate neoliberalism's progressively finance-led form via a state-led rescue. Following the rescue Turkey's new ruling elites and state authorities maintained their political commitments to internalizing the social logic of financial capital as the state's own social logic. The consolidation of Turkey's emerging finance capitalist state form has meant that the popular and laboring classes disproportionately bear the costs of this accumulation strategy without sharing in the benefits. This argument is developed in four sections. Section 7.1 examines the 2001 crisis and how the state-led rescue internalized new financial imperatives. Section 7.2 details how the incoming Adalet ve Kalkınma Partisi (AKP; Justice and Development Party) government continued to restructure the state apparatus in ways beneficial to financial capital in Turkey. Section 7.3 analyzes the changing structure of the banking sector from 2001 until the present, and Section 7.4 looks at how and why the Turkish banks weathered the 2008 crisis. A brief conclusion follows.

7.1 THE 2001 STATE-LED BANKING RESCUE: SAVING NEOLIBERALS FROM THEMSELVES, AGAIN

Far from severing ties to neoliberalism the state-led bank rescue of 2001 demonstrated a clear political commitment to underwriting and institutionalizing a new phase of finance-led capital accumulation premised on strengthening the state financial apparatus (Marois 2011a). This interpretation conflicts with, for example, mainstream interpretations that share an understanding of the 2001 crisis as being fundamentally a result of the failures of state authorities, which sidesteps questions of the profit-maximizing activities of financial capital (Yılmaz 2007; Steinherr et al. 2004).[1] The BRSA (Banking Regulation and Supervision Agency; Bankacılık Düzenleme ve Denetleme Kurumu) points to the private banks' mounting exchange rate and foreign capital risks but the BRSA is equally vigorous in blaming state bank duty losses on the failings of state institutional regulation (compare BRSA 2009a, 43). Finally, the Banks Association of Turkey (BAT; Türkiye Bankalar Birliği) offers what it refers to as the banking sector perspective. The BAT acknowledges the problematic build-up of private financial risks and even the excessive competition leading up to the 2001 crisis but, without a hint of irony, blames this on state authorities (BAT 2009c, 68–9, 71). Under what can be understood as the nascent post-Washington consensus discourse it seems that financial capitalism in the developing world needed the state but that the state was ill-equipped to manage their needs. Financial crisis has seemingly little to do with finance capital and everything to do with the state apparatus. As we will see Turkish authorities nonetheless recognized at the time of the 2001 crisis that they had to do something, notably institutionalize a more muscular state financial apparatus. Yet to get there state officials had first to halt the crisis, socialize the financial risks gone bad, and then begin re-regulating financial capital's activities. Let us start with what triggered the 2001 crisis.

In the volatile context that followed the November 2000 crisis, the immediate trigger to the 2001 crisis was a dramatic quarrel between Turkey's Prime Minister Ecevit and President Ahmet Necdet Sezer during a National Security Council meeting on 19 February 2001. Sezer accused Ecevit of not doing enough to combat government corruption, demanding an investigation into the BRSA and the workings of the Turkish state banks. Rejecting any investigation into the state banks, Ecevit criticized Sezer for undermining him and the Demokratik Sol Parti (DSP; Democratic Left Party) coalition government. Apparently incensed, Sezer literally threw the Turkish Constitution at Ecevit, who then walked out of the meeting. News of the political fallout spooked the ever-jittery financial markets, sparking massive capital flight. By the end of the day a quarter of Turkey's $20 billion in foreign reserves had vanished as the İstanbul Stock Exchange (İSE; İstanbul Menkul Kıymetler Borsası) fell by 63 per cent over the next two days. Two days later, on 21 February 2001 (ominously nicknamed Black Wednesday), overnight repurchase rates hit 3000 per cent and interest rates struck as high as 7500 per cent annually. With the sting of the 1997 East Asian and 1998 Russian crises still fresh on their faces, the international financial community feared the Turkish financial crisis might also spread. The first deputy director of the IMF, Stanley Fischer, happened to be in Turkey at the time. The Ecevit coalition called emergency meetings following which, on the advice of Fischer, the government abandoned Turkey's currency peg – the key to the IMF-sponsored 1999 disinflation program – in order to prevent the total collapse of Turkish banking. The government then allowed the price of the Turkish lira (TL) to be market-determined, which led to immediate domestic inflation. The Central Bank of Turkey (CBT; Türkiye Cumhuriyet Merkez Bankası) governor, Gazı Erçel, and head of the Secretariat of the Treasury, Selcuk Demiralp, resigned at once. The 1999 reforms meant to stabilize Turkey's market-oriented economy had instead wrought nationwide crisis.

Paradoxically, while the governing coalition had seemingly lost control of the Turkish economy, everyone understood that the government alone was capable of acting on behalf of financial capital in order to contain the crisis. As it had done during the 2000 crisis the DSP socialized the financial risks of the domestic private banks and the accumulated state bank duty losses. As detailed below, the social costs would reach over $47 billion, or about 30 per cent of GDP. The government socialized the losses, according to the BRSA, 'with the purpose of protecting the banking system' and to ensure continuity in the financial system (2003, 20; 2009a, 8).

The 2001 banking crisis sounded a wake-up call. The idealized Washington consensus approach had failed in Turkey as in so many other emerging capitalisms during the 1990s. Both IFI and state authorities recognized that they would have to do something or hazard the profligacy of financial capital causing systemic change. Simply socializing the financial risks of bankers, again, and to this extent, could not suffice politically or economically. Yet breaking from the pro-capital and anti-labor hard core of neoliberalism was not presented as an option by political forces. Rather, state authorities had to do something *for* finance-led neoliberalism. The post-Washington consensus showed the way by accepting a more active role for state institutions in promoting capitalist development. The beauty of it was that Turkey's pattern of capital accumulation and the state's role in it had already carved out this now legitimate path.

To push forward with the rescue and initiate state and bank restructuring without sacrificing Turkey's neoliberal orientation the DSP coalition named an unelected neoliberal technocrat, Kemal Derviş, as the new Minister of the Economy on 2 March 2001. The decision had followed after some debate but, as *The Economist* put it, Turkey's bickering coalition agreed to allow a technocrat to spearhead reform and restart the flow

of foreign capital.[2] As a longtime World Bank executive and capable neoliberal technocrat, the selection of Derviş appeased both financial investors
and IFIs (Chhibber 2004, 6). And this was vital as Derviş's most pressing
problem was to get international lenders like the European Union (EU),
US, IMF, and World Bank to lend more to Turkey. To help him along,
the government gave Derviş significant administrative powers including
control over the new BRSA. Financial capital responded favorably. The
İSE shot up 40 per cent, state bond interest rates dropped from 100 to 40
per cent, and the TL stabilized. The IMF gestured its approval by offering
another $8 billion in credits for an available total of $19 billion. In retrospect the 2001 banking crisis had opened an opportunity to push forward
with market-oriented reforms previously thought politically impractical,
and a range of social forces lined up behind Derviş's restructuring plans
to take advantage.

On taking office Derviş announced the Transition to a Strong Economy
(TSE) program. The TSE formed the legal and institutional framework
within which Derviş exercised his administrative, and ultimately political, power. The goal of the TSE, in the words of Derviş, was to institutionally 'separate the economic from the political' (quoted in BAT,
2001) – however improbable, even impossible, this formal separation is
in real world practice. The discourse around Derviş's 'de-politicization'
of Turkey's economic processes facilitated state restructuring under the
TSE. For example, changes to the Central Bank Law granted the institution formal independence from the Turkish government. The same law
granted the now formally independent CBT responsibility for maintaining price stability. A newly created monetary policy committee was then
given responsibility for implementing an inflation-targeting regime. In this
reconstitution of the state financial apparatus, the CBT can still pursue
other economic activities but only so long as its activities do not conflict
with the price stability imperative. To bolster institutional independence
and prevent political interventions (albeit in its institutionally-neoliberal
orientation), the government extended the rights and tenures of senior
CBT executives. In practice the changes removed many of the state-led
developmental powers exercised through central banks in the postwar
period. No more could the CBT extend loans or grant credit to the
Treasury or any other state institution and neither could it purchase any
state debt in the primary market. Financial capital had good reason to
celebrate the reforms. As one Deutsche Bank manager working in Turkey
put it, Derviş's reforms were praiseworthy *because* they were irrevers-
ible and immune to democratic revision (in Rhode 2001, 40). Now more
than ever the independence of financial authorities protects and manages
financial markets in the interest of financial capital while insulating flows

of money from popular oversight and the demands of labor. Viewed in this critical light neoliberal de-politicization is a chimera. Derviş's TSE program responded to crisis by restructuring the state in ways subordinate to financial profit imperatives. This is especially evident in the TSE-related banking reforms.

It should be pointed out that to argue that the reforms were in the interests of financial capital is different from asserting change was imposed on Turkish society from above by IFIs or financial capital. Before they can become institutionalized in the Turkish state, the interests of IFIs and needs of financial capital are always mediated by domestic politics, institutions, patterns of accumulation, and relations of class power. In this conceptualization, I agree with the former Subsecretary of the Treasury and architect behind the 2001 crisis restructuring plan, Faik Öztrak, that the TSE and associated banking reforms were not simply imposed by the IMF or financial capital but prepared in consultation with and implemented by the Turkish bureaucracy (Interview, CHP Member of Parliament, 27 August 2007). Öztrak suggests that the 2001 reforms were a Turkish affair, even though it is in the interests of Turkish politicians to suggest otherwise and to have the IMF absorb popular discontent. To be sure, changes in Turkey occurred within the structural context and constraints of world market competitive imperatives. It is nonetheless a conceptual and political error to argue that neoliberal reforms are merely imposed on society because this ignores and denies the role of struggle in national decision-making capacity, the historical contingencies of Turkish social relations of power and class, and the impact of preceding domestic patterns of accumulation. However universal neoliberal financial imperatives have become these imperatives are always differentiated nationally. This is evident in Turkey's restructuring of the banking sector.

7.1.1 The 2001 Banking Sector Restructuring Program

The May 2001 Banking Sector Restructuring Program (BSRP) was a cornerstone of Derviş's TSE project.[3] In the short term the BSRP aimed to restore banking stability and in the long term bring financial prosperity. State financial authorities claim the BSRP has proven capable of eliminating financial distortions and promoting an efficient, globally competitive, better regulated, and stable banking sector in Turkey (BRSA 2002; 2009a, viii). In many regards the BSRP is Turkey's contribution to the post-Washington consensus – or a blueprint for how to institutionally manage the practices of financial capital without sacrificing their profits or destabilizing underlying social relations of power.

With its unveiling, the 2001 BSRP targeted four areas for immediate banking reform and recovery. These included (1) regulatory and supervisory framework enhancement; (2) prompt Saving Deposit Insurance Fund (SDIF; Tasarruf Mevduatı Sigorta Fonu) bank resolution; (3) private bank and productive capital debt strengthening; and (4) state bank restructuring. The first target saw the BRSA undertake changes to the state's financial regulatory and supervisory framework. This involved restructuring aspects of the state financial apparatus to enhance its capacity to manage financial risks within Turkey's borders. For example, amendments to the 1999 Banking Law augmented the institutional powers of the BRSA and SDIF while bringing Turkey's financial regulations closer to EU standards. The list of specific reforms is extensive but included such things as higher capital requirements for Turkish banks, stiffer capital requirements for bank mergers and acquisitions, a fine-tuned determination of credit limits, new non-performing loan (NPL) provisions, harmonized accounts for the participation of banks in other companies, enhanced balance sheet reporting, and so on. Notably, the DSP altered corporate and tax legislation to transform Turkish financial-industrial groups into separate financial and corporate conglomerates. Whereas before 2001 the private banks had been at the core of holding group operations and profitability strategies, the banking affiliates would now have to become profit-seeking enterprises in their own right. According to one state bank manager, it was not until these changes were made that holding groups began to pursue banking as a separate business (Interview, Senior Manager, Halk Bank, 24 August 2007). The BSRP changes thus enhanced state regulatory capacity and the Turkish banks fell under greater state regulation – but without sacrificing their market-oriented accumulation strategy.

Further regulatory changes encouraged financial market deepening. The DSP authorized, for example, a series of tax incentives and new BRSA regulations to ease bank mergers and acquisitions beginning in June 2001. The goal was to increasingly centralize and concentrate bank capital in fewer banks in Turkey (see Section 7.3 below). The initial BSRP changes had also paved the way for compliance with the new Basel II Capital Accord requirements in 2002 (BAT 2009b, 6). The higher liquidity requirements (in a system where liquidity was low) compelled some private domestic banks to seek out foreign sources of bank capital and to establish joint banking ventures, which encouraged the internalization of foreign bank capital. Then in July 2001 the government allowed the Capital Markets Board of Turkey to establish a derivatives market under the İSE to expand domestic financial markets. Turkish state and government elites framed these changes as vital to enhancing efficiency and guarding against sectoral instability. In effect state authorities created new markets while forcing financial capital to better organize its accumulation activities in ways that would help protect financial markets from their own destabilizing practices. In official documents state authorities attribute no costs to themselves in institutionalizing these changes despite the fiscal outlay needed to cover the staff resources required of the process.

A second target of Derviş's BSRP involved the prompt resolution of the failed private banks held in the SDIF. From 1997 to 2001 the Turkish government had socialized eighteen collapsed banks by bringing them into the SDIF. Eleven failures had occurred since the 2000 crisis and constituted a fifth of all banking assets (BRSA 2009a, 15). Many of the failed private banks buckled because their owners had recognized that Turkey's liberalization process had made channeling large amounts of credit to themselves and to affiliated companies a successful, but ultimately unstable, accumulation strategy ($11 billion of these speculative dealings ended up under SDIF control (BRSA 2003, 24)). Others failed because liberalization had given them access to high levels of foreign money capital to service the state's lucrative debts. Both of these often-entangled strategies came crashing down in the late 1990s. The 2001 BSRP enabled state financial authorities to deal with this gaggle of banks gone bad by drawing their financial problems into the SDIF. This involved the Turkish Treasury transferring over $28 billion to the SDIF by July 2003 to cover not only the past bad debts and interest payments but also the mounting foreign exchange and interest accruals (BRSA 2003, 26–7). The process also involved finding some form of institutional resolution for the banks once rescued. This has involved such strategies as selling the bank (or its shares), selling its loan and deposit assets, and/or merging unsold failed banks. Institutional resolution has even involved forced mergers with the state banks, for example, when the state-owned Halk Bank was compelled to absorb the collapsed private Pamukbank in 2004. Within a year or so of the 2001 crisis the SDIF had reduced and consolidated the number of banks under its control to two: one bank that was up for sale and another to be held as a transitional bank (BRSA 2003, 19). It should be noted that even at the time of rescue state authorities saw little hope of recovering the state's socialization costs as a result of both private sector delay tactics and the fact that many socialized debts exceeded the debtor's wealth (BRSA 2003, 40). As of late 2009 only $13 billion has been recovered from the banks' shareholders with few realistic hopes of full recovery (BRSA 2009a, 17). Much as in Mexico, the Turkish state, and by extension the bulk of the working population in society, shoulders the burden.

A third target of Derviş's BSRP sought to strengthen the debt structures of the remaining private banks and troubled non-financial firms. In the case of the surviving private banks, state authorities opted to experiment with leaving recovery to financial capital and market-based mechanisms such as shareholder capital injections and voluntary mergers. However, the market-based strategy – much as it had prior to the 2001 crisis – proved unsuccessful in restoring stability. The extended recession and contraction in available loans forced state authorities to boost the capital base of private banks. Authorities pushed another $8 billion directly into the private banks, of which $5.2 billion was provided by the SDIF and only $2.7 billion demanded from the private sector. In addition, the BRSA in collaboration with the BAT and private sector representatives crafted a legal framework by the end of January 2002 that enabled the restructuring of private sector NPLs through the so-called 'İstanbul Approach' (BRSA 2003, 47–52). The İstanbul Approach constituted a voluntary program to assist insolvent firms regain solvency and to continue operations following the crisis by restructuring their bank loans. Private banks reduced perceived financial risk levels by, in essence, the government simply allowing them to redefine many NPLs as still operational.[4] The changes did little to improve the financial strength of the banks but rather reframed what risks state financial managers took as acceptable. About 100 small-scale and 208 large firms (controlled by no more than 32 Turkish holding groups) had taken advantage of the restructuring program by September 2003. The Central Bank reports that as of mid-2005, the holding group firms accounted for about $5.4 billion in restructured debt and small firms accounted for about $650 million (CBT 2005 (2005–10), 85). State authorities worked to facilitate, not restrict, capital accumulation. And again, authorities attributed no costs to themselves in coordinating this three-year program, despite the public staff hours consumed in its organization. The fourth target of the BSRP dealt with state bank restructuring, which I address in the next section.

7.1.1.1 The BSRP and the restructuring of the Turkish state banks

By the turn of the new millennium the Turkish state-owned banks' role in facilitating neoliberal transformation via mounting duty losses had come to threaten the underlying stability of neoliberalism in Turkey. While the ruling coalition attempted some initial changes in the late 1990s, the 2001 BSRP consolidated the neoliberal transformation of the state banks so that they were now institutionally compelled to operate as if they were private, profit-seeking banks. This qualitative privatization of the Turkish state banks has many parallels with the restructuring of Mexico's nationalized banks after 1982, albeit in ways unique to Turkey. Nonetheless, in both cases the political intention was to make the banks more attractive to private financial capital in preparation for eventual sell-off. The BAT wrote at the time that it was vital that the state banks operate on the basis of market rules and profitability imperatives (BAT 2001).

In retrospect the thrust of the 2001 BSRP state bank reforms had been anticipated in Turkey's December 1999 Letter of Intent to the IMF. Therein the DSP coalition had restated its commitment to state bank privatization and outlined a process of market-oriented restructuring. The 1999 Letter to the IMF is worth quoting at length (emphasis added).

> The long standing problems of the state-owned banks will be addressed by strengthening their oversight and developing strategic corporate plans, operational restructuring, and financial and capital restructuring plans with phased-in timetables, which will be initiated in year 2000. Pursuing actions will be taken to begin the *commercialization* of Ziraat Bank and Halk Bank with an eventual privatization goal. In the interim, in order to impose *financial discipline* on the operations of these banks, while improving their cash management, cash transfers to cover losses on subsidized lending have been specified in the 2000 budget. . . . these services will be *more properly priced* in the future. Management of the state-owned banks is expected to maintain the *profitability* of the state-owned banks under this tighter budget constraint.

Until the 2001 banking crisis hit, however, the DSP coalition had been politically unable to fully implement the desired changes. This is not to say the coalition lacked commitment. For example, in February 2000, nine months prior to the November 2000 crisis, the government set a new interest rate mechanism for Ziraat Bank and Halk Bank that eliminated any future duty losses accruing from credit subsidies. This move made the state banks' still legally mandated developmental missions effectively market-disciplined. The coalition had also tried to ram through state bank privatization but was halted first by a constitutional challenge and then by the instability caused by the 2000 banking crisis. Yet the outbreak of crisis in 2001 then helped the IFIs and government achieve what they previously could not. The BSRP provided the legal mandate and necessary fiscal resources for state authorities to undertake the politically difficult, risky, and costly process of state bank restructuring. This included setting the explicit goal of selling off the state banks by 2005. While the government's goals were ambitious, they were suddenly achievable – as a result of the crisis and because Derviş's BSRP was carried out largely outside of normal democratic processes.

As a first step towards transforming the state banks, state authorities transferred managerial control of Ziraat Bank, Emlak Bank, and Halk Bank to a joint board of directors chaired by bankers brought in from the private banking sector. Former Treasury Subsecretary Öztrak notes that new managers from the private sector and state development agencies were also drawn into the banks to facilitate market-oriented change (Interview, Ankara, 27 August 2007). The Turkish Council of Ministers then granted the joint board all necessary authority to restructure and prepare the state banks for privatization (BRSA 2003). This would be done in line with Turkey's commitments to the EU harmonization of banking regulations. To this end, the BRSA took charge of coordinating and implementing a two-phase project, involving, first, the immediate financial restructuring of the state banks (mostly completed by the end of 2001) and, second, their ongoing operational restructuring (BRSA 2002).

In the initial phase of immediate restructuring, the BRSA had first to contend with the accumulated state bank duty losses. As discussed in Chapter 5, the duty losses helped market-oriented governments sustain Turkey's socially volatile transition to neoliberalism in the late 1990s by channeling money into sensitive sectors of Turkish society. That is, the duty losses hid the government's budgetary deficits (BRSA 2003, 10). By 2000, the government had exhausted this resource by driving duty losses up to half the state banks' balance sheet. In reality the duty losses were always official debt, but now the government was forced to recognize this and formally draw the losses into the state apparatus. By the time the government had strengthened the state banks' capital base and covered the duty losses with applied interest, the Turkish Treasury had issued $21.9 billion in special government bonds (that is, bonds constituting forms of fictitious capital). This had a stabilizing effect on the sector by improving the state banks' capital adequacy ratios. This is especially so because the state bonds carry a very low credit risk weighting based, as they are, on the collective capacity of Turkish people to work and create value. The state banks then improved their own liquidity by selling off some of the state bonds they held through repurchase transactions with the CBT and by eliminating their short-term liabilities to the private sector. To cap off the duty loss problem, the DSP coalition canceled nearly 100 regulations so as to prevent any future political allocation of duty losses. Be they developmental or neoliberal in orientation, the possibility of any political channeling of state bank resources was arrested and the postwar institutional specificity of the Turkish state banks erased. Regulatory changes then required the state banks to price their deposit and loan interest rates according to market conditions so as to promote competition and profit-maximization (BRSA 2003, 12). In so doing the place of financial imperatives in Turkish state banking was bolstered.

The second phase of changes targeted the ongoing operational restructuring of the state-owned banks. This entailed restructuring state bank operations at all levels, including their institutional organization, technologies, human resources, financial control, planning, risk management, and services so that they could compete at home and abroad. The effects of these changes are detailed in Section 7.3 below, but each change was geared towards increasing the banks' profitability and market stability.

However, not all the state banks could be saved. Authorities targeted the troubled state-owned Emlak Bank, which had been driven into the ground as a consequence of government officials forcing the bank to offer real estate loans to the private sector in the 1990s – loans that carried little or no hope of being paid back (in 2000, Emlak had NPL levels of nearly 40 per cent (OECD 2002, 156)). However, because of the 2001 crisis and the banks' weak loan portfolio, the DSP was unable to sell Emlak. Instead, the BRSA dealt with Emlak by canceling its banking license and merging its operations into Ziraat Bank in July 2001 (BRSA 2009a, 3). Many of Emlak's branches and much of its foreign trade business were transferred to Halk Bank (Interview, Senior Manager, Halk Bank, 24 August 2007). The joint board at the same time reduced state bank employee numbers by half and closed a third of all state bank branches (BRSA 2003, 14–15).

The joint board, coalition government, and state authorities made these changes to the state banks with negligible, if any, input from the Turkish bank labor unions (Kibritçioğlu 2006, 23–5). This is not to say that the crisis resolution measures did not meet with resistance. Members of the more leftist bank workers' union, Bank-Sen, hotly contested the closure of Emlak via a series of actions including organizational meetings, demonstrations, and creative forms of workplace strikes. This culminated in the occupation of Emlak Bank's headquarters while the chair of the joint board, Vural Akışık, was inside. Unwilling to cede to the workers' demands, the DSP pushed forward and closed Emlak Bank, concerned, as it was, with reducing the financial costs of state bank restructuring rather than mitigating the problems facing workers. For their part, bank workers were unable to collectively force their own demands above those of financial capital.[5] Wider popular discontent followed over changes to the state banks. According to Öztrak, when the state bank credits dried up, and in particular small and medium-sized enterprise (SME) credits from Halk Bank, the scarcity of credit created hardships that led to popular demonstrations in Turkey (Interview, 27 August 2007). Many Turkish people took to the streets to protest against the corruption and the extraordinary profits accrued by financial capital prior to the 2001 crisis, the subsequent austerity measures, and the restructuring of the Turkish economy.

The 2001 state-led banking rescue was premised on socialized costs and particularized benefits. Overall estimates place the cost of the bank rescue at just over $47 billion, or about 30 per cent of 2002 GDP (BRSA 2003, 6). The Turkish state contributed $44 billion and the private sector $2.7 billion. At 30 per cent of GDP, the 2001 Turkish rescue was one of the most costly among emerging capitalisms. For example, Mexico's 1995 banking crisis cost about 20 per cent of GDP, Korea's 1997 crisis more than 20 per cent, and Malaysia's 1997 crisis about 5 per cent. Only

Thailand's 1997 meltdown was more costly at around 43 per cent of GDP (OECD 2002a, 91). Turkish state authorities do not deny the rescue's costliness, but they are unwilling to assess it critically. In the words of the BRSA, 'Although resolution of these banks within the SDIF has a cost to the public, it is believed that this option offered the least cost-solution when compared to the direct liquidation option' (BRSA 2003, 22).

However massaged in official discourse the DSP and Derviş's bank rescue strategy depended on transferring value and money resources from the wealth-creating majority of people and workers in society to the financial sector so as to protect finance-led neoliberal strategies of development in Turkey. The DSP could do this through the historically institutionalized capacity of the state financial apparatus to create state bonds in order to inject money capital into the private and state banks. As discussed in Chapter 2, state bonds are a particular form of fictitious capital, which are claims to the state's future annual tax yield convertible into money. The tax yield is the state's material foundation based on the capacity of the population to work, create wealth and value, and pay taxes. On this basis financial capital accepts the value of the state bonds with interest. To enhance the acceptability of the Turkish state bonds amidst the crisis (that is, their material foundations), the DSP moved to increase its tax revenue by increasing the standard VAT (value-added tax) rate from 10 per cent to 18 per cent. By even mainstream standards, VAT is the most regressive form of taxation, hitting the poor, lower, and middle-class workers hardest. The DSP had to go yet further to signal creditworthiness via working-class austerity measures that involved decreased social spending, lower public wages, higher income taxes, and so on, along with committing to more market-oriented reforms (notably privatizations to cover fiscal debts). There is thus a particularly class-based relationship between neoliberal crisis, Turkish working-class taxpayers, and the rescue of financial capital via socialization. Far from any euphemistic short-term pain for long-term gain, more than a decade later Turkish society is still responsible for servicing TL 20 billion (over $13 billion) in socialized bank losses from the 2001 crisis.[6] This includes the state bank duty losses that, by hiding fiscal expenses, facilitated the volatile transition to neoliberalism and the subordination of Turkish society to new competitive and financial imperatives.

Having initiated structural market-oriented changes, Derviş resigned from his unelected post as Minister of the Economy in August 2002 as did Akışık in 2002 after restructuring the state-owned banks. So too was the 'leftist' Ecevit DSP-led coalition government also on a short string after institutionalizing an 'unprecedented set of economic and political reforms' during its three-year term in power before, during, and after the 2001 crisis

(Öniş 2006, 253). The November 2002 Turkish elections would bring in a new era of one-party political stability but no change in Turkey's finance-led neoliberal orientation.

7.2 THE AKP AND EUROPE'S EMERGING CAPITALIST TIGER

Following the 2001 crisis and state-led recovery Turkey enjoyed a phase of rapid economic growth and rising financial profits amidst the global upswing. This led the World Bank Country Director for Turkey, Andrew Vorkink, in 2005 to hail the country as an 'emerging Euro Tiger'. Turkey's rise to 'emerging tiger' status has been overseen not by a string of unstable coalitions, as had been the case during the 1990s, but by one-party rule under the AKP, which continues to privilege finance-led neoliberal restructuring.

The AKP came to power in the aftermath of the 2001 banking crisis. National elections were called early, to be held in November 2002. The AKP came out the unexpected victor. The AKP had been established only in August 2001 from the remnants of the Islamist Refah Partisi (RP; Welfare Party), with the support of social and religious conservatives and representatives of Anatolian capital. In the context of crisis the AKP platform successfully targeted the excluded peoples in Turkish society (Keyder 2004, 70). By winning 34 per cent of the popular vote, the AKP defeated the crisis-worn DSP and formed one of Turkey's rare majority governments. Only the Cumhuriyet Halk Partisi (CHP; Republican People's Party) also secured enough votes to enter the Turkish Parliament, the result being that the AKP acquired 60 per cent of all seats. Under the leadership of Prime Minister Recep Tayyip Erdoğan AKP popularity has increased steadily. In the August 2007 national elections the AKP increased its popular vote to just under 47 per cent. The AKP leadership also survived a serious political crisis following charges of anti-secular activities in late July 2008. The Constitutional Court ruled against closing the AKP but imposed fines on the party. Emboldened by popular support the AKP called for a constitutional referendum to be held in September 2010. Again the AKP side garnered 58 per cent of the vote. This fed into the subsequent national elections in May 2011, which saw AKP support rise to 50 per cent of the popular vote. With each victory, US and EU leaders, international investors, and financial capital have enthusiastically welcomed AKP single-party rule and its pro-market orientation.

The AKP economic platform shifted from being initially 'domestic market' oriented to being 'world market' oriented on coming to political power – a transformation that accompanied a pragmatic switch from reactionary to progressive political Islam (Gunter and Yavuz 2007). The AKP victory also came at a time when Turkey could benefit from the global economic upturn along with the tailing off of regional uncertainty around the Iraq war. The 2005 opening of talks on Turkey's EU membership fed a sense of optimism in Turkey's economic prospects that, together with IMF policy prescriptions, have served as AKP policy anchors helping to hold Turkey politically in line with neoliberal post-Washington consensus imperatives (Öniş 2006, 254). In aggregate economic measures the AKP can claim success: Turkey's GNP growth reached 5.9 per cent in 2003, 9.9 per cent in 2004, 7.6 per cent in 2005, and 6 per cent in 2006 (BAT 2007 (1963–2010), vi). Inflation fell from 70 per cent in 2001 to 7.7 per cent by 2005. These aggregate successes have facilitated AKP popularity – despite Turkey ranking dead last in OECD 'social justice' indicators (2011b, 9).

As a majority government the AKP has not had to face many political barriers to continued neoliberal restructuring. This has been particularly evident in terms of SOE privatization. According to Tezcan Yaramancı, author of the 1994 Privatization Law, the legal infrastructure and the political will were finally combined under the AKP, enabling the move toward privatization (Interview, Investa Consulting, 21 August 2007). The AKP has earned more from privatization than all previous administrations combined. From 1985 to the end of 2002, for example, privatization receipts totaled just over $9 billion. The AKP surpassed this amount in the first three years of its administration and went on to earn a total of nearly $33 billion by the end of 2010.[7] The sell-offs have included real estate holdings, electrical plants, ports, and a wide range of state-owned industries. In certain cases, international public offerings of shares encouraged foreign participation, which has in turn bolstered the size of the İSE and its international integration. The partial privatization (through public offer) of two Turkish state banks contributed significantly to the AKP privatization receipts. For example, in November 2005 a 25 per cent block of Vakiflar Bank shares sold for $1.27 billion on the İSE, which was six times over book value. Then a 2007 Halk Bank IPO for nearly 22 per cent of its shares earned $1.9 billion. While partially privatizing these two state banks, the AKP did not comply with earlier promises to fully privatize Turkey's three state-owned banks by 2005. This, however, is by no means to suggest that the AKP is soft on financial reforms. Indeed, state and government elites have continued the restructuring of the state apparatus around financial imperatives initiated under the 2001 BSRP.

From the beginning Prime Minister Erdoğan signaled that the AKP would like to bring Turkey closer to EU financial standards. The EU standards were to replace the 1999 Bank Law via the new 2005 Bank Law

written explicitly with EU accession in mind (BRSA 2006a). Then managing director of the IMF, Rodrigo de Rato, praised AKP efforts to enhance
financial regulatory and supervisory capacity.[8] Part of the new 2005 Bank
Law entailed reversing certain liberalization measures, insofar as the law
gave state financial authorities greater power to manage the banking
sector by, for example, limiting the number of banks and new bank licens-
ing. The law also instituted new internal risk management practices and
bolstered corporate governance and auditing provisions. Regulations on
accounting and reporting were brought in line with international standards as capital adequacy and deposit insurance regulations tightened.
Taken out of the historical and political context in which the 2005 law was
enacted, one might have the impression of a return to the pre-neoliberal
era. Yet nothing is further from the reality. A clear political commitment
by state and government elites to a flexible, competitive, 'good governed',
and internationalized financial sector under the centralized and prudential
supervision of an equally internationalized state regulator, the BRSA,
and an independent CBT has guided each and every step of the financial
reform process (see BRSA 2009a, 27–8). By 2007 the BAT could report
that Turkish financial authorities had harmonized most banking activities
according to both EU directives and international best practices (2007
(1963–2010), I-8). While many of the ideal 'minimal state' neoliberal
approaches to banking and finance were effectively laid to rest, the practical institutional framework for enabling financial capital to prosper in the
long term over and above the interests of popular and working classes in
Turkey had been established.

Subsumed within the restructuring of the internal working of the financial apparatus was the responsibility to project Turkish finance into the
world market and initiate new activities on behalf of financial capital. To
this end, state authorities signed new memorandums of understanding
(MoUs) with other countries. The BRSA reports that to increase Turkey's
cross-border cooperation, evaluation, auditing, and information exchange
on banking operations and their associated domestic and foreign parent
companies, it accelerated efforts to establish new MoUs, which grew from
12 in 2005 to 18 by late 2009 (BRSA 2009a, 33).[9] The signing of MoUs are
not neutral events but institutionalize specific financialized international
relations between the Turkish BRSA and other foreign bank supervisory
agencies. In so doing the MoUs also embody prevailing political commitments. As an ideologically committed neoliberal and influential AKP
government minister, Ali Babacan, who is vehemently opposed to any
rejection of foreign capital in Turkey, puts it: 'we have to open to global
competition' and any political opposition to this is 'paranoid'.[10] It is on this
type of political authority that state financial authorities institutionalize

and enable new financial markets through such institutional means as MoUs. Thus, state and government elites augment the structural power of financial capital in the world market and at home.

In this the AKP government is like most of its contemporary emerging capitalist governments, which have also signaled their political commitments to an internationalized domestic financial sector. One of the most significant material forces behind this has been the systematic building up of foreign reserves (Akyüz 2008). A more detailed analysis is offered in Chapter 6, all of which is not necessary to repeat here. In brief, however, foreign reserves are financial assets, most often denominated in major foreign currencies like the US dollar and the euro, held by central banks to back the value of the local currency and to instill confidence in the economy more generally. It is widely recognized that these reserves have become much more significant for emerging capitalisms' financial stability since the mid-1990s as a signal of creditworthiness for financial capital (Rodrik 2006; Akyüz 2008; IMF 2009). Since 2001 the AKP has increased net foreign reserves nearly fourfold, or from about $29 billion (in constant dollars) to over $108 billion by late 2010.[11] The increase is even more dramatic when considered in relation to the initial transition to neoliberalism: in 1981, foreign reserves were only about $1.5 billion, while by 1990 (and following capital account liberalization in 1989) reserves hit $10 billion. Foreign reserves today are over 70 times larger than they were in the early 1980s, signaling not merely a quantitative but also a qualitative shift in Turkish political commitments to financial capitalism. As analysts recognize, however, there is a 'social cost' tied to reserve accumulation as a form of self-insurance historically specific to the current phase of financialization and recurrent crisis (Rodrik 2006, 254; Bakir and Öniş 2010). Because Turkey is subordinate within the international hierarchy of states, state agents are compelled to hold foreign reserves as a signal of stability and creditworthiness to globally mobile financial capital. Moreover, Turkish authorities must offer a higher rate of interest for Turkish state bonds than the rate of return earned by holding the bonds of states at the zenith of the hierarchy, such as US bonds. The difference between these rates is structural and is absorbed by the Turkish state as a fiscal loss (that is, as a socialized loss). Rodrik (2006) argues that the social cost of reserves accumulation now averages about 1 per cent of annual GDP for developing countries. Interpreted critically, foreign reserve accumulation constitutes a reconfiguration of institutionalized class relations in the Turkish state form in support of financial capital. The costs of self-insuring represent a transfer of value from Turkish taxpayers to financial capital.

Turkey's emergence as a European capitalist 'tiger' is the result of AKP commitments to continued market-oriented 'post'-Washington consensus reforms initiated under the 2001 TSE and 2001 BSRP. Yet the AKP has also accelerated these processes by further internationalizing the state apparatus in support of financial capital. The banking sector has benefited tremendously from these changes.

7.3 THE STRUCTURE OF NEOLIBERAL BANKING IN TURKEY, 2001 TO THE PRESENT

The structure of Turkish banking has shifted in accordance with prevailing strategies of neoliberal development and the associated material demands of the economy vis-à-vis political class compromises. Turkey's initial idealized faith in market discipline and the need to expand financial resources domestically led to a proliferation of new entrants, relative bank capital de-concentration and de-centralization, and excessive competition (read: speculative practices), which resulted in an unstable capitalist banking sector coming into the 1990s and leading to the 2001 crisis. The 2001 BSRP and subsequent AKP reforms have restructured the state apparatus so that authorities are better able to manage the market-oriented banking sector on behalf of financial capital. This has led the banking sector into a new phase of bank capital centralization and concentration, alongside the intensification of bank labor processes, from which financial capital has benefited.

The Turkish financial system remains bank-based and bank-dominated while becoming progressively more market-oriented (compare Bakir and Öniş 2010). Market-based finance has not replaced the dominance of banks, which hold 75 per cent of all financial assets in Turkey, including the assets held by the CBT (BRSA 2007, 61). Of this 75 per cent total, the universal commercial deposit banks dominate by controlling 97 per cent of all banking assets (the development and investment banks combined control the remaining 3 per cent) (BAT 2010 (1963–2010), I-37). During the last three decades the banking sector has also expanded. The ratio of total bank assets to GNP grew from 31 per cent in 1980 to 83 per cent in 2000 to 87 per cent in 2007 (BAT 2009c, 106). However, the nature and distribution of bank ownership and control has shifted.

Prior to the 2001 crisis there were over 60 commercial banks in Turkey (Table 7.1). Numbers fell quickly to 46 in 2001 and then to 40 in 2002, which represents a loss of over a third of the banks. The collapse in numbers resulted from state authorities dealing with the failed banks under SDIF, additional private domestic and foreign bank closures, and one state bank closure, Emlak. The impact of the 2001 crisis, however, had left government and state financial managers gun-shy of the more

Table 7.1   Turkish commercial banks, 1999–2011

	1999	2000	2001	2002	2003	2004	2005	2006	2007	2008	2009	2010	2011
State-owned	4	4	3	3	3	3	3	3	3	3	3	3	3
Private domestic	31	28	22	20	18	18	17	14	11	11	11	11	11
Foreign	19	18	15	15	13	13	13	15	18	17	17	17	16
SDIF	8	11	6	2	2	1	1	1	1	1	1	1	1
No. of commercial banks	62	61	46	40	36	35	34	33	33	32	32	32	31
ROA (%)	−0.96	−4.24	−6.37	1.32	2.33	2.31	1.53	2.43	2.68	1.96	2.52	n/a	n/a

Note: 2011 figures to March. Data do not include development, investment, and Islamic participation banks.

Sources: BAT (2009, 189); BAT / Statistical Reports / Banks, Branches and Employees / December (various years): available online: http://www. tbb.org.tr; OECD (2007, 522; 2010, 586).

idealized 'Washington consensus' approaches to banking. Instead, author-ities wanted to consciously craft a system with relatively fewer banks that were larger and hopefully more stable. This strategy fit comfortably with the interests of large Turkish holding groups and their associated banks, which also felt that there were too many banks and had already welcomed such government intervention.[12] In other words, both state managers and the larger bankers recognized that the competitive imperatives of a fully liberalized financial sector were not compatible with Turkey's periph-eral political economy. To rectify this, state authorities have held back on granting new bank licenses. Within a few years of the 2001 crisis the number of banks had fallen to the low 30s, hitting 31 banks by 2011 – or half the pre-crisis total. The private domestic banks experienced the most significant change as numbers fell from 22 in 2001 to 11 by 2007. Since 2007 the distribution of bank ownership has been relatively stable with three large state banks, 11 private domestic banks, and between 16 and 18 foreign banks. Under the AKP watch more banks have been centralized into fewer institutions as a concerted stabilization strategy.

The centralization of banking institutions has been matched by a greater concentration in bank assets. In 1999 the largest five banks controlled 46 per cent of total assets and the largest ten 68 per cent. Ten years later the largest five banks controlled 62 per cent and the largest ten 86 per cent (BAT 2000; 2009a, I-41). While fewer banks control more concentrated money assets, so too have these money assets become more concentrated under private control. In 1999 the four state banks controlled nearly 35 per cent of assets (already down from about 45 per cent in 1990) while the private sector banks (domestic and foreign combined) controlled nearly 55 per cent (BAT 2009c, 177–9). Ten years on state bank control fell to 30 per cent as private bank control increased to 63 per cent (BAT 2009c, 177–9; 2009b, 7). The escalating private control over money resources in Turkey has gone mostly to foreign banks. Prior to 2001 foreign capital owned just over 5 per cent of the sector's banks, which had actually fallen to about 3 per cent by 2004 (which is miniscule compared to the over 80 per cent foreign control at the time in Mexico) (BAT 2009c, 179). Foreign capital then increased its control to 5.2 per cent by 2005, to 12.2 per cent in 2006, and then to 15 per cent by 2007. When measured by the share of foreign stockholder ownership in the banking sector (so not necessarily implying majority control), the internalization of foreign bank capital reached nearly 24 per cent by 2009 (CBT 2010 (2005–10), 41). Over the last decade the control over money resources in Turkey has become more concentrated in fewer private banks, and increasingly so in foreign banks.

In brief, what has the internalization of foreign bank capital looked like? The UK-based giant HSBC, for example, had been in Turkey since the early 1990s, with a small investment of around $10 million dollars. HSBC then expanded its presence with the purchase of the failed private domestic Demirbank following the 2001 crisis, signaling a turning point for HSBC in Turkey. In early 2006 HSBC announced plans to double its number of branches and staff by 2010. In another example, the Dutch-Belgian Fortis Bank purchased the Turkish Dışbank in early 2005. At the same time the National Bank of Greece beat out the US-based Citibank giant with its $2.8 billion bid for a 46 per cent share in the Turkish Finansbank (whose profits have helped the Greek bank weather ongoing troubles today in Greece). By October 2006, however, Citibank had bought a 20 per cent share in Akbank for $3.1 billion. Akbank is part of the large Turkish Sabancı holding company and was the top-earning private domestic bank in 2005. In late 2005 Italy's Unicredit took part ownership of Yapi Kredi alongside another Turkish conglomerate, Koç. Most recently, in late 2010, the Spanish giant BBVA bought a 24.9 per cent stake in Garanti Bank for $5.8 billion, with future plans to internationalize the Turkish bank into North Africa and Russia. Indeed, *that* there has been an increased foreign bank presence is clear. But why? According to the BIS, the growing inter-est of major foreign banks is a result of Turkey's 'rehabilitation process' and 'increased soundness of the banking system' (2007, 6). The BAT sug-gests that the foreign and domestic interest has much to do with the size of the Turkish banking sector, which remains small relative to European Union countries. For example, in the EU-25 region there are fewer than 2300 people per branch but there are over 10000 people per branch in Turkey (BAT 2007, I-11). Global banks like HSBC and Citibank openly cite Turkey as a top priority for expansion because of the EU accession prospects, rapid development potential, and the AKP market-friendly reforms. Clearly the banks see vast potential for market expansion and capture. Let us be clear on this point, namely, that the only reason foreign banks are expanding into Turkey (and the private domestic banks are increasing their control of the sector) is to profit. The banks are not driven by any ideal-typical mission to open banking access to Turkey's unbanked population, to facilitate development, or even to channel funds into the so-called real sector. These activities are only considered viable to the extent they offer returns on investment.

In Turkish society the banks have not only the potential for profit, but for *high profits*. In the lead up to the 2001 crisis Turkish commercial banks posted collapsing after-tax return on assets (ROA) of –0.96 per cent of the balance sheet in 1999, –4.24 in 2000, and –6.37 in 2001 (Table 7.1). Since the state-led rescue, socialization of financial risks, and restructuring of the state financial apparatus the banks in Turkey have enjoyed a profita-bility renaissance. In 2002 after-tax ROA surged to 1.32 per cent and then continued to grow, staying in the 2 to 2.5 per cent range since 2006. It is no small matter, nor incidental to the growing interest of foreign banks, that the profit level in Turkey is double or more the average profits of banks in other OECD countries, such as the US, the UK, and Spain (which tend to be in the range of 1 per cent ROA) (OECD 2010). The current profits of Turkish banks are also double their average profits from the 1960s to 1980s, which approximated 1 per cent ROA (BAT 2009c, 98). The high profits gained in Turkey today are a consequence of the government and state's support for financial capital and in consequence of the premium that financial capital operating in emerging capitalisms like Turkey can demand in an open world market. Moreover, the Turkish banks reached this profit increase not in consequence of the government eliminating any lingering and so-called 'financial repression' legislation but as state authorities introduced more stringent requirements through the BSRP and 2005 Banking Law. For example, the banks now boast capital adequacy levels of nearly 19 per cent, which are well above the recommended BIS 8 per cent level (BRSA 2007, 72–3). Offsetting such increases in the costs of capital, bankers have enjoyed falling relative costs of labor (Section 7.3.1 below). Unsurprisingly the market value of banks traded on the İSE ballooned from about $7 billion in 2002 to a record high of $117 billion in late 2007 (BAT 2009c, 61). As the banks become more profitable and integrated into Turkish society, the more valuable they become in the eyes of investors.

What have been the sources of income for the banks? As with most banks, interest from loans has been the traditional source of income. Prior to the 1980s bank loans constituted about 50 per cent of assets and the lion's share of interest income. Since the 1990s the banks have looked more and more to dealing in state debt as the public sector borrowing requirement (PSBR) increased in line with Turkey's neoliberal growth strategy. By 2001 Turkey's PSBR had hit over 12 per cent of GDP and the ratio of gross public debt to GDP was nearly 58 per cent (BRSA 2009a, 37). As the banks have been the chief source of the state's finance capital needs, traditional loans consequently fell to 30 to 40 per cent of assets in the 1990s as income from securities neared 50 per cent by 2002 (BAT 2009c, 84, 96). As discussed in Chapter 5, moreover, these loans were often linked to the banks' related holding groups. The result was a general decline in finance capital availability to anyone but the state and large holding groups. Since 2001 public debt to GDP levels have stayed in the range of 40 to 50 per cent. Given the reluctance of the AKP governments to increase corporate tax to fund state activities, state debt recycling has remained a stable source of income for the banks (Yeldan 2006a). However, today's lower yielding state bonds have eaten into the banks' interest income, which has fallen from about 90 per cent of the total in the 1990s to just over 60 per cent since 2002 (BAT 2009c, 94–5).

Banks have therefore sought to diversify their sources of income. For one, banks have looked back to traditional loans for interest income, which had grown to 48 per cent of assets by 2007 (BAT 2009c, 63). The make up of these loans has also changed. In 2002, 86 per cent were corporate but this fell to 68 per cent by 2007. By contrast, consumer loans were only 12 per cent in 2002 but had nearly tripled to 33 per cent by 2007 (11 per cent of this total involved housing loans in addition to significant growth in vehicle loans) (BAT 2009c, 84). This points towards a general trend towards financialization, as noted in Chapter 2 (Lapavitsas 2009; compare Ertürk 2003). In advanced capitalisms, financialization has appeared historically and alongside the emergence of neoliberalism as larger enterprises turn away from traditional banks as a source of credit and towards more open market operations or retained earnings for self-financing. There is evidence of this occurring in ways specific to Turkey. The reduction in revenue derived directly from servicing state debt has impacted back on banks' accumulation strategies insofar as they must find new sources of profit, such as offering new financial services to individual workers (which, as in the Mexican case, fits nicely into the neoliberal argument for improved access to financial resources). As the real life situation of workers in Turkey worsens in consequence of neoliberal austerity, decreased social spending, downsizing, pension privatization, closing of public housing, and so on within an increasingly consumerist society, banks have found a growing market for lending to individuals directly (compare Erbaş and Turan 2009; Karaçimen 2011). Lapavitsas and dos Santos (2008) see this as a process of financial expropriation, which is the extraction of financial profits directly out of individual personal income. The banks in Turkey have also looked to other non-interest forms of income from fees and commissions, a source that has had a volatile history. Before 1980 fees and commissions comprised on average about 15 per cent of profits, with a massive spike occurring in the early 1980s to 24 per cent, which then fell back to the 5 to 9 per cent range for much of the 1990s (BAT 2009c, 95). New investments in information technologies in the 1990s, for which new service charges could be levied, then began to yield profits. Since the new millennium, income from fees and commissions has returned to pre-1980 levels of around 15 per cent (BAT 2009c, 95–6).

The banks in Turkey continue to earn significant income from state debts, but they are now more diversified in their revenue generating activities, which cut across all sectors of society, from consumer debt to corporate loans to fees and commissions, all of which are driven by profit imperatives. Private domestic, foreign, and state banks share this imperative regardless of ownership category. The banks have also shared a common strategy in terms of cutting labor costs.

7.3.1 The Intensification of Bank Labor

Since the 2001 crisis all the banks in Turkey have enjoyed a spectacular rebound in profitability. The rebound has involved strategies around profiting from different sources of interest income and by turning to fees and commissions. However, this is not the complete picture. The BAT also writes that holding down operating expenses, of which staff costs are the most significant element, has been a vital aspect of the banks' growth in earnings (BAT 2010 (1963–2010), I-45). As the BRSA puts it, competition between the banks has amplified the importance of worker productivity, and consequently bankers have had to reduce their operational costs (2006b, v). Banks that can reduce operational costs, argues the BRSA, can operate more efficiently and more profitably (2008, 42). Perhaps unsurprisingly, this too is the core message of a 2003 McKinsey Global Institute (MGI) report on Turkey. The report argues that the AKP could seize the opportunity presented by the 2001 crisis to institutionalize bank sector productivity imperatives through new regulations (and notably via state bank privatization) (MGI 2003, 191–2). These recommendations fit comfortably within wider neoliberal strategies premised on demanding productivity gains from labor but without redistributing the gains back to the workers. And this is precisely what has happened in the Turkish banking sector.

Most academic analyses have not appreciated the intensification of bank labor as a significant factor in Turkish banking or in the constitution of neoliberalism (for example, Akyüz and Boratav 2003; Erturk 2003; Eres 2005; Isık and Akçaoğlu 2006; Bakir and Öniş 2010). However, what bankers do (or do not do) with their income is important for understanding the banking sector and capital–labor relations. Labor costs *are* important to bank profitability (Hilferding 2006 [1910], 172). Under neoliberalism bank owners have sought and found means to *intensify* bank labor power. Why? Marx offers some guidance when he writes that the intensification of labor (in production) means enabling a worker 'to produce more in a given time with the same expenditure of labor'.[13] Analogously, Turkish bankers can increase profits by reducing staff costs (variable capital) while increasing the amount of work and money capital staff must handle. In other words, managers can make bank workers do more for less. Looking empirically at staff and branch numbers relative to staff costs reveals this tendency.

In Turkey the number of commercial bank workers reached its highest ever level in 1999 at just over 168 500.[14] Then in 2000 Turkey also reached its highest number of bank branches at 7808. Things changed with the 2001 crisis. By 2002 over 50 000 bank workers, comprising about a third of the total workforce, had been laid off or transferred out of the banking sector. At the same time just over 1700 branches evaporated as a result of bank failures and closures, as well as the merger of Emlak Bank into Ziraat Bank. The majority of the job losses occurred within the state-owned banks and the failed private banks under SDIF control. In a rare report on labor in banking, Aykut Kibritçioğlu reports that state authorities forced about 34 000 state employees to accept early retirement or to transfer out of the banking sector into another state institution (2006, 17–18). By 2003, over 17 500 Ziraat and Halk employees had retired and over 14 000 had been forced to move elsewhere in the state apparatus. About 2000 lost their jobs. State authorities also forced the remaining employees to convert from civil servant status to contract employees defined by a specific, if renewable, employment period and private sector regulations.[15] Then amidst the global economic upturn, Turkish banking began to recover. Between 2004 and 2009 the number of branch numbers exploded by nearly 50 per cent, or from 6088 in 2004 to 8983 by 2009. The number of staff likewise grew, but only by 36 per cent, or from 122 630 to 167 063 during this period. Not until 2010, however, did staff numbers surpass their 1999 levels. The central empirical and analytical point being that under neoliberalism state authorities and bank managers have treated bank staff and branch numbers as highly malleable factors in the maintenance of bank profitability.

The impact has been significant. First, while branch and staff numbers have returned to pre-crisis levels, bank managers have dramatically held down staff labor costs, which have fallen by about half between 1999 and 2009.[16] For example, in 1999 staff costs as a percentage of the banks' overall balance sheet totaled 2.65 per cent. In 2002, staff costs fell to 1.91 per cent. This drop did not merely constitute a one-off solution to the immediate threat of systemic banking crisis but in fact heralded a long-term profitability strategy. Despite recovery after 2003 bank managers squeezed down staff costs even further, to 1.58 per cent by 2005. By 2009, staff costs, at 1.35 per cent of the balance sheet, were nearly half their 1999 level. At the same time bank managers brought down the average number of employees per branch, which slid from 22 in 1999 to 19.2 in 2002 to 18.6 by 2009. As bank branches reopened in Turkey, they operated, on average, with about four fewer workers in 2009 than they did in 1999. Lest one think the state banks offered their workers any greater protection from such neoliberal restructuring processes, it should be noted that the state bank managers slashed average staff numbers even more aggressively than private ones. From 1999 to 2009 state bank staff averages fell from 25.1 employees per branch to 17.73, whereas private domestic averages fell from 19.3 to 18.74. Across the banking sector as a whole bank workers handled more money resources than ever before. Between 2002 and 2007 the average asset size per employee rose by 265 per cent, or from just over $1 million per employee to $3.1 million in the same period, and the average asset size per branch rose by 282 per cent to $63.5 million (BAT 2009c, 104–5). How significant are staff costs to the aggregate profit to loss balance of banks? Extremely. For the Turkish banks listed on the İSE in 2010, staff costs (at about 1.35 per cent of the balance sheet) came to over TL10.6 billion – a sum that equates to *over half* of the banks' total after-tax profits of TL20.5 billion. Staff costs, as bankers and regulators alike realize, underpin the profit performance of Turkish banks.

There is another process under way in Turkey, as in Mexico and elsewhere in the world, which has begun to play a significant part in holding down staff costs and increasing managerial flexibility – namely, outsourcing. According to an outsourcing firm, 'outsourcing' is a strategy that allows managers to increase the banks' bottom line through cost reductions and to avoid managerial problems associated with massive hirings (and firings).[17] The chief operating officer for technology at Deutsche Bank concurs, arguing that outsourcing has become a competitive imperative: 'The issue is that if you don't do it, you won't survive.'[18] In Turkey state authorities recognize that outsourcing has grown steadily since 2001. Indeed, authorities have facilitated the market insofar as the 2005 Bank Law and 2006 Outsourcing Regulation set out the necessary regulations and standards for outsourcing in banking. In line with market advocates, the BRSA sees outsourcing as a natural consequence of competition and new technologies which will help to increase productivity and efficiency insofar as it offers bankers more flexible and cost-effective solutions in the workplace (BRSA 2009a, 26). While the intentions are clear for labor, the impact of outsourcing has yet to be really studied and is in need of further research.

While under-appreciated in the literature, the intensification of bank labor in Turkey has formed a market-oriented response to crisis insofar as it serves to push the costs of economic adjustment and new profit imperatives onto the bank workforce (much as bank rescue and socialization pushes the costs of crisis onto society at large). The intensification of bank labor is constitutive of the current phase of emerging finance capitalism insofar as it represents the defeat of labor's collective capacity to resist the rise of financial capital's power. Where does this leave us in terms of understanding the current phase of accumulation and development in Turkey?

7.4 THE COSTS AND BENEFITS OF EMERGING FINANCE CAPITALISM IN TURKEY

With few exceptions outside of the liberal political economic tradition the transition to neoliberalism is seen to have brought few, if any, directly tangible benefits for the working classes in general (Cam 2002; Onaran 2008; Bedirhanoğlu and Yalman 2010). The 2001 crisis and recovery, moreover, brought no significant reversal of this tendency. Indeed, Turkish society has experienced growing inequality and the absence of redistributive gains for labor. The OECD, for instance, reports that the relative unit labor costs in Turkish manufacturing have been declining. Taking 2005 as the base year, the OECD reports labor costs fell to 94 per cent of 2005 levels by 2008 and during a period of strong economic expansion in Turkey. When the global financial crisis hit Turkey in 2009, labor costs collapsed to only 79 per cent of their 2005 levels, and they had only reached 87 per cent of their 2005 levels by the first quarter of 2011.[19] The OECD data reflect the findings of an academic study on the impacts of the 2001 crisis on small businesses and workers, which concludes that workers have borne the brunt of neoliberal restructuring, especially since the 2001 crisis (Erbaş and Turan 2009). The authors point to Turkey's jobless growth – to the fact that unemployment has risen to more than 10 per cent while the economy has been experiencing significant GDP growth levels (on GDP, see Table 1.1). According to their indicators, real wages by 2005 were only 92 per cent of wages in 1997 (2009, 86). While real wages have fallen, output and worker productivity have increased, yet without the gains accruing to the workers, who are working harder. As I discussed above, this too has been the case for bank workers who have seen the intensification of labor processes and falling labor costs amidst record bank profitability. This is indicative of highly unequal relationships of power between capital, labor, and the state apparatus. Inequality does not, however, explain why these relationships of power exist or how to overcome them. More particular to our problem at hand, why have Turkish state authorities privileged the profits and stability of finance over redistributive gains for labor?

The reasons 'why' are rooted in the material relationships between the Turkish state apparatus and the banks and the ways in which these are tied to labor, particularly through interest payments. As we know, the banks in Turkey earn significant income from servicing lucrative state debts. How is this linked to labor? The banks earn interest, the cost of borrowing money, which governments pay in exchange for an advance of money. Governments pay interest from the revenues taken in through income tax. When a government pays interest on a state bond, the interest payment represents a transfer of wealth from the Turkish taxpayers through the state apparatus to financial capital. Bakir and Öniş (2010, 98) recognize this process in terms of distributional effects, citing how the CBT has kept interest rates high (real interest rates on state bonds averaged over 15 per cent in the post-crisis period) to maintain the neoliberal imperatives of price stability and low inflation. Indeed, highlighting the systematic transfer of wealth from Turkish society to financial capital has been a constant critical theme of Turkish political economy throughout the neoliberal era (Keyder 2004, 76; Cizre and Yeldan 2005, 397). However, this is rarely posed as a class-based problem between capital, labor, and the state.

In Marxian terms, however, the interest earned by banks is a deduction from the surplus-value created by labor in the exploitative processes of capitalist production (Hilferding 2006 [1910], 172). So, the interest paid by states is, of course, a transfer of wealth from workers to financial capital through the state, but it is also indicative of historically specific social relations of power and class that have become crystallized in the state apparatus. There has solidified now a structural relationship of interdependence between the banks (and their capacity to profit) and the state (and its capacity to service debts) – neither of which could exist without labor working, creating value, and losing a portion of this value to capital and another portion to income taxes. Just to emphasize the point by example, should labor refuse to pay taxes then the material capacity of the state to pay interest would all but evaporate. By contrast, capital in general has been able to resist paying higher taxes, and this too necessitates constant state borrowing to cover fiscal shortfalls (Keyder 2004, 76–7; Yeldan 2006a). There is an inescapable structural and class-based relationship underpinning financial capitalism.

Yet while the state and banks depend on surplus-value and labor in these ways, organized labor has not been able to collectively assert power to their own benefit. Over the last three decades, and especially since the 2001 crisis, Turkish government and state elites have institutionally subordinated the state apparatus to financial imperatives. Financial capital, moreover, has at the same time been able to sever any need to conduct its activities in the interests of social development and fiscal discipline. Why? On the one hand, there is a structural tendency for economic and social reproduction under capitalism to become progressively articulated through the financial system (which is historically evident, as we have seen in the development of Turkey). According to Ben Fine (2010), the logic and imperatives of interest-bearing capital have extended across all economic activity, and this has intensified under neoliberalism making financialization necessary to the continuation of this phase of capital accumulation.

On the other hand, the agents and agencies of financial capital have militated on their own behalf to create and institutionalize the conditions for their own prosperity and reproduction. This has led to the present phase of accumulation wherein the state needs financial capital to service debts, financial capital benefits from state debt and the construction of an extensive financial apparatus designed to protect the financial system, and all this is premised on labor's capacity to work and create value. In the current phase of capital accumulation, each and every Turkish government that comes to power immediately confronts the necessity to recycle debts and secure recurrent flows of finance capital because everyday state operations depend on these flows of money. Because financial capital can threaten to withhold money resources and seek other sources of profit in an open world market, financial capital has been able to present its needs to state authorities, which are constrained by the financial requirements of the state apparatus, as general social imperatives. Organized labor, by contrast, has been unable to articulate its collective interests as forcefully, and it is for this reason that labor has become institutionally subordinated to financial capital.

These relationships of power and subordination are realized within the borders of Turkey, but they also occur within the world market. Because the banks can draw on international flows of capital in an open world market, this exposes the banks in Turkey, the state, and society at large to financial risks and relationships of power in the world market. At the same time, by internalizing foreign financial capital within its borders Turkish society, like all emerging capitalisms, is exposed to financial imperialism (Kiely 2007; Marshall 2010). Turkey has become a site of foreign bank earnings, which can be repatriated without being invested in Turkish society, just as domestic capital can spirit money resources abroad in times of crisis or in search of higher returns. This, too, is shaped by Turkey's still-subordinate position within a hierarchical interstate system and world market that is still dominated by the US. This structural relationship does not determine the options and choices made within Turkey, but like the growing power of financial capital, it imparts a certain social logic on state and government elites, pressing them in a certain direction. Such an interpretation runs contrary to neoclassical 'revealed preference' approaches which refuse to integrate historical-structural explanations for why the world is as it is today. So too does this Marxian interpretation run at odds with institutionalist and Weberian accounts which criticize the current era as a 'distortion' or 'perversion' of an ideal-typical form of capitalism wherein independent states better regulate banks in ways that ensure funding for productive development and a lessening of social inequality (compare Bakir and Öniş 2010). As laudable as these social goals are in the immediate term, one needs to look at the actually-existing institutionalized social logic of state, bank, and labor relationships based on their historically specific and structured material foundations conditioned by Turkey's subordinate position within the world market, which are legitimized by official pro-capitalist discourses. It is in this light that one needs to read the assessment of the 2001 crisis and state-led recovery of Durmuş Yılmaz, governor of the CBT, as expressed in a June 2007 speech, 'As we all know, tough times call for tough decisions. The collapse of the exchange rate-based stabilization program in 2001 was, in one sense, an opportunity for Turkey to put her house in order.' Less euphemistically, this has meant in practice the institutionalized privileging of financial imperatives over those of labor and the working majority. This social logic has also conditioned the government's response to the Great Recession.

7.4.1 The Great Recession and Emerging Finance Capitalism in Turkey

In the years following the 2001 crisis the AKP-led recovery piggybacked on a global expansionary phase. However, the AKP faced a new challenge in 2008 as the US sub-prime crisis took a turn for the worse and spread globally following the collapse of the US investment bank giant Lehman Brothers in late September 2008. In the words of the then IMF Chief Strauss-Kahn, the world economy neared 'total collapse'.[20] Until that point international commentators had optimistically hoped the sub-prime crisis would skirt emerging capitalisms like Turkey. By New Year 2009, however, it was clear to the IMF, OECD, and World Bank that the developing world too would be engulfed and face serious economic and social difficulties.[21] Turkey would be no exception. Many academics now refer to the prolonged global crisis as the 'Great Recession' (Albo et al. 2010). And so it began in Turkey. Inflows of financial capital slowed dramatically, income fell, foreign trade volumes diminished as world trade and industrial output plummeted. Unemployment shot up to over 10 per cent in 2008 then to over 13 per cent by mid-2009. The budget deficit increased to over 6.5 per cent in 2009. Recession set in as the Turkish economy could only muster 0.7 per cent GDP growth for 2008, which then plummeted to –4.7 for 2009. As a result of the slowdown, Turkey's current account deficit found some respite, falling from 47 billion to 20 billion between late 2008 and mid-2009. However, at the same time, capital inflows of $48 billion turned into outflows of $2 billion. Turkey had entered into a period of economic volatility with uncertain outcomes (see Yörüğlu and Atasoy 2010).

Yet in contrast to the wider Turkish economy and in stark contrast to previous neoliberal crises in Turkey, the banks have been a source of financial, economic, and even political stability. According to the BAT, the banking sector is 'the best story of Turkey' (2010 (1963–2010), I-6). Even at the beginning of global uncertainty in late 2008, World Bank president Zoellick suggested that the Turkish banking industry was 'shock-proof'.[22] Two years into the Great Recession, the banks in Turkey have seemingly fulfilled this prophecy. A July 2010 Deloitte Turkey report praised the banks' seemingly unshakable resilience, as they have continued to post record profits while earning an upgrade in credit ratings.[23] The reasoning behind Turkey's 'shock-proof' banking has involved a celebratory acceptance of the reforms since 2001 (Yılmaz 2011). For some, the 2001 crisis provided an opportunity to overcome past patterns of unstable capitalist development by instituting more competitive and market-oriented policies once thought improbable in Turkey (Öniş 2009). For others, more effective state supervision has ensured that the banks maintain sound balance sheets and undertake successful risk diversification and management strategies (compare BAT 2010, I-6).[24] To be sure, the reforms have been vital to this resilience. Immense political and social resources have been dedicated to re-aligning the relationships between the state apparatus, the banks, and Turkish labor so that they better support finance-led strategies of development. As a result of this convergence around financial imperatives, the banks have been able to prosper before, after, and during the crisis. As the BAT reports, this has resulted from lower official interest rates and greater loan volumes (BAT 2010 (1963–2010), I-45). More specifically, the CBT authored a fall in interest rates that enabled a widening differential between the price banks paid for money and the price they could charge to lend it out (due to the absence of any extra-market coordination to ensure otherwise). As a result, the banks' interest expenses fell by 22 per cent in 2009 and net interest income grew by 36 per cent. At the same time, income from fees and commissions grew by 10 per cent. Both increases occurred with only limited increases in operating and staff expenses. The banks' net income exploded by 52 per cent to TL 19.5 billion in 2009 (BAT 2010 (1963–2010), I-46). Amidst the worst global crisis since the Great Depression of the 1930s, financial capital in Turkey has become as rich as Croesus.

How can we understand or interpret the social logic of the government's actions? Let us look at some of the immediate measures undertaken in the face of the 2008 crisis and some longer-term responses as the Great Recession took hold. As an immediate response, the AKP and state managers aimed first and foremost to quell financial instability and to restore the confidence of capital in Turkish society. For one, the Central Bank intervened in late 2008 to support the foreign exchange market by increasing its transaction limits and by extending lending maturities from one week to one month (BAT 2009b). Authorities then began selling off foreign reserves in order to support foreign exchange liquidity (that is, the capacity for financial capital to exit the Turkish market or, by extension, feel secure in staying on). To further increase liquidity, the CBT reduced the banks' foreign exchange liability reserve requirements from 11 to 9 per cent. The AKP also directly intervened on several fronts in 2008. Circumventing established laws, the government offered a two year period of unlimited deposit insurance backed by the Treasury's direct guarantee, understanding that the SDIF lacked sufficient resources to insure financial capital. Recognizing that the self-interest of banks would not prove sufficient to ensure the banking sector's best interests, the BRSA intervened by monitoring the distribution of banks' earnings in 2008 to ensure sufficient capital adequacy levels while allowing the reclassification and restructuring of certain securities and loans.

Wider supports were also rolled out to support Turkey's market-oriented strategy of development. On the one hand, the Finance Ministry offered favorable tax advantages to industry and, on the other hand, the CBT increased the availability and eased the terms of export credits. More controversially, the AKP allowed individuals and corporations to repatriate foreign assets subject to a minimal tax of 2 per cent (assets that in all likelihood had escaped legal taxation to begin with). Likewise, those in Turkey who had failed to register certain assets and securities in Turkey would be allowed to do so with a tax of 5 per cent. In both instances the crisis offered an opportunity for the AKP to legalize what the wealthy classes had been doing illegally and in so doing to draw in some much needed, if truncated, money revenues. As the crisis persisted into 2009, however, the AKP had to roll out some assistance to workers by extending unemployment fund coverage from three to six months, while increasing compensation by 50 per cent (that is, cover the minimum costs required to stem wider social unrest). In March 2009 the AKP introduced some stimulus packages. To encourage consumption, and indirectly stimulate industrial capital, VAT was lowered from 18 per cent to 8 per cent for three months alongside other tax reductions in large item consumption and real estate dealings. The reduction in interest rates by the CBT, moreover, has facilitated consumer loans and consumption. In consequence of the government's crisis support programs, the public sector borrowing requirement increased to about 5 per cent of GDP. However, the combination of government stimulus, the availability of cheap money from the US (quantitative easing), and low growth rates in most advanced capitalisms has led to inflows of capital into Turkey. As a result, Turkey enjoyed a stronger than expected economic recovery (Yılmaz 2011, 11). This is not without complications, though, as authorities have had to increase foreign reserves (that is, socialize some of the risks faced by financial capital) to offset the rising potential for instability should investors decide to reverse the flow of funds suddenly (which, in fact occurred in August 2011).

It is important to recall that the reason that the AKP has the material capacity to undertake these measures is because the banking sector did not collapse. Furthermore, the banking sector did not collapse because of the state financial apparatus' support for financial capitalism since 2001 and for allowing very profitable interest differentials in the midst of crisis in 2008. In other words, state reforms enabled the banks to be profitable, and in return the banks are able and willing to fund the state's stimulus activities so long as they also remain profitable. It is in this way that the banking sector and the Turkish economy have been able to maintain relative stability, even in the face of record unemployment and falling standards of living. Indeed, for Yılmaz, 'social welfare' derives from ongoing structural reforms that reinforce fiscal discipline and from keeping interest rates low (2011, 16). In the absence of a strongly articulated alternative political program, financial imperatives will continue to dominate and the needs of labor continue to be subordinated.

7.5   CONCLUSION

The specific content of the AKP response to the Great Recession since 2008 has varied from the coalition government's response to the 2001 crisis. However, in essence, there is a singular underlying social logic. State authorities react by first ensuring the protection of financial capital without privileging the needs of labor. This does not suggest that state authorities act simply at the behest of financial capital. Rather, through the historical evolution of material constraints and institutionalizations of power relations beneficial to financial capital and debt-led neoliberal strategies of growth in Turkey, there has been a fusion of the interests of financial capital into the state apparatus. This may at times involve specific actions that do not benefit any individual bank, for example, when state agencies act to protect the general interests of financial capitalism. This is a foundational lesson learned in the wake of the 2001 crisis, and which has proven valuable to state and banks alike in the current crisis. Notably, the Turkish state has developed unprecedented capacity to supervise and regulate financial capital while being able to socialize financial risks if and when necessary. Labor, by contrast, has had to absorb the costs of socialization through the state apparatus, while bank workers have been directly impacted by intensified work conditions.

The social consequences of this finance-led process have reached so far as to reconstitute the operations of the state banks. Not only have their postwar developmental missions been stripped but state authorities have reorganized their operations so that they conform to world market financial and neoliberal competitive imperatives. In terms of efficiency, profitability, and productivity (that is, the measures that concern global capital), emerging finance capitalism in Turkey is an example of success. Besides being more profitable than ever, the banking sector is seemingly shock-proof to even global financial crisis. Yet this resilience has relied on the exploitation of labor and the transfer of wealth from the working majority to the more powerfully organized financial capitalists. Only a sustained political and collectively-driven challenge strategically oriented towards breaking the exploitative social relations of power now evident between the state, banks, and labor will lead to substantive democratic changes and social development.

NOTES

1. For example, much of the debt the state had amassed at the time was due to the excessive interest rates demanded by money dealers in the 1990s (Keyder 2004, 76).
2. 8 Dec 2001, Vol. 361, Issue 8251: 86.
3. The TSE and the BSRP formed part of a broader restructuring strategy not limited to these programs. In December 2001 the government also launched the 'Principle Decision on the Reform Program for Improving the Investment Climate in Turkey' to enhance state capacity to manage greater inflows of foreign financial capital. The same initiative likewise centralized and insulated decision-making power in the Coordination Council, an official body composed of government officials and the private sector, which was to identify and remove barriers to investments in Turkey.
4. The BRSA reports that the level of NPLs had reached nearly 30 per cent by late 2001. Moreover, many of the NPL included illegal related loans given by banks to their shareholders or affiliated holding companies in excess of legal limits.
5. Since then, there have been instances of collective bank worker actions. In 2004 the 'Platform for State-Bank Employees' formed to monitor the state bank privatization process, to militate on behalf of former state bank employees to return to their jobs, and to contest the merger of the private Pamukbank with Halkbank in 2004. The platform, led by ex-employees, argued, among other things, that the criteria used to lay off state workers was unclear and that transfers within the state had been unfair, often leaving senior employees in junior positions and unable to receive pay raises for long periods (Kibritçioğlu 2006, 18–19). More radical unions have also tried to organize in the banking sector. For example, Bank-Sen has been trying to increase membership in the state banks to mobilize against further plans for privatization, and its 2011 Congress focused on the two biggest threats it perceives to bank workers, bank privatization and outsourcing.
6. 'Turkey Moves on Own Initiative, Vows to Stick to Fiscal Discipline', *Today's Zaman*, online, 21 March 2010.
7. See http://www.oib.gov.tr/index_eng.htm.
8. 'Statement by IMF Managing Director Rodrigo de Rato on Turkey', Press Release No. 04/265, 14 December 2004.

9. The countries that have financial MoUs with Turkey include TRNC, Albania, Romania, Bahrain, Indonesia, Kazakhstan, Pakistan, Malta, Greece, Kirghizstan, Azerbaijan, Bulgaria, China, Dubai, Georgia, Kosovo, United Arab Emirates, and Luxembourg.
10. 'Babacan Accuses Opposition of being "paranoid"', *Turkish Daily News*, online, 6 February 2007.
11. Data available at: http://evds.tcmb.gov.tr/yeni/cbt-uk.html.
12. Suzan Sabancı Dincer, managing Director of Akbank, 'Tougher Stance against Failure', *Banker*, 2 October 2000.
13. See Marx, Karl (1867). *Economic Manuscripts: Capital Vol. I*, Chapter Fifteen, available at http://www.marxists.org/archive/.
14. Bank branch and employee numbers from BAT 2005 (1963–2010), 5; BAT online Statistical Reports, December 2010; BAT 2009c, 189.
15. A clause within the new contract states the employees must be able to work in any of the banks' branches. In confidential interviews in 2010 and 2011, Ziraat employees report that this has been used as a mechanism to fire otherwise protected workers or to force more active union employees out of the bank.
16. Aggregate staff costs data from OECD 2007, 523; OECD 2010, 586–7. Since 2001, the BAT does not report on real wages in banking. Data for 2001, however, shows wages beginning to fall (Kibritçioğlu 2006, 15). Kibritçioğlu also reports that in some cases managerial wages had been cut in half after 2001. Moreover, about 70 per cent of employees report being unhappy because of their lower earnings after 2001.
17. Steve Martin, 'Is Banking Ripe for Outsourcing?', 24 February 2010, www.banktech. com.
18. 'Deutsche Bank's Outsourcing Imperative', www.BusinessWeek.com, 30 January 2006.
19. Data extracted on 14 June 2011 from OECD.Stat.
20. 'World Faces Deepening Crisis, IMF Chief Warns', *IMF Survey Magazine*, online, 21 January 2009.
21. 'IMF-OECD-WB Seminar on the Response to the Crisis and Exit Strategies – Joint Statement', World Bank, online, 4 February 2009.
22. 'WB Says Turkey has Shock-Proof Financial System', *Hurriyet,* online, 14 October 2008.
23. 'Turkish Finance Proves Resilient', *Hurriyet,* online, 8 July 2010.
24. Ironically just before crisis unfolded in Turkey in 2008, Tezcan Yaramancı and BRSA analysts each suggested that the post-2001 regulatory changes had been too reactionary and alarmed private investors, and therefore should be relaxed somewhat (Interview, Investa Consulting, 21 August 2007; Interviews, BRSA, 14 August 2007).

8. Comparing alternatives in an era of emerging finance capitalism

It has taken sustained political will and dedicated material state resources for financial capital to secure the benefits it enjoys today. Reaching this point has not been the natural consequence of individual human nature, the outcome of agent-less markets, or simply derived from overarching structures. Individual and collective agents have brought about emerging finance capitalism within a historical-structural context of a system of social reproduction that is increasingly articulated through finance and subject to competitive imperatives. The benefits have fallen disproportionately to financial capital. This is the wrong dream, the wrong ambition. Yet to make a break in these institutionalized social relationships of power economic crisis alone is insufficient. Just as it led to the current era, so too must sustained political will and collective action lead to change. In this chapter we explore the argument that any substantive alternative cannot simply modify the form of capitalism but must institutionalize a radically different and democratized social economy wherein the financial system is subordinated to collective ownership and developmental goals. I develop this argument by way of three concluding sections. Section 8.1 offers a comparative summary of the evolution of relations between the states and banks in Mexico and Turkey, which have shown aspects of universalization around financial imperatives differentiated by the institutional forms, operational strategies, and ownership patterns specific to each country's historical patterns of accumulation. Section 8.2 looks at the state of mainstream alternatives to the current crisis, wherein innovative thinking is restricted to how to have more capitalism by subordinating society yet further to financial imperatives. Section 8.3 then sketches out more radical analytical premises of what constitutes a substantive break with emerging finance capitalism and a move towards a democratized social economy. I then offer some final remarks in the last section.

8.1 EMERGING FINANCE CAPITALISM IN COMPARISON: UNIVERSALIZATION AND DIFFERENTIATION

We have come a long way in the study of states, banks, and crisis in Mexico and Turkey, and it is important now to draw their shared yet distinct experiences into a succinct comparison. Thinking back to Philip McMichael's incorporated comparison model introduced at the start of the book, recall that it seeks to integrate theory and history such that both abstract individuality and abstract generality are avoided. The basic idea for McMichael is to 'try to perceive the unity in diversity without reifying either' (1990, 395). Preserving the specificity of emerging capitalisms analytically and empirically in comparison is not necessarily a straightforward task. However, Przeworski and Teune (1970) suggest that constructing general conceptual categories to build meaningful comparisons can do this. I suggest that through comparing Mexico and Turkey's interrelated and historically specific material, institutional, spatial, and discursive dynamics we can better grasp how and why individual and collective agencies are collectively influenced and shaped by the universalized and structured social logic of neoliberal and finance-led capitalist development (compare Greenfield 2004; Albo 2005; Marois 2011a).

8.1.1 Material Dynamics

The comparative material dynamic looks at how the social relations of banking are historically shaped, reproduced, and changed. At its most general level capitalism in Mexico and Turkey consolidated in the postwar period and has transitioned into a more finance-led neoliberal form since the 1980s. The banks have survived largely on interest income as a share of the surplus-value created by labor in both phases of accumulation. However, under emerging finance capitalism capitalist banking relations are more volatile and dependent on the state financial apparatus not only as a source of profit but also as a source of stability for financial capital's risky accumulation strategies. Likewise, emerging capitalist states are dependent on financial capital for recurrent flows of money to service deficits and debts. When state authorities are unable to smoothly secure such funds, the results are crisis and working-class austerity measures.

As explored in Chapter 3, the material foundations of Mexico and Turkey's postwar banking systems are rooted in pre-existing colonialist and imperialist banking relations, national independence struggles, and the consolidation of capitalism. In both cases their financial systems took root as bank-based because of the scarcity of domestic savings and capital. In Mexico after the 1910–17 revolution the ruling Sonora gang elite returned control of the appropriated banks to private Mexican ownership. This was followed by a political commitment to ensuring Mexican bank ownership and control. The banks in return helped to finance Mexican industrialization through official reserves held in the Bank of Mexico, which state authorities then channeled into priority economic sectors (often through the state development banks). The Mexican commercial banks, insulated as they were from world market competition, survived by expanding national branch coverage to augment deposit collection as well as by targeting specific sectors and industries for credit and loan allocation. Turkey likewise developed a bank-based system. After the collapse of the Ottoman Empire, the legacy of the imperialist 'odious debt administration' and scarcity of domestic money resources formed the material basis of Turkey's bank-based system, but its development took a form different from Mexico's. The decisions taken by the nascent Turkish capitalists and state elites during the 1923 İzmir Congress articulated a system of state and privately-owned Turkish commercial banks, which would co-exist alongside the ongoing presence of foreign banks. As the Great Depression hit Turkey the state commercial banks assumed greater significance as agents of domestic industrialization acting in tandem with the Central Bank of Turkey which allocated official reserves for national development. In Turkey, as in Mexico, state authorities channeled state financing into areas of the economy in which the private sector could not or would not invest (infrastructure, heavy industry, and so on). Thus, the state financial apparatus socialized many of the investment risks of peripheral postwar state-led capitalist development through official financing. In both Mexico and Turkey the largest private domestic banks came to be owned by family-based holding groups that secured privileged positions of power both in the domestic market and the state. At this historical phase of peripheral capitalist development it is pure fantasy to suggest that the liberalized financial markets of today could possibly have led to more rapid development then – let alone have survived without the intervening decades of state-led capacity building.

Mexico and Turkey's postwar state-led strategies encouraged capitalist development but not without putting growing pressure on state finances. By the late 1970s serious fiscal and financial barriers emerged creating tensions between financial capital and national governments, which could not be overcome easily within the confines of state-led development. Mexican bankers reacted via capital flight and investment strikes, which resulted in the 1976 and 1982 crises. To protect Mexican capitalism the Partido Revolucionario Institucional (PRI; Institutional Revolutionary

Party) government nationalized the domestic private banks and then used the banks to usher in neoliberalism. Despite similar foreign exchange and debt crises in Turkey the predominance of no single bank ownership group meant that the control over domestic money resources was less concentrated in private hands. This reduced the likelihood of a Mexico-like investment strike leading to bank nationalization – if for no other reason than that the Turkish state banks controlled about half the banking sectors' assets. Nonetheless, the social and economic instability arising in Turkey, as in Mexico, from the US Volcker shock-induced peripheral debt crisis gave pretext to the 1980 military regime. Turkey, too, underwent an initial period of rapid and authoritarian neoliberal structural adjustment processes but not of a kind leading to any major swing in bank ownership.

Through the 1980s and 1990s neoliberal governments supplanted state-led development strategies with market-oriented ones (Chapters 4 and 5). Domestic capitalists argued that the postwar material gains of organized labor had to be broken to restore waning profit levels, competitiveness, and growth. Financial restructuring was at the center of this transformation premised upon debt-led growth. Subsequently, world market flows of money, credit, and capital have become increasingly determinant factors of capitalist development, and this change is closely related to each state's restructuring and class reformation processes around finance-led accumulation. International financial institutions (IFIs) such as the IMF and World Bank have encouraged and given financial support to these processes. However, their market-oriented 'Washington consensus' advice led to further crises by promoting idealized neoliberalism as a panacea for peripheral development. Like-minded state elites and fractions of capital in Mexico and Turkey supported processes of internationalization and world market integration as the basis of accumulation (institutionalized in Mexico via NAFTA and in Turkey via the European Union Customs Union and the promise of European Union membership).

The material reproduction of each society's banking system consequently has converged around world market competitive and financial imperatives. Banks operating in Mexico and Turkey are more than ever exposed to free-flowing international capital that demands high levels of creditworthiness and profitability. The money resources controlled by the banks allow owners to profit from the lucrative recycling of state debts. The banks' interest income constitutes a stable transfer of wealth to the banks from Mexican and Turkish people via the state's taxation revenues. Much as a brewery has no interest in reducing the consumption of beer from whence its profits flow, neither do the banks desire any end to state debt and the income tax revenues covering interest payments. Traditional loan activity remains but the process is market-determined rather than determined by developmental priorities in agriculture and industry. There is also mounting evidence that the neoliberal rollback in social supports has opened a new market for banks to service high-interest consumer debts and also to earn significant returns from new fees and commissions.

While financial income generating activities have become more speculative and global in scope, the process has also exposed new threats to the material reproduction of financial and bank capital. The intensification of bank labor and the state's socialization of financial risks have evolved as two specific responses. In the first case, the intensification of bank labor works as both an immediate response to crisis and as a long-term profitability strategy premised on productivity gains. Current world market competitive imperatives compel all banks – be they private domestic, foreign, or state banks – to reduce labor costs and outsource non-essential services. In the second case, the state's socialization of risks has worked as an immediate response to financial crises (insofar as financial risks are drawn into the state apparatus) and long-term profitability strategy (insofar as the state absorbs the costs of financial regulation while building up fiscally costly foreign reserves to protect financial capital flows). In both types of response the centralization and concentration of all bank and financial operations into fewer and more powerful financial groups has magnified the scope of the banks' market power and their capacity to extract these benefits from labor, society, and state and government elites. This has facilitated most of the banks operating in Mexico and Turkey to become more profitable than many other OECD banks despite the impact of the Great Recession.

While the material foundations of Mexico and Turkey's state and banking relations have both converged towards privileging the needs of financial capital, they have also evolved differently in many respects. In Mexico the exigencies of debt, competition, and emerging finance-led accumulation strategies have resulted in dramatic bank ownership swings. The 1991–92 bank privatizations concentrated bank ownership within a small fraction of Mexican capitalists, which led to the 1995 banking crisis. Following the state-led rescue, Mexican bankers then sold the banks to powerful global financial groups operating in Mexico. Only one major domestic bank remains, Banorte, whose basic profit-maximizing operations illustrate little qualitative difference from the dominant foreign banks. Turkish banking has never experienced such dramatic ownership shifts. Only since the mid–late 1990s has there been a trend towards increased private domestic bank control and only recently towards foreign ownership. Whereas in Mexico neoliberal finance-led restructuring in the 1990s demanded the formal privatization of the nationalized banks and the subsequent internalization of foreign capital in response to the volatility of the 1990s, in Turkey the volatile 1990s and the 2001 crisis instead resulted in regulatory changes to help 'de-politicize' state bank operations and reverse their idealized approach to neoliberalism. Market-oriented reforms offered a modus vivendi for continued state bank viability within a neoliberal finance-led strategy of accumulation because the reforms qualitatively privatized the Turkish state banks by institutionalizing, among other things, new profit imperatives.

The material dynamics of banking in Mexico and Turkey have thus converged around world market-oriented competitive and profit imperatives but in ways unique to the historical social, political, and developmental patterns of each society. Yet this has not necessarily meant any reduction in the scope of the state's responsibility for institutionally organizing financial capital within their borders.

8.1.2   Institutional Dynamics

The institutional dynamics of Mexico and Turkey's postwar banking operations were shaped through each state's national developmental frameworks which supported a national bourgeoisie while making specific concessions to a growing and organized working class. Different institutional arrangements between the central banks, commercial banks, and development banks achieved the goal of channeling money into developmental priorities. The financial apparatus and policy measures thus regulated flows of capital to facilitate economic growth and capital accumulation, but in ways that did not repress private banking profits. Moreover, state and government elites institutionalized tight relations formed between the bankers, represented by the national bankers' associations, and the government. Private bankers often assumed important positions in the state financial apparatus and influenced policy decisions. Nonetheless, the state financial apparatus was not as dependent then on bankers, foreign or domestic, for the state's debt requirements as it is now.

New policy formation and state institutions have emerged out of the 1980s debt crises. Significantly, the internationalization of the state's financial apparatus has resulted from successive governments accepting the responsibility and developing the capacity to manage international debt and mounting financial risks in their societies. The form taken by the restructured state institutions has involved the concentration of political and state power around each state's financial agencies, such as the state treasury, the central bank, and the banking regulators as typically 'formally' independent institutions. These independent institutions have taken on the task of reforming each country's financial adequacy and accounting standards in line with international best practices. At the same time, the state apparatus coordinates new bilateral banking agreements to facilitate the internationalization of bank capital. While uneven in their scope, range, and timing the Mexican and Turkish financial authorities have helped to construct a world market for financial capital by ensuring their own market-oriented institutional frameworks at home. International institutions like the OECD, World Bank, IMF, and BIS help to coordinate and shape these national regulatory changes, which intensifies financial imperatives. As and when crises emerge these same institutions help to overcome the instability without sacrificing the benefits won by financial capital. Equally importantly, the international financial institutions help to absorb the popular discontent that arises in response to subsequent austerity and restructuring measures undertaken within national borders.

The internationalization of the state financial apparatus has also been premised on the idea of formal institutional independence. In neoliberal theory state financial institutions such as central banks must be free from political interference to approximate price stability and inflation targeting as a credibility signal to financial capital. In practice, there have been fewer conflicts than collusions between neoliberal governments and the financial apparatus staffed by neoliberal technocrats. Institutional independence has emerged more as a strategy to silence the demands of labor while better enabling accumulation for foreign and domestic financial capital alike. Indeed, governments since the 1980s have crafted new bank regulatory and financial insurance institutions based solely on the need to contain and control the now inevitable yet still unpredictable financial crises. Financial capital constantly impresses the need to remove any vestige of the state's direct presence in the economy, the regulation of finance, and the apparent 'politicization' of market processes. Yet the benefits enjoyed by financial capital today have depended on the politicization of banks by states as a constitutive element of the transition to neoliberalism in both Mexico and Turkey. The nationalized Mexican banks saved the economy from collapse, acted as agents of neoliberalism from 1982 to 1992, and then opened a speculative opportunity for domestic capital. In Turkey the state bank duty losses smoothed the volatile 1990s transition to neoliberalism until the 2001 banking crisis. While formal independence and 'de-politicization' have carried on in theory within the state apparatus and mainstream discourse, strategic interventions to socialize financial risks at times of crisis demonstrate the state's ongoing political presence in each country's capitalist economy.[1] Indeed, emerging finance capitalism cannot survive without the robust capacity of the state apparatus to make constant interventions on behalf of financial capital.

8.1.3   Spatial Dynamics

The spatial dynamics of postwar banking created patterns of uneven and combined capitalist development. As peripheral states, and in comparison to colonial periods, Mexico and Turkey achieved significant levels of capitalist industrialization and integrated into world market flows of money. Despite this the barriers presented by state-led capitalist developmental strategies meant that the two societies continued to exist at the margins of the world market and as subordinate within the hierarchy of inter-state relations. International banks and foreign governments advanced money capital that returned from Turkey and Mexico with their values augmented, reinforcing patterns of uneven exchange. State-led strategies also created patterns of uneven and combined development within Mexico and Turkey. Postwar development brought the generalized expansion of money relations and the state-led coordination of internal production in both societies. Capital, finance, and production, however, became concentrated within a few urban centers at the expense of rural areas as regional development split from north to south in Mexico and from east to west in Turkey. The banking systems, geared as they were to capitalist industrialization rather than to equitable social development, pooled resources and channeled money capital from capital poor to capital rich areas. Turkey differed insofar as the state banks were able to modestly counteract these patterns, but the state banks alone could not prevent them.

The spatial dynamics of emerging finance capitalism are tied to Mexico and Turkey's pre-existing patterns of subordinate integration into world market flows of capital and credit. Lacking the material and institutional power of the advanced capitalisms at the center of the financial world market, Mexico and Turkey must constantly prove their creditworthiness and offer lucrative conditions to draw recurrent flows of financial capital into their borders. Each society has transformed into a 'staging post' for financial capital within a world market organized around finance-led and neoliberal imperatives (compare Cerny 2000). One particular interrelated and socially costly manifestation of this has been the massive accumulation of foreign reserves within emerging capitalisms, which constitutes a direct transfer of money capital from the poor to rich countries. So too are there interrelated spatial dynamics vis-à-vis the commercial banks. For example, many large Mexican and Turkish banks have internationalized to some degree to service the credit requirements of domestic capitalists and to capture lucrative foreign worker remittances. Yet there are no Mexican or Turkish banks that seek to capture foreign markets like Spain's BBVA or Santander, the US Citibank, or the UK HSBC. Mexican and Turkish banks remain at the periphery of international banking despite the inclusion of their state regulators in the Group of Twenty (G-20). Mexico differs from Turkey insofar as the PAN government has facilitated the use of Mexico as a platform for foreign bank expansion into Central America. The internalization of foreign bank capital has been much slower in Turkey. Foreign banks may soon find Turkey to be a useful platform for expansion into surrounding regions, especially if the AKP can successfully fashion Istanbul as a regional financial hub. The crafting of Mexico and Turkey as international staging posts has done little to counteract the regional divide and dominance of large cities that remains unchecked in Mexico and Turkey. The only significant form of decentralization occurs through free trade zones characterized by highly exploitative production relations in the north of Mexico and the west and south of Turkey.

8.1.4 Discursive Dynamics

The discursive and ideational dynamics of postwar banking involved the commitment of the Turkish and Mexican governments to subordinating the banking systems and foreign capital flows to domestic stability, development priorities, and domestic capital accumulation. State elites promoted the Mexican Revolution and Turkey's independence struggles as national legacies within each state's developmental discourse. The Turkish state banks, in particular, were associated with Kemalist modernization and westernization ideologies. The importance of having the banks be Mexican or Turkish owned, rather than foreign owned, went almost unquestioned. The national bourgeoisie accepted the political orientation of domestic money savings towards national development as legitimate, necessary, and profitable.

The discursive dynamics of emerging finance capitalism in Mexico and Turkey evolved into the unquestioned need for everyone to be individually and nationally competitive, productive, and efficient. Finance-led pressures have helped intensify, deepen, and reproduce this discourse through various Mexican and Turkish state agencies and in government discourse. State financial managers advocate and domestic banks practice competitive austerity as the only effective way to encourage domestic development and profitability. At no time is this more evident than at times of crisis when working-class austerity measures become seemingly inevitable. At the same time it is said that politicians ought to leave financial regulation to independent and prudential state agencies (except, however, at times of crisis). The protection of private property has been elevated to paramount importance within state discourses so that even bank nationalizations in response to financial crises are framed as necessary to preserve market discipline. No longer is it legitimate for the state to take a direct role in providing finance to priority sectors or poorer segments of society. Now states need only ensure Mexican and Turkish people have *access* to financial services (that is, that states create the parameters of a stable market for financial capital).

In comparative perspective we can see the complexity of historical change insofar as individual and collective agencies together shape and are shaped by the structured social logic of capitalist development across the material, institutional, spatial, and discursive dynamics that constitute Mexican and Turkish society. In the most recent phase of capital accumulation, these dynamics have been predominantly influenced by the universalization of financial and competitive imperatives across the world market in ways differentiated by domestic accumulation patterns, institutions, struggles, crises, and so on, which define historical change. Thus, we see the institutionalization of a certain social logic of material reproduction and form of discipline generated by the consolidation of emerging finance capitalism that favors the needs of financial capital. This, however, has been far from contradictory and crisis-free to which the Great Recession testifies.

8.2   MAINSTREAM CONTINUITY IN AUSTERE ALTERNATIVES

> We commit to take all necessary actions to preserve the stability of banking systems and financial markets as required. We will ensure that banks are adequately capitalized and have sufficient access to funding to deal with current risks and that they fully implement Basel III along the agreed timelines. Central Banks will continue to stand ready to provide liquidity to banks as required. Monetary policies will maintain price stability and continue to support economic recovery. (G-20 Washington September 2011 Communiqué)

The responses of global authorities and mainstream economists to recurrent financial crises in emerging capitalisms, widening social inequality, the disciplinary power of financial capital over all aspects of social life, and the persistent global instability of the Great Recession have lacked imagination and progressive ambition (notably, Mishkin 2009). As Alfredo Saad-Filho writes, 'two years after the collapse of Lehman Brothers very little of substance has actually happened' (2010, 251). Rather, the collective output of the world's international forums, IFIs, financial regulators, and economic experts has only arrived at the most austere alternatives premised, as they are, on state authorities better safeguarding financial capitalism through permanent working-class austerity measures.

Perhaps the foremost international expression of this lack of alternative initiatives is the recurrent G-20 summit forum. Since the first crisis-instigated meeting in November 2008 in Washington subsequent G-20 summits have been held in London in April 2009, Pittsburg in September 2009, Toronto in June 2010, and Seoul in November 2010. According to the G-20, the summits are meant to tackle the financial and economic crisis that spread across the globe in 2008 via further international cooperation. If judged solely on its capacity to stem crisis, then G-20 efforts have been a manifest failure as fears of a double-dip recession remain pervasive three years on. However, in terms of crystallizing agreement for national authorities to act to preserve the international capitalist financial system, then the G-20 has had more success. Governments everywhere agreed to intervene in their economies through monetary and fiscal policies, by central banks reducing interest rates in support of local banks' profit margins and providing liquidity to financial markets, and, of course, by governments offering financial resources to troubled institutions. The G-20 has also successfully provided a forum to legitimize what is already being done in practice and to suggest new practices representing radically little substantive change. At the fifth summit, the 2010 Seoul Summit, the G-20 announced the direction of reforms that should act as fortifying pillars of a sound financial system: stronger regulation; more effective supervision; development of a resolution mechanism for systemically important financial institutions; improving the process for assessing the implementation of new standards; the creation of a level regulatory playing field among countries; and resolving other critical cross-border issues.[2] Lest there be any doubt, the reforms are intended to be anything but market constraining. A February 2011 G-20 communiqué reaffirmed its commitment to free trade and investment as the basis of global recovery while opposing any introduction of protectionist measures.[3] At this time, the so-called 'Seoul Development Consensus for Shared Growth', set up in apparent contrast to the first Washington consensus, recognizes the need for domestic policy space, greater country fit, and the ownership of development strategies – so long as these remain subordinate to market-oriented development. In this the G-20 only acknowledged what is already being done in practice. Where the G-20 suggests it has made the most significant progress, that is, in the gaining of agreement to the Basel III reforms meant to enhance the supervisory oversight of international finances, this too has been conservative at best.

This is evident in the October 2010 Basel Committee on Banking Supervision's Report to the G-20 (BIS 2010). The report recognizes that the depth and severity of the current crisis is the result of specific weaknesses in the banking sector, such as excessive leveraging, low levels and quality of capital, and inadequate liquidity. Rather than dealing with the problem of financial capitalism, however, the committee was charged with crafting new regulations capable of improving the banks' and the system's capacity to absorb shocks at times of crisis. The new standards, developed between July 2009 and September 2010, have come to be called Basel III – the regulations on which the G-20 has staked its claim to progress. In brief, Basel III seeks the following changes: to enhance the quality of capital in banks so banks can better absorb losses; to increase risk coverage especially vis-à-vis trading, securities, off-balance sheet vehicles, and derivatives; to increase minimum capital requirements; to introduce an international harmonized leverage ratio; to enhance standards of supervisory review and public disclosures; to introduce global liquidity standards; to promote the amassing of capital buffers during periods of stability; and to address problems of systemically important banks. The national implementation of Basel III, however, is proving to be limited and only to involve a small number of capital and leverage requirements. For example, the risk-based capital requirements are to begin on 1 January 2013 – over four years after the Lehman collapse – and to be phased in slowly until the end of 2018. Leverage ratios are also to begin in January 2013 with full disclosure by January 2015. The remainder – review of trading, ratings and securitizations, systemically important banks, contingent capital, large exposures, cross-border bank resolution, review of Core Principles for Effective Banking Supervision, and standards implementation – remain as future work. Evidently, the G-20 is in no immediate rush. The report and the Basel III regulations ultimately retain their faith in better-regulated market processes, while accepting that financial crises are inevitable but manageable. As such, states must increase their material and institutional capacity to manage financial capitalism. How has this translated into policy advice for the world's developing countries?

Senior World Bank economist, F. Halsey Rogers, has synthesized a series of lessons that developing countries should learn from the current crisis that reflect much of the G-20 and Basel III sentiments (2010, 15–22). First, regardless of whether they have sound policies and good performance environments developing countries need to be realistic about their ability to moderate global economic swings within their national economies (that is, crisis is inevitable, if unpredictable, so get used to it). Second, as a result of integration and the increasing frequency of crises developing countries must factor in the impacts of crises originating from developed countries (that is, poorer countries share responsibility for managing the financial world market). Third, in order to rebalance the global economy developing countries may need to rethink export-oriented growth strategies and their over-reliance on portfolio investment funds (that is, the export-orientation mantra of the Washington consensus may be wrong, and global capitalism will need more capitalist markets in developing countries to protect global demand). Fourth, developing country governments must reinforce greater fiscal health in order to allow for a greater range of responses to crisis when it arises and, fifth, governments should therefore reinforce the quality and efficiency of public spending (that is, state authorities must develop greater institutional and material capacity to support finance and self-insure against crisis, and this depends on minimizing all other fiscal commitments to society). The alternative to current instability and crisis, then, includes committing greater material social resources to private profit-oriented banking and finance and institutionalizing narrowly delimited domestic regulatory and supervisory changes that maintain the spatial internationalization of the state and capital. These are framed in a discourse that, first, rejects as legitimate any alternative that does not reproduce competitive profit-oriented capitalist behavior and, second, promotes the fantastic idea that the post-Washington consensus itself represents a qualitative break with the Washington consensus.

There should be no confusion over the fact that most of the world's most powerful agents and agencies do not seek any substantive change. In 2009 shortly after the collapse of Lehman Brothers the chair of the US Federal Reserve Ben Bernanke warned that reform must not 'forfeit the economic benefits of financial innovation and market discipline'.[4] Senior World Bank economists caution that the crisis must not spark a permanent deviation from hitherto sacred cows of market-oriented financial policy (Demirgüç-Kunt and Servén 2009, 45). International authorities have taken this to heart. According to a 2011 OECD report on better policy, the pre-crisis supply-side structural policies, monetary policy geared towards price stability, rules-based fiscal policy to ensure fiscal sustainability, the benefits of globalization, and the need to ease rigidities in labor and product markets all remain valid (OECD 2011a, 15, 19). The IMF World Economic Outlook 2011 report emphasizes two main points: (a) repair and reform the financial sector, and (b) fiscal adjustment. Underneath all this mainstream analysts continue to see humanity's best hopes as resting in capitalist markets and the private control of finance, albeit better regulated insofar as individual self-interest needs state regulation (Acemoglu 2009). Indeed, mainstream economists warn authorities not to overreact and take a populist turn against market systems.

Dissenting mainstream critics of today's open finance systems have attempted to push for reforms that constrain financial capital in ways that reduce inequality and enhance stability. As a 2010 report by the United Nations Department of Economic and Social Affairs (DESA) observes, 'instead of increasing investment and growth, capital and financial market liberalization had the opposite effect by increasing volatility and uncertainty' (2010, 103). The DESA report goes on to criticize the G-20 crisis summits as ad hoc consultations likely unable to coordinate a long-term plan to restore global stability (2010, 124). Because the G-20 relies on the OECD and IMF for technical and staff support, a continued reliance on neoclassical orthodoxy is likely (DESA 2010, 148). Indeed, many of the 'new' reforms under G-20 consideration following the crisis were already under consideration beforehand (Helleiner and Pagliari 2009). Despite such heterodox dislike for orthodox policy, the terms of disagreement are limited to the legitimate role and extent of extra-market coordination over financial markets needed to moderate the ebbs and flows of development, support the private sector, foster economic stability, and reduce social inequalities (Carvalho 2009–10; Stiglitz 2010).[5] Yet as Ben Selwyn suggests, such mainstream policy-based critiques are weakened by their under-theorization of the state and of the exploitative class relations specific to capitalism (2009, 162). The alternatives remain within the confines of capitalist social relations. In this tradition, the struggle – as articulated by Hall and Soskice (2009) – is for an alternative variety of capitalism.

The underlying social power and class dynamics of emerging finance capitalism, however, have not been addressed as the competitive reproduction of the banks and financial capital remains constant. To survive banks must operationally earn income and compete by facilitating the transformation of money savings into money capital in the service of the exploitation of labor and the extraction of surplus-value, with the end goal being the amassing of individual hoards of money wealth. In so doing the banks facilitate the reproduction of emerging finance capitalism and, by extension, the class-based power to exploit. Moreover, by transforming money into money capital banks distribute purchasing power by lending it and exercise discipline by potentially refusing to lend it. Because of society's dependence on financial capital and financial capital's dependence on profit, society becomes institutionally subordinate to the social logic of financial profit imperatives. State financial managers and government elites have crafted powerful institutions designed to manage financial capitalism and committed unprecedented state resources to upholding emerging finance capitalism. At times of financial crisis state-led recovery corrects for the failure of atomistic financial decisions by socializing the risks of financial capital through the state apparatus and the taxation system. This state restructuring and class reformation around financial capitalism have institutionalized a structurally profound role for money capital in the state apparatus and everyday life. This has led to the severing of legitimate democratic control over money flows within spatial borders. As Harvey points out, 'the raw money power wielded by the few undermines all semblances of democratic governance' (2010, 220). At the same time financial capital has used this domestic power to facilitate the internationalization of capital and the state. As a result the needs and interests of financial capital have come to seemingly represent a common sense social logic and to seemingly embody the collective aspirations of all. Everyday discourse is imbued with ideas that the financial market made governments introduce this or that policy and, indeed, that there is no alternative to the present situation since globally mobile finance capital can always go to other countries where institutional constraints are fewer and their capacity to invest, or not, is untrammeled. Breaking with emerging finance capitalism means moving beyond, indeed burying, these social dynamics and relations of power and institutionalizing new democratic social ones. Otherwise societies risk reconstituting precisely the underlying exploitative relationships they hope to overcome (Biewener 1988).

8.3 BREAKING FROM EMERGING FINANCE CAPITALISM, MOVING TOWARDS A DEMOCRATIZED SOCIAL ECONOMY

There is an urgent need to articulate a new research agenda based on an epistemological concern for human emancipation and anti-capitalist social goals – one which breaks with the exploitative social relations of emerging finance capitalism (compare Freire 1970; Lipietz 1987; Wood 1988; Harvey 1998). Therein, alternative policy formation and institution building confront existing unequal social relations of power in ways that challenge competitive individualism and international competitiveness strategies as universalized through international financial institutions and as particularized in national states and local workplaces (compare Albo 2003, 110). Such a research agenda and institution-building project, much like the neoliberal revolution, is rooted in political and social processes insofar as popular, labor, and class mobilizations are vital to emancipatory and anti-capitalist struggles (Ercan and Oguz 2007; Saad-Filho 2003; Veltmeyer 2010). To become a revolutionary practice these struggles must involve self-change wherein society itself collectively assumes responsibility for being democratic, participatory, and protagonistic (Lebowitz 2006, 70–1). For radical policymakers in the global South this involves insurgent planning, defined as 'purposeful actions that aim to disrupt domineering relationships of oppressors to the oppressed, and to destabilize such a status quo through consciousness of the past and imagination of an alternative future' (Miraftab, in Irazábal and Foley 2010, 109). The critical academic and analyst's part in change involves researching and theorizing in ways that help expose dominant power structures and forms of oppression while articulating possible alternative demands. The following sketches out some general material, institutional, spatial, and discursive premises and interrelated practices that begin to constitute an alternative to financial capitalism in ways that open up the possibility of a democratized social economy.[6]

The most significant obstacle to the effective realization of human potential and the substantive democratic development of society is the material reproduction of society under capitalist social relations shaped by the primacy of private property, competition, and capitalist class rule (Devine 1988, 121). It follows that an alternative social banking and credit system must not reproduce these forms of exploitation but be premised on different means of sustainable self-existence (and ones not restricted to state directed capitalist development). One of the first steps, as Hilferding understood a century ago, involves society making the political demand to take control of the banks (2006 [1910], 367–8). People must be able to exercise discretion over the employment of society's collective money resources. This involves an immediate struggle to dispossess financial capital of their institutions, amassed property, wealth, and social power (Harvey 2010, 248). While the social ownership of the banks is necessary, so too must their operational bases of sustainability be restructured away from profit imperatives that encourage private speculation, economic volatility, and irrational behavior. This means reconstituting banking around a form of socialist or labor money rather than capitalist money.[7] In a non-capitalist social economy labor time can serve as the unit of accounting such that the prices of products in 'labor money' are proportionate to the hours worked in the product. This also ensures that no social surplus is allocated in money to an individual who has not earned it and that any surpluses amassed for individual or social needs will be based on labor time rather that surplus-value extraction. As such, the material elements necessary for a social credit system based on the management of idle labor money resources exist. Worker controlled firms will need to accumulate reserves of labor money to expand operations, replace or upgrade equipment, and to cover unexpected expenditures. Individual workers will also want to save for a whole range of costly life events, such as marriage, travel, large consumption items, and so on. These savings will need to be kept in banks, which can be mobilized to meet needs in society. Worker controlled firms will periodically need to borrow from the banks to manage their operations as will individuals want to have the flexibility to borrow to manage large expenses over a long period of time. Similarly, the state apparatus will have to borrow from the banks or sell state bonds to them in order to finance expenditures, promote social development, build infrastructure, and so on. The sustainability of the credit system can be based on charging interest, defined as the cost of loanable funds in a social economy. A society can manage the interest rate and credit allocation in ways that increase flexibility of production and consumption, encourage the efficient use of resources, and regulate the pace of growth. Yet because the labor money used to create such funds has a fundamentally different non-exploitative material basis and mode of distribution, so too are the credit and banking institutions responsible for the pooling, management, and allocation of labor money in society constituted under different non-capitalist social relationships.

The material basis of non-capitalist banking and finance also needs to be set on institutionally democratized footings such that their operations facilitate domestic monetary and financial autonomy along collectively determined social priorities (compare Albo 1997, 32; Saad-Filho 2010, 253). Indeed, new institutional mechanisms are required to militate against the wasting of social energies on amassing huge individual fortunes and instead to encourage social wealth being channeled into worker self-development, democratic participatory mechanisms, and collectively determined developmental priorities (compare Selwyn 2009, 175). This involves, on the one hand, crystallizing new relationships between states and banks. Socially interdependent decisions will need to be nationally coordinated in ways that are more efficient, effective, stable, and beholden to a participatory self-governed social economy (Devine 1988, 121–2; Irazábal and Foley 2010; Harvey 2010, 225). On the other hand, banks will need to be reconfigured as semi-autonomous worker collectives within this collective paradigm. As a matter of right individuals in the workplace will be involved in decisions relevant to their work. This encourages individual and collective professionalization and responsibility. Rather than passively performing duties and seeking individual gain alone workers are responsible for being actively involved in their place of work in ways consistent with and complementary to the self-development of their community and society. In banking this would involve, for example, such things as agricultural banks funding decisions around sustainable farming and food security, 'green' banks targeting priorities around sustainable energy and industrial production, and people's banks supporting local worker-controlled firms, housing development, and so on. Rather than prioritizing the needs of private financial capital the central bank is responsible for the overall continuity and sustainability of collective priorities (compare Marshall 2010). It should be clear that the institutional basis of a democratized social economy does not envision setting up the state apparatus and state elites as the vanguard owners and controllers (Veltmeyer 2010). Any such structure will necessarily reproduce a passive and less protagonistic role for people in the economy and in society. Rather, the goal is the substantive democratization of politics in ways that underpin egalitarian economic processes, collective decision-making, and self-development (Brus 1975 in Devine 1988, 128). Political and economic democracy are integrated directly into people's working plans (Irazábal and Foley 2010).

The possibility of an alternative democratized social economy and financial system must also be premised on not only capturing but also on producing new territorially defined social spaces within which communities can collectively manage their democratic affairs. On this it is worth quoting Henri Lefebvre (1991, 54):

> A revolution that does not produce a new space has not yet realized its full potential; indeed it has failed in that it has not changed life itself, but has merely changed ideological superstructures, institutions or political apparatuses. A social transformation, to be truly revolutionary in character, must manifest a creative capacity in its effects on daily life, on language and on space.

In terms of money and finance, democratic authorities and financial workers must secure the autonomous capacity to influence monetary relations within their borders to break with emerging finance capitalism. It is, as Benjamin Cohen argues, impossible to think of influencing monetary matters without such domestic autonomy (2008, 456). A necessary first step means slapping down capital controls, without which there can be no substantively democratic development process (compare Crotty and Epstein 1996; Soederberg 2004; Saad-Filho 2010). The material and institutional changes above will then be able to reconstitute a national space. However, an alternative social economy must facilitate new opportunities vis-à-vis finance and banking within its borders. This will involve, for example, finding financial mechanisms for reversing the centralization and concentration of money resources in urban centers in ways that allow for viable and sustainable livelihoods in rural areas. At the other end of the spatial scale, social forces will need to craft alternative interstate monetary relations that enable societies to equitably integrate yet insulate themselves internationally. The new regional Banco del Sur (Bank of the South) is one such alternative experiment that is now under way (compare Marshall 2010). However, much more will need to be done to create space for anti-capitalist financial alternatives.

Part of the challenge of democratizing and reining in the more destructive than creative power of financial capital involves exposing false claims and creating new legitimizing and enabling discourses. Critical scholars need to render 'transparent what political power always wants to keep opaque' as internal to any revolutionary strategy (Harvey 2010, 241). Critical scholars also need to examine how everyday practices and organized collective resistances have been legitimized to help us understand how 'non-elite agents are able to transform their own political, social and economic environments, with consequences for hegemonic or imperialist influence in the international political economy' (Seabrooke 2007, 2, 14). At the level of money and finance this involves breaking with the discourse that finance is productive in and of itself and subordinating the idea of finance to its being a social utility in the service of collective goals rather than individual profit. It also means challenging the chimera of neoliberal 'de-politicization' and central bank independence, both of which in their constitution are already beholden to the interests of financial capital. Rather, new discourses must connect the financial workplace to larger social aspirations. As Michael Lebowitz argues, social forces need to craft a new common sense of equality and fairness, of human family over the individual, of collective well-being, of solidarity, and of the idea of the fully developed human being (2006, 65).

In their generality, these are some material, institutional, spatial, and discursive premises needed to break from emerging finance capitalism and to forge alternative social relations of financing and development, which, of course, because of the historical specificities of different societies can assume a variety of concrete expressions.

8.4 FINAL REMARKS: THE FUTURE OF EMERGING FINANCE CAPITALISM DEPENDS. . .

Capitalism, as Leo V. Panitch writes, is '"the wrong dream," and . . . only an alternative that is just as universal and ambitious, but rooted in our collective liberating potentials, can replace it' (2001, 225–6). Yet to articulate such faith in our collective capabilities is not, as Sam Gindin reminds us, 'to assert that their realization is *guaranteed*; only that because of such potentials, the future is *not closed* – it "depends"' (2002, 13; emphasis in original). The idea that the future is open and 'depends' is the revolutionary idea that defenders of emerging finance capitalism most fear and do not want to see examined. As Gindin also reminds us, one of neoliberalism's greatest victories has been the suppression of people's expectations and the belittling of our collective ambitions (2002, 13). Indeed, even in the face of the Great Recession and the unprecedented social costs of rescuing global financial capital within the confines of mainstream media it seems only that the interests of financial capital prevail as our own.

What critical scholars, policymakers, and social forces can be sure of, and need to acknowledge, is that economic crisis alone is insufficient to break the foundations of emerging finance capitalism. Over the last 30 years and across repeated financial crises the most revolutionary class has not been workers but foreign and domestic financial capital. There is nothing automatic, predetermined, and inevitable about the process of social change (Devine 1988, 130). And while the recurrence of financial crises and the persistence of the Great Recession provide an opportunity for thinking and acting beyond emerging finance capitalism, there are no necessary causal relationships between the deepening contradictions of capitalism, crisis, and revolutionary change. We have seen time and again – not only in Mexico and Turkey, but everywhere – that so long as the majority of people are willing to sacrifice the fruits of their labor to working-class austerity and state-led crisis rescue and recovery then financial capital can find innumerable ways of reproducing its hegemonic power in society. Only a direct political confrontation will lead to change.

What social forces might lead this political confrontation? Experience shows us that we can, and must, rule out any support from or compromise with financial capital, international financial institutions, and most state authorities. For all intents and purposes these social forces will be antagonistic to progressive change and form the object, rather than subject, of popular struggles for change. Fortunately this leaves the overwhelming majority of people in society. This opens the very real and practical possibility of organizing collectively around a politics of taking effective ownership and control of finances to institutionalize a democratized financial system. While the scope must be society wide, it is imperative that the labor movement, for all of its fractions, contradictions, problems, and diversity, be at the heart of this change. It is still today only labor movements that have the material resources, organizational capacity, and unique ability to shut down the economy, and banks, in ways that can force change: 'without the radicalization of working people and without a working class with a universal sense of social justice – without all of this no movement can sustain hopes of transforming the world' (Gindin 2002, 9). To this end, a revitalized bank labor union movement will need to assume a central place in articulating and putting into practice new demands by building on and transforming their existing capacities and expertise in managing society's money resources in line with democratic social aspirations. There is, of course, no escaping the bleak reality that given the institutionalized power of money, financial capital, and credit in society today that even the most meager collective challenge to emerging finance capitalism by financial workers would be met by a savage coordinated response. Workers' demands within the financial sector will need to be matched by much broader collective demands, for example, to dismantle the state's capacity to support financial capital, to refuse to socialize private financial risks, and to nationalize and restructure all financial institutions in line with democratic social control. This opens the door to subordinating the activities of financial institutions to social priorities, such as sustainable green productive investment, education, housing, and welfare, that fulfill human needs.

In the absence of such a collective anti-capitalist political challenge to financial capital amidst the Great Recession it is most probable that we will see a reconfiguration of society around financial capital's interests. Such a reconfiguration will involve some reining in of certain financial practices but no fundamental challenge to the collective power of financial capital. We are thus at a crossroads – but we are always at a crossroads. It is as important today as it was ten, twenty, or fifty years ago to collectively articulate and organize for democratic changes that break with the exploitative social conditions of capitalism – social conditions that stifle and suppress the great potential of so many and from which so few profit. This is where the frontiers of research into finance and development must reach.

NOTES

1. As this book was going to print in August 2011, Turkey's AKP government passed a new law that subordinates some previously independent state agencies to ministerial control, including the banking regulator BDDK. Neoliberal commentators fear this represents a digression. While it is too early to tell definitively, this does not represent a threat to financial capital or a break in the internationalization of the state, and it is certainly is not a progressive move towards democratizing finance. The AKP has so far signaled the change is about ministers enhancing their power to push forward with difficult reforms (including, I suspect, state bank privatization and the centralization of the state financial apparatus in Istanbul).
2. 'The Post-Summit Prospects for Policy Cooperation', an Address to the Economic Club of New York by John Lipsky, First Deputy Managing Director, International Monetary Fund, 23 November 2010.
3. Communiqué Meeting of Finance Ministers and Central Bank Governors, Paris, 18–19 February 2011.
4. 'The Crisis and the Policy Response', Stamp Lecture at the London School of Economics, 13 Jan 2009: available online: http://www.federalreserve.gov/newsevents/ speech/bernanke20090113a.htm.
5. For a fascinating discussion of Stiglitz and the limits to legitimate dissent, see Fridell 2011.
6. I beg the pardon of my readers, friends, and colleagues for footnoting this point, but it is beyond my expertise and the scope of the book's analysis to comment on the necessarily gendered and racialized dynamics of any progressive social alternative.
7. Except where noted, the following draws from Itoh and Lapavitsas 1999, Chapter 11, 'Money and Credit in a Socialist Economy', pp. 246–57.

Bibliography

PRIMARY SOURCES

ABM (Asociación de Bancos de México; Banks' Association of Mexico) (2006a), 'Historia 1982–1996', Mexico City: available online: http://www.abm.org.mx/banca_mexico/historia.htm.
—— (2006b), 'Proceso de Desincoporación', Mexico City: available online: http://www.abm.org.mx/banca_mexico/historia.htm.
—— (2008), 'Estructura del Systema Bancario, 1982–1992', Mexico City: available online: http://www.abm.org.mx/banca_mexico/historia.htm.
—— (2008b), 'La Reforma Financiera', Mexico City: available online: http://www.abm.org.mx/banca_mexico/historia.htm.
BAT (Banks Association of Turkey; Türkiye Bankalar Birliği;) (1963–2010), *Banks in Turkey*, Istanbul: available online: http://www.tbb.org.tr.
—— (1999a), *In its 40th Year: The Banks Association of Turkey and the Turkish Banking System, 1958–97*, Istanbul: available online: http://www.tbb.org.tr/english/40.htm.
—— (1999b), *Recent Developments Related to the Banking Sector and the Financial System 1999–2000*, Istanbul: available online: http://www.tbb.org.tr/english/v12/research.htm.
—— (2000), *The Turkish Banking System*, Istanbul: available online: http://www.tbb.org.tr/english/v12/research.htm.
—— (2001), *Recent Developments Related to the Banking Sector and the Financial System*, Istanbul: available online: http://www.tbb.org.tr/english/developments.htm.
—— (2005), *The Financial Sector and Banking System in Turkey*, Istanbul: available online: http://www.tbb.org.tr/english/TBBBrosur10032005englishi.pdf.
—— (2009a), *The Banking System in Turkey, Quarterly Statistics by Banks, Branches and Employees,* June 2009, Istanbul: available online: http://www.tbb.org.tr.
—— (2009b), *The Financial Sector and Banking System in Turkey*, Istanbul: available online: http://www.tbb.org.tr.

—— (2009c), *50th Anniversary of the Banks Association of Turkey and Turkish Banking System 1958–2007*, Istanbul: available online: http://www.tbb.org.tr

BdeM (Banco de México) (1990–2006), *Informe Annual*, Mexico City: Banco de Mexico.

—— (2007–10), *Financial System Report*, Mexico City: Banco de Mexico.

BIS (Bank for International Settlements) (2004), 'Foreign Direct Investment in the Financial Sector of Emerging Market Economies', Committee on the Global Financial System, Basel, Switzerland: BIS.

—— (2007), 'Payments Systems in Turkey', Committee on Payment and Settlement Systems, Basel, Switzerland: BIS.

—— (2010), 'The Basel Committee's Response to the Financial Crisis: Report to the G20', Bank for International Settlements, Basel, Switzerland, available online at www.bis.org.

BRSA (Banking Regulation and Supervision Agency; Bankacılık Düzenleme ve Denetleme Kurumu) (2001a), *Towards a Sound Turkish Banking Sector*, Ankara: available online: www.bddk.org.tr.

—— (2001b), *Banking Sector Reform: Progress Report*, 2 August, Ankara: available online: www.bddk.org.tr.

—— (2001c), *Banking Sector Restructuring Program Action Plan*, 25 September, Ankara: available online: www.bddk.org.tr.

—— (2002), *Banking Sector Reform: Progress Report*, July, Ankara: available online: www.bddk.org.tr.

—— (2003), *Banking Sector Restructuring Program Progress Report – (VII)*, October, Ankara: available online: www.bddk.org.tr.

—— (2004–2006), *BRSA Annual Report*, available online: www.bddk.org.tr.

—— (2004), *Banking Sector Evaluation Report*, Ankara: available online: www.bddk.org.tr.

—— (2006a), *Strategic Plan, 2008–2008*, Ankara: available online: www.bddk.org.tr.

—— (2006b), *Structural Developments in Banking*, Issue 1, Ankara: available online: www.bddk.org.tr.

—— (2007), *Financial Markets Report*, Issue 6, Ankara: available online: www.bddk.org.tr.

—— (2008), *Structural Developments in Banking*, Issue 3, Ankara: available online: www.bddk.org.tr.

—— (2009a), 'From Crisis to Financial Stability', Working Paper, 2nd edn, Ankara: available online: www.bddk.org.tr.

—— (2009b), *Financial Markets Report*, Issue 16, Ankara: available online: www.bddk.org.tr.

BYEGM (2005), *Banking in Turkey*, Office of the Prime Minister,

Directorate General of Press and Information (BYEGM): available online: http://www.byegm.goc.tr/REFERENCES/banking/htm.

CBT (Central Bank of Turkey; Türkiye Cumhuriyet Merkez Bankası) (2005–10), *Financial Stability Report*, Ankara.

CNBV (Comisión Nacional Bancaria y de Valores) (2001–2010), *Boletín Estadístico Banca Múltiple Diciembre*, Mexico City: CNBV.

—— (2005), *Boletín Estadístico Grupos Financieros Diciembre 2004*, Mexico City: CNBV.

ERF (Economic Research Forum) (2005), *Turkey Country Profile: The Road Ahead for Turkey*, Cairo: ERF.

IDB (Inter-American Development Bank) (2004), *Unlocking Credit: The Quest for Deep and Stable Bank Lending*, Washington, DC, Inter-American Development Bank.

IMF (International Monetary Fund) (2005), *Turkey: Letter of Intent and Memorandum of Economic and Financial*, 26 April 2005, Washington, DC: IMF.

—— (2006), *Mexico: Financial System Stability Assessment Update*, IMF Country Report No. 06/350, Washington, DC: IMF.

—— (2007a), *Mexico: Financial Sector Assessment Program Update – Detailed Assessment of Compliance with the Basel Core Principles for Effective Banking Supervision and Transparency of Banking Supervision*, IMF Country Report No. 07/172, Washington, DC: IMF.

—— (2007b), 'IMF Executive Board Concludes 2007 Article IV Consultation with Turkey', *Public Information Notice*, No. 07/66, 12 June, Washington, DC: IMF: available online: http://www.imf.org/external/np/sec/pn/2007/pn0766.htm.

—— (2009), *World Economic Outlook: Crisis and Recovery*, April, Washington, DC: IMF.

—— (2010a), 'Mexico: 2010 Article IV Consultation', IMF Country Report, No. 10/71, Washington, DC: IMF.

—— (2010b), 'IMF Executive Board Concludes 2010 Article IV Consultation with Mexico, Public Information Notice (PIN) No. 10/39, Washington, DC: IMF.

NAFTA (North American Free Trade Agreement) (1994), *NAFTA Text, including Supplemental Agreements: Final Version*, USA: CCH Incorporated.

OECD (1991), *Bank Profitability: Financial Statements of Banks 1981–1989*, Paris: OECD.

—— (1992), *OECD Economic Surveys: Mexico 1991/1992*, Paris: OECD.

—— (1993), *Bank Profitability: Financial Statements of Banks 1982–1991*, Paris: OECD.

—— (1994), *Bank Profitability: Financial Statements of Banks 1983–1992*, Paris: OECD.

—— (1995), *OECD Economic Surveys: Mexico 1995*, Paris: OECD.

—— (1996), *Bank Profitability: Financial Statements of Banks 1985–1994*, Paris: OECD.

—— (1998a), *Bank Profitability: Financial Statements of Banks 1998*, Paris: OECD.

—— (1998b), *OECD Economic Surveys: Mexico 1998*, Paris: OECD.

—— (1999), *OECD Economic Surveys: Turkey 1998–1999*, Paris: OECD.

—— (2000), *OECD Economic Surveys: Mexico 2000*, Paris: OECD.

—— (2001a), *Bank Profitability: Financial Statements of Banks 2000*, Paris: OECD.

—— (2001b), *OECD Economic Surveys: Turkey 2000–2001*, Paris: OECD.

—— (2002a), *OECD Economic Surveys: Turkey 2001–2002*, Paris: OECD.

—— (2002b), *OECD Economic Surveys: Mexico 2002*, Paris: OECD.

—— (2004), *Bank Profitability: Financial Statements of Banks 1994–2003*, Paris: OECD.

—— (2005), *Bank Profitability: Financial Statements of Banks 1994–2003*, Paris: OECD.

—— (2007), *Bank Profitability: Financial Statements of Banks 1995–2005*, Paris: OECD.

—— (2009), *OECD Economic Surveys: Mexico 2009*, Paris: OECD.

—— (2010), *Bank Profitability: Financial Statements of Banks 2000–2009*, Paris: OECD.

—— (2011a), *OECD AT 50: Evolving Paradigms in Economic Policy Making*, Paris: OECD.

—— (2011b), *Social Justice in the OECD – How Do the Member States Compare? Sustainable Governance Indicators 2011*, Gütersloh: Bertelsmann Stiftung.

SHCP (Secretario de Hacienda y Crédito Público; Ministry of Finance and Public Credit) (1994), *The Divestiture Process in Mexico,* Mexico City: SHCP Office of Privatization.

—— (1998), *Fobaproa: La Verdadera Historia*, Mexico, DF: SHCP.

—— (2005), *Equilibrio y Responsibilidad en las Finanzas Públicas*, Mexico, DF: Fondo de Cúltura Económica.

—— (2008), 'Sociedades Controladoras', SHCP Financial System Catalogue, Mexico City: available online: http://www.apartados.hacienda.gob.mx/casfim/index.html.

World Bank (1990), *Trends in Developing Economies 1990*, Washington, DC: The World Bank.

—— (2000), *Turkey Country Economic Memorandum, Structural Reforms for Sustainable Growth*, Report No. 20657-TU, Washington, DC: The World Bank.

—— (2003), *Turkey Country Economic Memorandum, Towards Macroeconomic Stability and Sustained Growth*, Report No. 26301-TU, Washington, DC: World Bank.

—— (2005), *The World Bank in Turkey, 1993–2004, Country Assistance Evaluation*, Report No. 34783, Independent Evaluation Group, Washington, DC: World Bank.

—— (2008), 'Privatization Database, Mexico 2000 to 2006', Washington, DC: available online: http://rru.worldbank.org.

—— (2011), *Global Development Horizons 2011, Multipolarity: The New Global Economy*, Washington, DC: World Bank.

YASED (International Investors Association of Turkey) (2003), *The New Turkish Investment Environment*, Foreign Investors Association, Istanbul: available online: www.yased.org.tr.

SECONDARY SOURCES

Acemoglu, Daron (2009), 'The Crisis of 2008: Lessons for and from Economics', *Critical Review*, **21** (2–3), 185–94.

Adamson, Michael R. (2006), 'Debating Sovereign Bankruptcy: Postrevolutionary Mexico, 1919–1931', *Financial History Review*, **13** (2), 197–215.

Aguilar Monteverde, Rubén (2005), 'La Banca y Los Banqueros antes de 1982', in *Cuando el Estado se Hizo Banquero: Consequencias de la Nacionalizacion*, ed. Gustavo A. del Ángel-Mobarak, Carlos Bazdrech Parada, and Francisco Suarez Parada, Colecion Lecturas de El Trimestre Economico, 96, Mexico: Fondo de Cultura Economica.

Ahmad, Feroz (2003), *Turkey: The Quest for Identity*, Oxford: Oneworld Publications.

Akçaoğlu, Emin (1998), *Financial Innovation in Turkish Banking*, Ankara: Capital Markets Board.

Akkaya, Yüksel (2002), 'The Working Class and Unionism in Turkey under the Shackles of the System and Developmentalism', in *The Ravages of Neo-Liberalism*, ed. Neşecan Balkan and Sungur Savran, Huappauge, NY: Nova Science Publishers.

Akyüz, Yılmaz (2008), 'Managing Financial Instability in Emerging Markets: A Keynesian Perspective', *METU Studies in Development*, **35**, 177–207.

Akyüz, Yılmaz and Korkut Boratav (2003), 'The Making of the Turkish Financial Crisis', *World Development*, **31** (9), 1549–66.

Alavi, Hamza (1982), 'State and Class under Peripheral Capitalism', in *Introduction to the Sociology of Developing Societies*, ed. H. Alavi and T. Shanin, New York: Monthly Review Press.

Albo, Gregory (1994), '"Competitive Austerity" and the Impasse of Capitalist Employment Policy', in *The Socialist Register 1994: Between Globalism and Nationalism*, ed. Ralph Miliband and Leo Panitch, London: The Merlin Press.

—— (1997), 'A World Market of Opportunities? Capitalist Obstacles and Left Economic Policy', in *Socialist Register 1997: Ruthless Criticism of all that Exists*, ed. Leo Panitch, London: Merlin Press.

—— (2003), 'The Old and New Economies of Imperialism', in *The Socialist Register 2004: The New Imperial Challenge,* ed. L. Panitch and C. Leys, London: The Merlin Press.

—— (2005), 'Contesting the "New Capitalism"', in *Varieties of Capitalism, Varieties of Approaches*, ed. David Coates, New York: Palgrave Macmillan.

—— (forthcoming 2012) 'Contemporary Capitalism', in *The Elgar Companion to Marxist Economics*, ed. Ben Fine and Alfredo Saad Filho, Cheltenham, UK and Northampton, MA, USA: Edward Elgar.

Albo, Gregory, Sam Gindin, and Leo Panitch (2010), *In and Out of Crisis: The Global Financial Crisis and Left Alternatives*, Oakland, CA: PM Press.

Allegret, J.P, B. Courbis, and Ph. Dulbecco (2003), 'Financial Liberalization and Stability of the Financial System in Emerging Markets: The Institutional Dimension of Financial Crises', *Review of International Political Economy*, **10** (1), 73–92.

Alper, C.E. and Ziya Öniş (2003), 'Financial Globalization, the Democratic Deficit, and Recurrent Crises in Emerging Markets', *Emerging Markets Finance and Trade*, **39** (3), 5–26.

Altvater, Elmar (1993), *The Future of the Market*, trans. Patrick Camiller, New York: Verso.

Álvarez Béjar, Alejandro and Gabriel Mendoza Pichardo (1993), 'Mexico 1988–1991: A Successful Economic Adjustment Program?', trans. John F. Uggen, *Latin American Perspectives*, issue 78, **20** (3), 32–45.

Álvarez Béjar, Alejandro and Mariana Ortega Breña (2006), 'Mexico's 2006 Elections: The Rise of Populism and the End of Neoliberalism?', *Latin American Perspectives*, **33** (2), 17–32.

Amable, Bruno (2003), *The Diversity of Modern Capitalism*, Oxford: Oxford University Press.

Andrade, Luis, Sarah Huber, and Antonio Martinez (2009), 'How Latin American Banks are Performing in the Crisis', *McKinsey Quarterly*, July 2009, 1–7.

Andrews, Michael A. (2005), 'State-Owned Banks, Stability, Privatization, and Growth: Practical Policy Decisions in a World without Empirical Proof', IMF Working Paper, WP/05/10, Washington, DC: IMF.

Ankarloo, Daniel (2002), 'New Institutional Economics and Economic History,' *Capital and Class*, Autumn, **78**, 9–36.

Ankarloo, Daniel and Giulio Palermo (2004), 'Anti-Williamson: A Marxian Critique of New Institutional Economics', *Cambridge Journal of Economics*, **28**, 413–29.

Arestis, Philip and Luiz Fernando de Paula (eds) (2008), *Financial Liberalization and Economic Performance in Emerging Markets*, New York: Palgrave Macmillan.

Arestis, Philip and Ajit Singh (2010), 'Financial Globalisation and Crisis, Institutional Transformation and Equity', *Cambridge Journal of Economics*, **34**, 225–38.

Arregui Koba, Edur (1990), 'El Resurgimiento del Cuarto Estado: Los Asalariados y su Ciclo', in *La Clase Obrera y el Sindicalismo Mexicano*, ed. Álejandro Alvarez Béjar, Mexico City: UNAM.

Arrighi, Giovanni (2002 [1994]), *The Long Twentieth Century*, New York: Verso.

Aspe, Pedro (1993), *Economic Transformation the Mexican Way*, Cambridge, MA: MIT Press.

Atasoy, Yıldız (2007), 'The Islamic Ethic and the Spirit of Turkish Capitalism Today', in *Socialist Register 2008: Global Flashpoints, Reactions to Imperialism and Neoliberalism*, ed. L. Panitch and C. Leys, Halifax: Fernwood Publishing.

Aubey, Robert T. (1971), 'Regional Credit and the Mexican Financial System', *Growth and Change*, **2** (4), 25–33.

Avalos, Marcos and Fausto Hernández Trillo (2006), 'Competencia Bancaria en México', Santiago de Chile: Comisión Económica Para América Latina y el Caribe (CEPAL),

Aybar, Sedat and Costas Lapavitsas (2001), 'Financial System Design and the Post-Washington Consensus', *Development Policy in the Twenty-First Century: Beyond the Post-Washington Consensus*, ed. Ben Fine, Costas Lapavitsas, and Jonathan Pincus, London: Routledge.

Aydın, Zulkuf (2005), *The Political Economy of Turkey*, London: Pluto Press.

Babatz Torres, Guillermo E. (2010), 'Problemas en Banca y Valores: Soluciones Inteligentes Adoptadas', Presentación en el Congreso Nacional IMEF Universitario, available online: http://www.cnbv.gob. mx.

Babb, Sarah (2005), 'The Rise of the New Money Doctors in Mexico', in

Financialization and the World Economy, ed. G.A. Epstein, Cheltenham, UK and Northampton, MA, USA: Edward Elgar.

Bahmani-Oskooee, Mohsen and Ilker Domaç (2003), 'On the Link between Dollarisation and Inflation: Evidence from Turkey', *Comparative Economic Studies*, **45**, 306–28.

Bakır, Caner (2006), 'Governance by Supranational Interdependence: Domestic Policy Change in the Turkish Financial Services Industry', *International Financial Review*, **6**, 179–211.

—— (2009), 'Wobbling but Still on its Feet: The Turkish Economy in the Global Financial Crisis', *South European Society and Politics*, **14** (1), 71–85.

Bakır, Caner and Ziya Öniş (2010), 'The Regulatory State and Turkish Banking Reforms in the Age of Post-Washington Consensus', *Development and Change*, **41** (1), 77–106.

Balassa, Bela (1981), *The Newly Industrializing Countries in the World Economy*, New York: Pergamon Press.

—— (1982), 'Structural Adjustment Policies in Developing Economies', *World Development*, **10** (1), 23–38.

Balkan, Erol and Erinç Yeldan (2002), 'Peripheral Development under Financial Liberalization: The Turkish Experience', in *The Ravages of Neo-Liberalism*, ed. Neşecan Balkan and Sungur Savran, Huappauge, New York: Nova Science Publishers.

Balkan, Neşecan and Sungur Savran (2002), 'Introduction', in *The Politics of Permanent Crisis: Class, Ideology and State in Turkey*, ed. N. Balkan and S. Savran, New York: Nova Science Publishers, Inc.

Barth, J.R., G. Caprio, Jr, and R. Levine (2006), *Rethinking Bank Regulation: Till Angels Govern*, New York: Cambridge University Press.

Bátiz-Lazo, Bernardo and Gustavo A. Del Angel (2003), 'Competitive Collaboration and Market Contestability: Cases in Mexican and UK Banking, 1945–75', *Accounting, Business, and Financial History*, **13** (3), 339–68.

Bayliss, Kate and Ben Fine, eds (2008a), *Privatization and Alternative Public Sector Reform in Sub-Saharan Africa: Delivering on Electricity and Water*, New York: Palgrave Macmillan.

—— (2008b), 'Privatization in Practice', in *Privatization and Alternative Public Sector Reform in Sub-Saharan Africa: Delivering on Electricity and Water*, ed. K. Bayliss and B. Fine, New York: Palgrave Macmillan.

Beaud, Michel (2001), *A History of Capitalism, 1500–2000*, trans. Tom Dickman and Anny Lefebvre, New York: Monthly Review Press.

Beck, Thorsten and Maria Soledad Martinez Peria (2010), 'Foreign Bank Participation and Outreach: Evidence from Mexico', *Journal of Financial Intermediation*, **19**, 52–73.

Beck, Thorsten, Aslı Demirgüç-Kunt, and Ross Levine (2006), 'Bank Supervision and Corruption in Lending', *Journal of Monetary Economics*, **53**, 2131–63.

Bedirhanoğlu, Pınar and Galip Yalman (2010), 'State, Class and the Discourse: Reflections on the Neoliberal Transformation in Turkey', *Economic Transitions to Neoliberalism in Middle-Income Countries: Policy Dilemmas, Economic Crises, Forms of Resistance*, ed. Alfredo Saad-Filho and Galip Yalman, Abingdon: Routledge.

Bello, Walden (2006), 'The Capitalist Conjuncture: Over-Accumulation, Financial Crises, and the Retreat from Globalisation', *Third World Quarterly*, **27** (8), 1345–67.

Bennett, Douglas and Kenneth Sharpe (1980), 'The State as Banker and Entrepreneur: The Last-Resort Character of the Mexican State's Economic Intervention, 1917–76', *Comparative Politics*, **12** (2), 165–89.

Bieler Andreas, Ingemar Lindberg, and Werner Sauerborn (2010), 'After 30 Years of Deadlock: Labour's Possible Strategies in the New Global Order', *Globalizations*, **7** (1), 247–60.

Biewener, Carole (1988), 'Keynesian Economics and Socialist Politics in France: A Marxist Critique', *Review of Radical Political Economics*, **20** (2 & 3), 149–55.

—— (1989), 'Socialist Politics and Theories of Money and Credit', *Review of Radical Political Economics*, **21** (3), 58–63.

Biles, James J. (2010), 'Chronicle of a Debt Foretold: Mexico's FOBAPROA Debacle and Lessons for the US Financial Crisis', *Progress in Development Studies*, **10** (3), 261–6.

Boehmer, Ekkehart, Robert C. Nash, and Jeffry Netter (2005), 'Bank Privatization in Developing and Developed Countries: Cross-Sectional Evidence and the Impact of Economic and Political Factors', *Journal of Banking and Finance*, **29**, 1981–2013.

Bonefeld, Werner (1999), 'Notes on Competition, Capitalist Crises, and Class', *Historical Materialism*, **5** (1), 5–28.

Boratav, Korkut and Erinc Yeldan (2002), 'Turkey, 1980–2000: Financial Liberalization, Macro-Economic (In)-Stability, and Patterns of Distribution', Ankara: available online: www.bilkent.edu. tr/~yeldane/B&YCEPA2002.PDF.

Bortolotti, Bernardo and Enrico Perotti (2007), 'From Government to Regulatory Governance: Privatization and the Residual Role of the State', *World Bank Research Observer*, **22** (1), 53–66.

Bortz, J.L. and S. Haber (2002), 'The New Institutional Economics and Latin American Economic History,' in *The Mexican Economy, 1870–1930*, ed. J.L. Bortz and S. Haber, Chicago: Stanford University Press.

Boubakri, Narjess, Jean-Claude Cosset, Klaus Fisher, and Omrane

Guedhami (2005), 'Privatization and Bank Performance in Developing Countries', *Journal of Banking and Finance*, **29**, 2015–41.

Boubakri, Narjess, Jean-Claude Cosset, and Omrane Guedhami (2008), 'Privatisation in Developing Countries: Performance and Ownership Effects', *Development Policy Review*, **26** (3), 275–308.

Bouzas Ortíz, José Alfonso (2003), *Democracia sindical en el sector bancario*, Mexico City: Plaza y Valdés.

Brenner, Robert (1998), 'The Looming Crisis of World Capitalism: From Neoliberalism to Depression?' *Against the Current*, **13** (5), 22–6.

—— (2007) 'Property and Progress: Where Adam Smith Went Wrong', in *Marxist History-Writing for the Twenty-First Century*, ed. C. Wickham, Oxford: Oxford University Press.

Buffie, Edward F. (1989), 'Mexico 1958–86: From Stabilizing Development to the Debt Crisis', in *Developing Country Debt and the World Economy*, ed. J.D. Sachs, Chicago: University of Chicago Press.

Bustamante, Patricio (2000), 'Mexico: Evolution of the Financial System and its Supervisory Structure', *Reform of Latin American Banking Systems,* ed. E. Aguirre and J. Norton, London: Kluwer Law International.

Cam, Surhan (2002), 'Neo-Liberalism and Labour within the Context of an "Emerging Market" Economy – Turkey', *Capital and Class*, **77**, 89–114.

Cammack, Paul (1992) 'The New Institutionalism: Predatory Rule, Institutional Persistence, and Macro-Social Change', *Economy and Society*, **21** (4), 397–429.

Caprio, Gerard, J.L. Fiechter, R.E. Litan, and M. Pomerleano, eds (2004), *The Future of State-Owned Financial Institutions*, Washington, DC: Brookings Institution Press.

Caprio, Gerard, J.A. Hanson, and R.E. Litan, eds (2005), *Financial Crises: Lessons from the Past, Preparation for the Future*, Washington, DC: Brookings Institution Press.

Cardero, María Elena (1984), *Patrón Monetario y Accumulación en México: Nacionalización y Control de Cambios*, Mexico City: Siglo Veintiuno Editores.

Carnoy, Martin (1984), *The State and Political Theory*, Princeton, NJ: Princeton University Press.

Carroll, William K. (1989), 'Neoliberalism and the Recomposition of Finance Capital in Canada', *Capital and Class*, **13** (2), 81–112.

Carvalho, F.J.C. (2009–10), 'Financing Development: Some Conceptual Issues', *International Journal of Political Economy*, **38** (4), 5–24.

Cerny, Philip (1999), 'Globalising the Political and Politicising the Global: Concluding Reflections on International Political Economy as a Vocation', *New Political Economy*, **4** (1), 147–62.

—— (2000), 'Structuring the Political Arena: Public Goods, States, and Governance in a Globalizing World', in *Global Political Economy: Contemporary Theories*, ed. Ronen Palan, New York: Routledge.

Chang, Dae-Oup (2009), *Capitalist Development in Korea: Labour, Capital and the Myth of the Developmental State*, London: Routledge.

Chhibber, Ajay (2004), 'The Economic Policy Reform of Turkey', Stanford Center for International Development Lecture Series, 26 October.

Chong, Alberto and Florencio López-de-Silanes (2004), 'Privatization in Mexico', Research Department Working Papers, 513, Washington, DC: Inter-American Development Bank.

Christiansen, Lone, Martin Schindler, and Thierry Tressel (2009), 'Growth and Structural Reforms: A New Assessment', IMF Working Paper, WP/09/284, Washington, DC: IMF.

Christophers, Brett (2011), 'Making Finance Productive', *Economy and Society*, **40** (1), 112–40.

Cizre Sakallıoğlu, Ümit (1991), 'The State and Interest Groups with Special Reference to Turkey', in *Strong State and Economic Interest Groups: The Post-1980s Turkish Experience*, ed. M. Heper, New York: Walter de Gruyter.

Cizre, Ümit and Erinç Yeldan (2005) 'The Turkish Encounter with Neo-Liberalism: Economics and Politics in the 2000/2001 Crises', *Review of International Political Economy*, **12** (3), 387–408.

Clarke, George R.G., Robert Cull, and Mary M. Shirley (2005), 'Bank Privatization in Developing Countries: A Summary of Lessons and Findings', *Journal of Banking and Finance*, **29**, 1905–30.

Clarke, Simon (1988a), *Keynesianism, Monetarism, and the Crisis of the State*, Brookfield, VT: Gower Publishing.

—— (1988b), 'Overaccumulation, Class Struggle and the Regulation Approach', *Capital and Class*, **36**, 59–92.

Coates, David (2005), 'Paradigms of Explanation', in *Varieties of Capitalism, Varieties of Approaches*, ed. David Coates, New York: Palgrave Macmillan.

Cockcroft, James D. (1998), *Mexico's Hope: An Encounter with Politics and History*, New York: Monthly Review Press.

—— (2010), *Mexico's Revolution Then and Now*, New York: Monthly Review Press.

Cohen, Benjamin J. (2008), 'The International Monetary System: Diffusion and Ambiguity', *International Affairs*, **84** (3), 455–70.

Cokgezen, Murat (2000), 'New Fragmentations and New Cooperations in the Turkish Bourgeoisie', *Environment and Planning C: Government and Policy*, **18**, 525–44.

Correa, Eugenia (2004), 'Reforma Financiera en México', *Economía*

Financiera Contemporánea IV, Mexico City: Miguel Angel Porrua Grupo Editorial.

Cosar, Nevin (1999), 'Demirbank: The History of a Small Commercial Turkish Bank', *Business and Economic History*, **28** (2), 125–32.

Crane, D.B. and Ulrike Schaede (2005), 'Functional Change and Bank Strategy in German Corporate Governance', *International Review of Law and Economics*, **25**, 513–40.

Crespo, José Antonio (1992), 'Crisis Económica. Crisis de Legitimidad', in *México Auge Crisis, y Ajuste, Lecturas de El Trimestre Económico*, No. 73, ed. Carlos Bazdrech, México, FCE.

Crotty, James and Gerald Epstein (1996), 'In Defense of Capital Controls', in *Socialist Register: Are There Alternatives?*, ed. Ralph Miliband and Leo Panitch, London: The Merlin Press.

Crouch, Colin (2009), 'Typologies of Capitalism', in *Debating Varieties of Capitalism: A Reader*, ed. Bob Hancké, Oxford: Oxford University Press.

Cypher, James M. (1989), 'The Debt Crisis as "Opportunity": Strategies to Revive U.S. Hegemony', *Latin American Perspectives*, **16** (1), 52–78.

—— (1996), 'Mexico: Financial Fragility or Structural Crisis?' *Journal of Economic Issues*, **30** (2), 451–61.

—— (2001), 'Developing Disarticulation within the Mexican Economy', *Latin American Perspectives*, **28** (3), 11–37.

de Brunhoff, Suzanne (2003), 'Financial and Industrial Capital: A New Class Coalition', in *Anti-Capitalism: A Marxist Introduction*, ed. Alfredo Saad-Filho, London: Pluto Press.

De Rato, Rodrigo (2005), 'Globalization and the New Priorities of the IMF', Managing Director, IMF, Círculo de Economía, Barcelona, Spain, 20 October: available online: http://imf.org/external/np/speeches/2005/102005a.htm.

De Roover, Raymond (1971), 'Early Banking before 1500 and the Development of Capitalism', *International Review of the History of Banking*, **4**, 1–16.

Del Ángel-Mobarak, Gustavo A. (2005), 'La Banca Mexicana antes de 1982', in *Cuando el Estado se Hizo Banquero: Consequencias de la Nacionalizacion*, ed. Gustavo A. del Ángel-Mobarak, Carlos Bazdrech Parada, and Francisco Suarez Parada, Colecion Lecturas de El Trimestre Economico, 96, Mexico: Fondo de Cultura Economica.

Delgado Wise, Raúl and Rubén Del Pozo Mendoza (2005), 'Mexicanization, Privatization, and Large Mining Capital in Mexico', *Latin American Perspectives*, issue 143, **32** (4), 65–86.

Demirgüç-Kunt, Aslı and Luis Servén (2009), 'Are All the Sacred Cows

Dead? Implications of the Financial Crisis for Macro and Financial Policies', *Policy Research Working Paper*, 4807, World Bank.

Demirgüç-Kunt, Aslı, Ross Levine, and Hong-Ghi Min (1998), 'Opening to Foreign Banks: Issues of Stability, Efficiency, and Growth', in *The Implications of Globalization of World Financial Markets*, ed. Seongtae Lee, Seoul: The Bank of Korea.

DESA (2010), *World Economic and Social Survey 2010: Retooling Global Development*: available online: http://www.un.org/en/development/desa/policy/wess/index.shtml.

Detragiache, Enrica and Giang Ho (2010), 'Responding to Banking Crises: Lessons from Cross-Country Evidence', IMF Working Paper, WP/10/18, Washington, DC: IMF.

Devine, J. (1987), 'An Introduction to Radical Theories of Economic Crises', in *The Imperiled Economy: Volume One*, ed. R.Cherry et al., New York: URPE.

Devine, Pat (1988), *Democracy and Planning*, Cambridge: Polity Press.

Duman, Anil, Hakki C. Erkin, and Fatma Gül Unal (2005), 'The Determinants of Capital Flight in Turkey, 1971–2000', in *Capital Flight and Capital Controls in Developing Countries*, ed. G.A. Epstein, Cheltenham, UK and Northampton, MA, USA: Edward Elgar.

Duménil, Gerard and Dominique Lévy (2004), 'The Economics of US Imperialism at the Turn of the 21st Century', *Review of International Political Economy*, **11** (4), 657–76.

—— (2005), 'Costs and Benefits of Neoliberalism: A Class Analysis', in *Financialization and the World Economy*, ed. G.A. Epstein, Cheltenham, UK and Northampton, MA, USA: Edward Elgar.

—— (2011), *The Crisis of Neoliberalism*, Cambridge, MA: Harvard University Press.

Dussel Peters, Enrique (2000), *Polarizing Mexico: The Impact of Liberalization Strategy*, Boulder, CO: Lynne Rienner.

Elizondo, Carlos (1994), 'In Search of Revenue: Tax Reform in Mexico under the Administrations of Echeverria and Salinas', *Journal of Latin American Studies*, **26** (1), 159–90.

Engels, Friedrich (1959 [1888]), 'Ludwig Feuerbach and the End of Classical German Philosophy', in *Marx and Engels: Basic Writings on Politics and Philosophy*, ed. L.S. Feuer, New York: Anchor Books.

Epstein, G.A., ed. (2005), *Financialization and the World Economy*, Cheltenham, UK and Northampton, MA, USA: Edward Elgar.

Epstein, G.A. and A. Erinç Yeldan (2009), 'Beyond Inflation Targeting: Assessing the Impacts and Policy Alternatives', in *Beyond Inflation Targeting: Assessing the Impacts and Policy Alternatives*, ed. G.A.

Epstein and A.E. Yeldan, Cheltenham, UK and Northampton, MA, USA: Edward Elgar.

Epstein, Keith and Geri Smith (2007), 'The Ugly Side of Microlending', 13 December, available online: www.businessweek.com.

Erbaş, Hayriye and Feryal Turan (2009), 'The 2001 Crisis, its Impacts and Evaluations: The Case of Workers and Small Employers in Ankara', *Review of Radical Political Economics*, **41** (1), 79–107.

Ercan, Fuat (2002), 'The Contradictory Continuity of the Turkish Capital Accumulation Process: A Critical Perspective of the Internationalization of the Turkish Economy', in *The Ravages of Neo-Liberalism*, ed. Neşecan Balkan and Sungur Savran, Huappauge, NY: Nova Science Publishers.

Ercan, Fuat and Sebnem Oguz (2006), 'Rescaling as a Class Relationship and Process: The Case of Public Procurement Law in Turkey', *Political Geography*, **25** (6), 641–56.

—— (2007), 'Rethinking Anti-Neoliberal Strategies through the Perspective of Value Theory: Insights from the Turkish Case', *Science & Society*, **71** (2), 173–202.

Erçel, Gazı (1997), 'Turkey: Business, Finance, and Investment', Keynote Address, Euromoney Conference, 14 May, Istanbul: available online www.tcmb.gov.tr.

Eres, Benan (2005), 'Capital Accumulation and the Development of a Financial System: The Turkish Example', *Review of Radical Political Economics*, **37** (3), 320–8.

Ertürk, Ismail (2003), 'Governance or Financialisation: The Turkish Case', *Competition and Change*, **7** (4), 185–204.

Evans, Peter (1995), *Embedded Autonomy: States and Industrial Transformation*, Princeton, NJ: Princeton University Press.

Evans, Trevor (2009), 'Forum: The 2002–2007 US Economic Expansion and the Limits of Finance-Led Capitalism', *Studies in Political Economy*, **83**, 33–59.

Evrensel, Ayşe Y. (2004), 'IMF Programs and Financial Liberalization in Turkey', *Emerging Markets Finance and Trade*, **40** (4), 5–19.

Fine, Ben (2008), 'Privatization's Shaky Theoretical Foundations', in *Privatization and Alternative Public Sector Reform in Sub-Saharan Africa: Delivering on Electricity and Water*, ed. Kate Bayliss and Ben Fine, New York: Palgrave Macmillan.

—— (2010) 'Locating Financialisation', *Historical Materialism*, **18**, 97–116.

Fine, Ben and Kate Bayliss (2008), 'Rethinking the Rethink: The World Bank and Privatization', in *Privatization and Alternative Public Sector Reform in Sub-Saharan Africa: Delivering on Electricity and Water*, ed. Kate Bayliss and Ben Fine, New York: Palgrave Macmillan.

Fine, Ben and Alfredo Saad-Filho (2004), *Marx's Capital*, 4th edn, London: Pluto Press.

FitzGerald, E.V.K. (1981), 'Recent Writing on the Mexican Economy', *Latin American Research Review*, **16** (3), 236–44.

—— (1985), 'The Financial Constraint on Relative Autonomy: The State and Capital Accumulation in Mexico, 1940–82', in *The State and Capital Accumulation in Latin America, Vol.1: Brazil, Chile, Mexico*, ed. C. Anglade and C. Fortin, London: Macmillan Press.

Foster, J.B. (2008), 'The Financialization of Capital and the Crisis', *Monthly Review*, **11**, 1–19.

Freire, Paulo (1970), *Pedagogy of the Oppressed*, trans. Myra Bergman Ramos, New York: Continuum.

Fridell, Gavin (2011), 'Joseph Stiglitz: The Citizen-Bureaucrat and the Limits of Legitimate Dissent', *New Political Science*, **33** (2), 169–88.

Frieden, Jeff (1981), 'Third World Indebted Industrialization: International Finance and State Capitalism in Mexico, Brazil, Algeria, and South Korea', *International Organization*, **35** (3), 407–31.

Furceri, Davide and Annabelle Mourougane (2009), 'Financial Crises: Past Lessons and Policy Implications', OECD Economics Department Working Papers, No. 668.

Galindo, Luis Miguel and Jaime Ros (2009), 'Alternatives to Inflation Targeting in Mexico', in *Beyond Inflation Targeting: Assessing the Impacts and Policy Alternatives*, ed. G.A. Epstein and A.E. Yeldan, Cheltenham, UK and Northampton, MA, USA: Edward Elgar.

Garrido, Celso (2005), *Desarrollo Económico y Procesos de Financiamento en México: Transformaciones Contemporáneas y Dilemas Actuales*, Mexico City: Siglo XXI Editores/Universidad Autónoma Metropolitana.

Gerschenkeron, A. (1962), *Economic Backwardness in Historical Perspective: A Book of Essays*, Cambridge, MA: Belknap Press of Harvard University Press.

Gindin, Sam (2002), 'Anti-Capitalism and the Terrain of Social Justice', *Monthly Review*, **53** (9), 1–14.

Girón, Alicia and Noemí Levy (2005), *Mexico: Los Bancos que Perdimos: De la Desregulación a la Extranjerización del Sistema Financiero*, Mexico City: UNAM.

Glyn, Andrew (2006), *Capitalism Unleashed: Finance, Globalization and Welfare,* Oxford: Oxford University Press.

González, Humberto (2004), 'Convergence: Social Movements in Mexico in the Era of Neoliberal Globalism', in *Mexico in Transition: Neoliberal Globalism, the State and Civil Society*, ed. G. Otero, Black Point, Nova Scotia: Fernwood Publishing.

Gowan, Peter (1999), *The Global Gamble: Washington's Faustian Bid for World Domination*, New York: Verso.

Greenfield, Gerard (2004), 'Bandung Redux: Imperialism and Anti-Globalization Nationalisms in Southeast Asia', in *The Socialist Register 2005: The Empire Reloaded,* ed. L. Panitch and C. Leys, London: The Merlin Press.

Guillén Romo, Héctor (2005), *México frente a la Mundialización Neoliberal*, Mexico City, Ediciones Era.

Guislain, Pierre (1997), *The Privatization Challenge: A Strategic, Legal, and Institutional Analysis of International Experience*, Washington, DC: IBRD/The World Bank.

Gültekin-Karakaş, Derya (2008), *Global Integration of Turkish Finance Capital*, Saarbrücken: Verlag Dr Mueller.

Gunter, Michael M. and M. Hakan Yavuz (2007), 'Turkish Paradox: Progressive Islamists versus Reactionary Secularists', *Critique: Critical Middle Eastern Studies*, **16** (3), 289–301.

Guttmann, Robert (1994), *How Credit-Money Shapes the Economy: The United States in a Global System*, New York: M.E. Sharpe.

Haber, Stephen (1992), 'Assessing the Obstacles to Industrialisation: The Mexican Economy, 1830–1940', *Journal of Latin American* Studies, **24** (1), 1–32.

—— (2005a), 'Mexico's Experiments with Bank Privatization and Liberalization, 1991–2003', *Journal of Banking and Finance*, **29**, 2325–53.

—— (2005b), 'La Importancia de los Derechos de Propiedad', in *Cuando el Estado se Hizo Banquero: Consequencias de la Nacionalizacion*, ed. Gustavo A. Ángel-Mobarak, Carlos Bazdrech Parada, and Francisco Suarez Parada, Colecion Lecturas de El Trimestre Economico, 96, Mexico: Fondo de Cultura Economica.

Hall, Peter and David Soskice, eds (2001), *Varieties of Capitalism: The Institutional Foundations of Comparative Advantage*, New York: Oxford University Press.

—— (2009), 'An Introduction to Varieties of Capitalism', in *Debating Varieties of Capitalism: A Reader*, ed. Bob Hancké, Oxford: Oxford University Press.

Halsey Rogers, F. (2010), 'The Global Financial Crisis and Development Thinking', Policy Research Working Paper, No. 5353, World Bank.

Hancké, Bob, Martin Rhodes, and Mark Thatcher (2009), 'Beyond Varieties of Capitalism', in *Debating Varieties of Capitalism: A Reader*, ed. Bob Hancké, Oxford: Oxford University Press.

Hanieh, Adam (2009), 'Hierarchies of a Global Market: The South and the Economic Crisis', *Studies in Political Economy*, **83**, 61–84.

—— (2011), *Capitalism and Class in the Gulf Arab States*, New York: Palgrave Macmillan.

Hanioğlu, M. Sükrü (2001), *Preparation for a Revolution: The Young Turks, 1902–1908*, Oxford: Oxford University Press.

Hanlon, Joseph (2009), 'Debt and Development', in *Introduction to International Development*, ed. Paul A. Haslam, J. Schafer, and P. Beaudet, Oxford: Oxford University Press.

Harmes, Adam (2001), *Unseen Power: How Mutual Funds Threaten the Political and Economic Wealth of Nations*, Toronto: Stoddart.

Hart-Landsberg, Martin (2002), 'Challenging Neoliberal Myths: A Critical Look at the Mexican Experience', *Monthly Review*, **54** (7), 14–27.

Harvey, David (1998), 'The Practical Contradictions of Marxism', *Critical Sociology*, **24** (1–2), 1–36.

—— (1999 [1982]), *The Limits to Capital*, New York: Verso.

—— (2005), *A Brief History of Neoliberalism*, New York: Oxford University Press.

—— (2010), *The Enigma of Capital and the Crises of Capitalism*, London: Profile Books.

Hay, Colin (2002), *Political Analysis: A Critical Analysis*, New York: Palgrave.

Hayek, F.A. (1967 [1944]), *The Road to Serfdom*, Chicago: University of Chicago Press.

Helleiner, Eric and Stefano Pagliari (2009), 'Towards a New Bretton Woods? The First G20 Leaders Summit and the Regulation of Global Finance', *New Political Economy*, **14** (2), 275–87.

Hellman, Judith Adler (1978), *Mexico in Crisis*, New York: Holmes and Meier Publishers.

Henry, Clement M. (1996), *The Mediterranean Debt Crescent: Money and Power in Algeria, Egypt, Morocco, Tunisia, and Turkey*, Gainesville: University of Florida Press.

Hilferding, Rudolf (2006 [1910]), *Finance Capital: A Study in the Latest Phase of Capitalist Development*, ed. with an introduction by Tom Bottomore, trans. Morris Watnick and Sam Gordon, London: Routlege.

Himmelweit, Susan and Simon Mohun (1981), 'Real Abstractions and Anomalous Assumptions', in *The Value Controversy*, ed. Ian Steedman, London: Verso.

Honohan, Patrick (1997), 'Banking System Failures in Developing and Transition Countries: Diagnosis and Prediction', *BIS Working Papers*, **39**, 1–45.

Huber, Evelyne and Fred Solt (2004), 'Successes and Failures of Neoliberalism,' *Latin American Research Review*, **39** (3), 150–64.

Irazábal, Clara and John Foley (2010), 'Reflections on the Venezuelan Transition from a Capitalist Representative to a Socialist Participatory Democracy: What Are Planners to Do?', *Latin American Perspectives*, issue 170, **37** (1), 97–122.

Isık, İhsan and Emin Akçaoğlu (2006), 'An Empirical Analysis of Productivity Developments in "Traditional Banks": The Initial Post-Liberalization Experience', *Central Bank Review*, **1**, 1–35.

Itoh, Makoto and Costas Lapavitsas (1999), *Political Economy of Money and Finance*, New York: St Martin's Press.

Jessop, Bob (1982), *The Capitalist State: Marxist Theories and Methods,* Oxford: Martin Robertson and Company.

—— (1990), *State Theory: Putting the Capitalist State in its Place*, University Park, PA: Pennsylvania State University Press.

—— (2010), 'The "Return" of the National State in the Current Crisis of the World Market', *Capital & Class*, **34** (1), 38–43.

Judson, Fred (1993), 'The Making of Central American National Agendas under Adjustment and Restructuring', *Labour, Capital and Society*, **26** (2), 148–80.

Kapstein, E.B (2000), 'Winners and Losers in the Global Economy', *International Organization*, **54** (2), 359–84.

Karaçimen, Elif (2011), 'Financialisation of Workers' Income in Turkey: An Exploratory Study', paper presented to 2nd International Conference, International Initiative for the Promotion of Political Economy, Istanbul, Turkey, 20–22 May.

Karadag, Roy (2010), 'Neoliberal Restructuring in Turkey: From State to Oligarchic Capitalism', Max Planck Institute for the Study of Societies, Discussion Paper 10/7.

Karataş, Cevat (1995), 'Fiscal Policy in Turkey: Public Debt and the Changing Structure of Taxation and Government Expenditure, 1980–1993', in *Turkey: Political, Social and Economic Challenges in the 1990s*, ed. C. Balim et al., New York: Brill.

—— (2001), 'Privatization in Turkey: Implementation, Politics of Privatization and Performance Results', *Journal of International Development*, **13**, 93–121.

Keyder, Çağlar (2004), 'The Turkish Bell Jar', *New Left Review*, **28**, 65–84.

Kibritçioğlu, Aykut (2006), 'The Labour Market Implications of Large-Scale Restructuring in the Banking Sector in Turkey', MPRA Paper No. 2457.

Kiely, Ray (2007), *The New Political Economy of Development: Globalization, Imperialism, Hegemony*, New York: Palgrave Macmillan.

Knight, Alan (1992), 'The Peculiarities of Mexican History: Mexico

Compared to Latin America, 1821–1992', *Journal of Latin American History*, **24**, 99–144.

Knuttila, Murray (1987), *State Theories: From Liberalism to the Challenge of Feminism*, Toronto: Garamond Press.

Konings, Martijn (2008), 'The Institutional Foundations of US Structural Power in International Finance: From the Re-Emergence of Global Finance to the Monetarist Turn', *Review of International Political Economy*, **15** (1), 35–61.

Kosebalaban, Hasan (2007), 'The Rise of Anatolian Cities and the Failure of the Modernization Paradigm', *Critique: Critical Middle Eastern Studies*, **16** (3), 229–40.

Kregel, Jan (2000), 'Banks, Stockmarkets and Financial Resources for Business under the Economic Reform in Developing Countries', *Emerging Markets: Past and Present Experiences, and Future Prospects*, ed. S. Motamen-Samadian and C. Garrido, New York: St Martin's Press.

Kus, Basak and Isik Ozel (2010), 'United we Restrain, Divided we Rule: Neoliberal Reforms and Labor Unions in Turkey and Mexico', *European Journal of Turkish Studies*, available online: http://ejts.revues.org/index4291.html.

La Porta, Rafael, Florencio Lopez-de-Silanes, and Andrei Shleifer (2002), 'Government Ownership of Banks', *Journal of Finance*, **57** (1), 265–301.

Lapavitsas, Costas (2003), 'Money as Money and Money as Capital in a Capitalist Economy', in *Anti-Capitalism: A Marxist Introduction*, ed. Alfredo Saad-Filho, London: Pluto Press.

—— (2009), 'Financialised Capitalism: Crisis and Financial Expropriation', *Historical Materialism*, **17**, 114–48.

Lapavitsas, C. and P.L. dos Santos (2008), 'Globalization and Contemporary Banking: On the Impact of New Technology', *Contributions to Political Economy*, **27**, 31–56.

Lapavitsas, Costas, Annina Kaltenbrunnera, Duncan Lindo, J. Michella, Juan Pablo Painceira, Eugenia Pires, Jeff Powell, Alexis Stenfors, and Nuno Teles (2011), 'Eurozone Crisis: Beggar Thyself and thy Neighbour', *Journal of Balkan and Near Eastern Studies*, **12** (4), 321–73.

Lebowitz, Michael A. (2006), *Build it Now: Socialism for the Twenty-First Century*, New York: Monthly Review Press.

Lefebvre, Henri (1991), *The Production of Space*, trans. D. Nicholson-Smith, Oxford: Wiley-Blackwell.

Legorreta Chauvet, Agustín (2005), 'Transformaciones en la Banca Mexicana en los Años Ochenta', in *Cuando el Estado se Hizo Banquero: Consequencias de la Nacionalizacion*, ed. Gustavo A. del Ángel-Mobarak, Carlos Bazdrech Parada, and Francisco Suarez Parada,

Colecion Lecturas de El Trimestre Economico, 96, Mexico: Fondo de Cultura Economica.

Lenin, V.I. (1974 [1939]), *Imperialism: The Highest Stage of Capitalism*, New York: International Publishers.

Levy, Noemí Orlik (2003), 'Los Cambios Institucionales y su Efecto sobre la Estructura Financiera: Modificación de los Agregados Monetarios', in *Hacia una Política Monetaria y Financiera para el Cambio Estructural y el Crecimiento*, ed. E. Ortiz Cruz, Mexico City: UAM y Plaza y Valdes Editores.

Lewis, Bernard (1961), *The Emergence of Modern Turkey*, London: Oxford University Press.

Leys, Colin (1996), *The Rise and Fall of Development Theory*, Bloomington, IN: Indiana University Press.

Lipietz, Alain (1987), *Miracles and Mirages: The Crises of Global Fordism*, London: Verso.

—— (1997), 'Warp, Woof and Regulation: A Tool for Social Science', in *Space and Social Theory*, ed. G. Benko and U. Strohmayer, Oxford: Blackwell.

Lukauskas, Arvid and Susan Minushkin (2000), 'Explaining Styles of Financial Market Opening in Chile, Mexico, South Korea, and Turkey', *International Studies Quarterly*, **44**, 695–723.

MacLeod, Dag (2005), 'Privatization and the Limits of State Autonomy in Mexico', *Latin American Perspectives*, **32** (4), 36–64.

Mannsberger, Jörg and J. Brad McBride (2007), 'The Privatization of the Mexican Banking Sector in the 1990s: From Debacle to Disappointment', *International Journal of Emerging Markets*, **2** (4), 320–34.

Marchini, Geneviève (2004), 'Financial Liberalisation, the Banking Crisis and the Debtors' Movement in Mexico' *Portal*, **1** (2), 1–27.

Marini, Francois (2005), 'Banks, Financial Markets, and Social Welfare, *Journal of Banking and Finance*, **29**, 2557–75.

Marois, Thomas (2005), 'From Economic Crisis to a "State" of Crisis?: The Emergence of Neoliberalism in Costa Rica', *Historical Materialism*, **13** (3), 101–34.

—— (2008), 'The 1982 Mexican Bank Statization and Unintended Consequences for the Emergence of Neoliberalism', *Canadian Journal of Political Science*, **41** (1), 143–67.

—— (2009), 'Un Modelo Neoliberal para Institutionalizar el Desacuerdo Social: La Comisión de Cooperación Ambiental del TLCAN', *Revista Vetas*, **12** (3), 54–64.

—— (2011a), 'Emerging Market Bank Rescues in an Era of Finance-Led Neoliberalism: A Comparison of Mexico and Turkey', *Review of International Political Economy*, **18** (2), 168–96.

—— (2011b), 'The Socialization of Financial Risk in Neoliberal Mexico', Research on Money and Finance Discussion Paper, 25: available online: http://www.researchonmoneyandfinance.org/discussion-papers/.

—— (forthcoming 2012) 'Finance, Finance Capital, and Financialisation', in *The Elgar Companion to Marxist Economics*, ed. Ben Fine and Alfredo Saad Filho, Cheltenham, UK and Northampton, MA, USA: Edward Elgar.

Marshall, Wesley C. (2010), 'Banco del Sur and the Need for Downstream Linkages: The Role of National Publicly Owned Banks', *International Journal of Political Economy*, **39** (3), 81–99.

Martinez-Diaz, Leonardo (2009), *Globalizing in Hard Times: The Politics of Banking-Sector Opening in the Emerging World*, Ithaca: Cornell University Press.

Marx, Karl (1849), *Wage Labour and Capital*, trans. F. Engels, Original pamphlet 1891, available online: http://www.marxists.org/archive/marx/works/1847/wage-labour/index.htm.

—— (1959 [1869]), 'The Eighteenth Brumaire of Louis Bonaparte', in *Marx and Engels: Basic Writings on Politics and Philosophy*, ed. L.S. Feuer, New York: Anchor Books.

—— (1959), 'Theses on Feuerbach', in *Marx and Engels: Basic Writings on Politics and Philosophy*, ed. L.S. Feuer, New York: Anchor Books

—— (1970), *A Contribution to the Critique of Political Economy*, Moscow: Progress Publishers.

—— (1973), *Grundrisse*, trans. Martin Nicolaus. London: Allen Lane.

—— (1990 [1976]), *Capital: A Critique of Political Economy*, Vol. III, trans. David Fernbach, Harmondsworth: Penguin Classics.

—— (1991 [1981]), *Capital: A Critique of Political Economy*, Vol. I, trans. Ben Fowkes, Toronto: Penguin Classics.

Maxfield, Sylvia (1992), 'The International Political Economy of Bank Nationalization: Mexico in Comparative Perspective,' *Latin American Research Review*, **27** (1), 75–103.

Maxfield, Sylvia and James H. Nolt (1990), 'Protectionism and the Internationalization of Capital: U.S. Sponsorship of Import Substitution Industrialization in the Philippines, Turkey and Argentina', *International Studies Quarterly*, **34** (1), 49–81.

McDonald, David and Greg Ruiters (2006), 'Rethinking Privatization: Towards a Critical Perspective', in *Beyond the Market: The Future of Public Services*, ed. Daniel Chavez, Amsterdam: TNI/Public Services International Research Unit.

McKeen-Edwards, Heather, Tony Porter, and Ian Roberge (2004),

'Politics or Markets? The Determinants of Cross-Border Financial Integration in the NAFTA and EU', *New Political Economy*, **9** (3), 325–40.

McKinnon, Ronald I. (1973), *Money and Capital in Economic Development*, Washington, DC: The Brookings Institution.

McMichael, Philip (1990), 'Incorporating Comparison within a World-Historical Perspective: An Alternative Comparative Method', *American Sociological Review*, **55**, 385–97.

McNally, David (2009), 'From Financial Crisis to World-Slump: Accumulation, Financialisation, and the Global Slowdown', *Historical Materialism*, **17**, 35–83.

Megginson, William L. (2005a), 'The Economics of Bank Privatization', *Journal of Banking and Finance*, **29**, 1931–80.

—— (2005b), *The Financial Economics of Privatization*, New York: Oxford University Press.

MGI (McKinsey Global Institute) (2003), *Turkey: Making the Productivity and Growth Breakthrough*, McKinsey & Company: available online: http://www.mckinsey.com/mgi/publications/turkey/index.asp.

Micco, Alejandro, Ugo Panizza, and Monica Yañez (2007), 'Bank Ownership and Performance: Does Politics Matter?', *Journal of Banking and Finance*, **31**, 219–41.

Mihaljek, Dubravko (2010), 'Domestic Bank Intermediation in Emerging Market Economies during the Crisis: Locally Owned versus Foreign-Owned Banks', *BIS Papers*, **54**, 31–48.

Miliband, Ralph (1974 [1969]), *The State in Capitalist Society: The Analysis of the Western Power System*, London: Quartet Books.

Minsky, Hyman P. (1992), 'The Financial Instability Hypothesis', Working Paper, No. 74, The Jerome Levy Economics Institute of Bard College, New York.

—— (1994), 'Financial Instability and the Decline (?) of Banking: Public Policy Implications', Working Paper No. 127, The Jerome Levy Economics Institution of Bard College, New York.

Minushkin, Susan (2005), 'De Banqueros a Casaboleros: La Transformación Estructural del Sector Financiero Mexicano', in *Cuando el Estado se Hizo Banquero: Consequencias de la Nacionalizacion*, ed. Gustavo A. del Ángel–Mobarak, Carlos Bazdrech Parada, and Francisco Suarez Parada, Colecion Lecturas de El Trimestre Economico, 96, Mexico City: Fondo de Cultura Economica.

Mishkin, Frederic S. (2009), 'Why We Shouldn't Turn Our Backs on Financial Globalization', *IMF Staff Papers*, **56** (1), 139–70.

Morera, Carlos (1998), *El Capital Financiero en Mexico y la Globalizacion*, Mexico City: Ediciones Era.

Morgan, Glenn (2007), 'The Theory of Comparative Capitalisms and the Possibilities for Local Variation', *European Review*, **15** (3), 353–71.

Morton, Adam David (2003), 'Structural Change and Neoliberalism in Mexico: "Passive Revolution" in the Global Political Economy', *Third World Quarterly*, **24** (4), 631–53.

—— (2010), 'Reflections on Uneven Development: Mexican Revolution, Primitive Accumulation, Passive Revolution', *Latin American Perspectives*, issue 170, **37** (1), 7–34.

Motamen-Samadian, Sima (2000), 'Mexican Banking Crisis: Causes and Consequence', in *Emerging Markets: Past and Present Experiences, and Future Prospects*, ed. S. Motamen-Samadian and C. Garrido, New York: St Martin's Press.

Munck, Ronaldo (2010), 'Globalization, Crisis and Social Transformation: A View from the South,' *Globalizations*, **7** (1), 235–46.

Munoz-Martinez, Hepzibah (2008), 'The Global Crisis and Mexico: The End of Mexico's Development Model?' *Relay*, **24**, 18–20.

Myrdal, Gunnar (1963 [1957]), *Economic Theory and Under-Developed Regions*, London: Gerald Duckworth & Co. Ltd.

Nachtwey, Oliver and Tobias ten Brink (2008), 'Lost in Translation: The German World-Market Debate in the 1970s', *Historical Materialism*, **16**, 37–70.

Neiman Auerbach, Nancy (2001), *States, Banks, and Markets: Mexico's Path to Financial Liberalization in Comparative Perspective*, Boulder, CO: Westview Press.

Newfarmer, Richard S. and Willard Mueller (1975), *Multinational Corporations in Brazil and Mexico: Structural Sources of Economic and Noneconomic Power*, Report to the US Senate, Committee on Foreign Relations, Subcommittee on Multinational Corporations, Washington, DC: Government Printing Office.

Nissanke, M. and E. Thorbecke (2006), 'Channels and Policy Debate in the Globalization-Inequality-Poverty Nexus', *World Development*, **34** (8), 1338–60.

—— (2010), 'Globalization, Poverty, and Inequality in Latin America: Findings from Case Studies', *World Development*, **38** (6), 797–802.

North, Douglass C. (1981), *Structure and Change in Economic History*, New York: W.W. Norton & Co.

—— (1990), *Institutions, Institutional Change and Economic Performance*, New York: Cambridge University Press.

Núñez Estrada, Héctor Rogelio (2005), *Reforma y Crisis del Sistema Bancario 1990–2000: Quiebra de Banca Serfin*, Mexico City: Plaza y Valdés.

O'Connor, James (2009 [1973]), *The Fiscal Crisis of the State*, New Brunswick, NJ: Transaction.

O'Toole, Gavin (2003), 'A New Nationalism for a New Era: The Political Ideology of Mexican Neoliberalism', *Bulletin of Latin American Research*, **22** (3), 269–90.

Ocampo, Jose Antonio, Jan Kregel, and Stephany Griffith-Jones, eds (2007), *International Finance and Development*, London: Zed Books.

Ocampo, Jose Antonio, Shari Spiegel, and Joseph E. Stiglitz (2008), 'Capital Market Liberalization and Development', in *Capital Market Liberalization and Development*, ed. J.A. Ocampo and J.E. Stiglitz, Oxford: Oxford University Press.

Ollman, Bertell (1993), *Dialectical Investigations*, New York: Routledge.

Onaran, Özlem (2002), 'Adjusting the Economy through the Labor Market: The Myth of Rigidity', in *The Ravages of Neo-Liberalism*, ed. Neşecan Balkan and Sungur Savran, Huappauge, NY: Nova Science Publishers.

—— (2008), 'Life after Crisis for Labor and Capital', in *Neoliberal Globalization as New Imperialism: Case Studies on Reconstruction of the Periphery*, ed. E. Yeldan, A. Kose, and F. Senses, Huappauge, NY: Nova Scientific Publishers.

Öncü, Ayse and Deniz Gokçe (1991), 'Macro-Politics of De-Regulation and Micro-Politics of Banks', in *Strong State and Economic Interest Groups: The Post-1980s Turkish Experience*, ed. M. Heper, New York: Walter de Gruyter.

Öniş, Ziya (2003), 'Domestic Politics versus Global Dynamics: Towards a Political Economy of the 2000 and 2001 Financial Crises in Turkey', in *The Turkish Economy in Crisis*, ed. Ziya Oniş and Barry Rubin, Portland, OR: Frank Cass.

—— (2004), 'Turgut Özal and his Economic Legacy: Turkish Neoliberalism in Critical Perspective', *Middle Eastern Studies*, **40** (4), 113–34.

—— (2006), 'Varieties and Crises of Neoliberal Globalisation: Argentina, Turkey and the IMF', *Third World Quarterly*, **27** (2), 239–63.

—— (2009), 'Beyond the 2001 Financial Crisis: The Political Economy of the New Phase of Neo-Liberal Restructuring in Turkey', *Review of International Political Economy*, **16** (3), 409–32.

Öniş, Ziya and Ahmet Faruk Aysan (2000), 'Neoliberal Globalisation, the Nation-State and Financial Crises in the Semi-Periphery: A Comparative Analysis', *Third World Quarterly*, **21** (1), 119–39.

Orhangazi, Özgür (2008), *Financialization and the US Economy*, Cheltenham, UK and Northampton. MA, USA: Edward Elgar.

Ortiz Martínez, Guillermo (1993), 'The Modernization of the Mexican Financial System', in *Financial Sector Reforms in Asian and Latin*

American Countries: Lessons of Comparative Experience, ed. Shakil Faruqi, Washington, DC: The World Bank.

Otero, Gerardo (2004), 'Mexico's Double Movement: Neoliberal Globalism, the State and Civil Society', in *Mexico in Transition: Neoliberal Globalism, the State and Civil Society*, ed. G. Otero, Black Point, Nova Scotia: Fernwood Publishing.

Oyan, Oğuz (2002), 'From Agricultural Policies to an Agriculture without Policies', in *The Ravages of Neo-Liberalism*, ed. Neşecan Balkan and Sungur Savran, Huappauge, NY: Nova Science Publishers.

Özince, Ersin (2005), 'Turkish Banking System', Presentation by the Chair of the Turkish Banks Association of Turkey, Istanbul: available online: http://www.turkisheconomy.org.uk/banking.html#.

Ozkan-Gunay, E. Nur and Arzu Tektas (2006), 'Efficiency Analysis of the Turkish Banking Sector in Precrisis and Crisis Period: A DEA Approach', *Contemporary Economic Policy*, **24** (3), 418–31.

Panitch, Leo (1994), 'Globalisation and the State', in *The Socialist Register 1994: Between Globalism and Nationalism*, ed. L. Panitch and C. Leys, London: The Merlin Press.

—— (2001), *Renewing Socialism: Democracy, Strategy, and Imagination*, Boulder, CO: Westview Press.

—— (2002), 'Impoverishment of State Theory', in *Paradigm Lost*, Minneapolis: University of Minnesota Press.

Panitch, Leo and Sam Gindin (2003), 'Global Capitalism and American Empire', in *The Socialist Register 2004: The New Imperial Challenge*, ed. L. Panitch and C. Leys, London: The Merlin Press.

—— (2003/04), 'American Imperialism and Eurocapitalism: The Making of Neoliberal Globalization', *Studies in Political Economy*, **71–72**, 7–38.

—— (2004), 'Finance and American Empire', in *The Socialist Register 2005: The Empire Reloaded,* ed. L. Panitch and C. Leys, London: The Merlin Press.

—— (2005), 'Euro-Capitalism and American Empire', in *Varieties of Capitalism, Varieties of Approaches*, ed. David Coates, New York: Palgrave Macmillan.

Patomäki, Heikki (2001), *Democratising Globalisation: The Leverage of the Tobin Tax*, New York: Zed Books.

Peck, J. and A. Tickell (2002), 'Neoliberalizing Space', *Antipode*, **34** (3), 380–404

Poulantzas, Nicos (1974), *Classes in Contemporary Capitalism*, London: NLB.

—— (2000 [1978]), *State, Power, Socialism*, New York: Verso Classics.

Prasad, Eswar and M. Ayhan Kose (2010), *Emerging Markets Resilience and Growth Amid Global Turmoil*, Washington, DC: Brookings Institution Press.

Przeworski, Adam (2004), 'The Last Instance: Are Institutions the Primary Cause of Economic Development?', *European Archives of Sociology*, **45** (2), 165–88.

Przeworski, Adam and Henry Teune (1970), *The Logic of Comparative Social Inquiry*, New York: Wiley-Interscience.

Radice, Hugo (2010), 'Confronting the Crisis: A Class Analysis', in *Socialist Register 2011: The Crisis this Time*, ed. Leo Panitch, Greg Albo, and Vivek Chibber, London: Merlin Press.

Ramírez, Miguel D. (1994), 'Privatization and the Role of the State in Post-ISI Mexico', in *Privatization in Latin America: New Roles for the Public and Private Sectors*, ed. W. Baer and M.H. Birch, London: Praeger.

—— (2001), 'The Mexican Regulatory Experience in the Airline, Banking and Telecommunications Sectors', *Quarterly Review of Economics and Finance*, **41**, 657–81.

Rhode, William (2001), 'Dervis Takes the Economy by Storm', *Global Finance*, **16** (6), 36–42.

Richmond, D.W. (1987), 'Nationalism and Class Conflict in Mexico, 1910–1920', *The Americas*, **43** (3), 279–303.

Robertson, Justin, ed. (2007), *Power and Politics after Financial Crises: Rethinking Foreign Opportunism in Emerging Markets*, Basingstoke: Palgrave Macmillan.

Robinson, W.I. (2003), *Transnational Conflicts: Central America, Social Change, and Globalization*, New York: Verso.

Rodríguez Araujo, Octavio (2010), 'The Emergence and Entrenchment of a New Political Regime in Mexico', *Latin American Perspectives*, issue 170, **37**(1), 35–61.

Rodríguez, Javier and Javier Santiso (2007), 'Banking on Development: Private Banks and Aid Donors in Developing Countries', OECD Development Centre Working Papers, No. 263, OECD, Paris.

Rodrik, Dani (2006), 'The Social Costs of Foreign Exchange Reserves', *International Economic Journal*, **20** (3), 253–66.

—— (2008), 'Second-Best Institutions', NBER Working Paper, No. 14050, National Bureau of Economic Research, Cambridge, MA.

Rogozinski, Jacques (1998), *High Price for Change: Privatization in Mexico*, Washington, DC: Inter-American Bank.

Roman, Richard and Edur Velasco Arregui (2007), 'Mexico's Oaxaca Commune', in *Socialist Register 2008: Global Flashpoints, Reactions to Imperialism and Neoliberalism*, ed. L. Panitch and C. Leys, Halifax: Fernwood Publishing.

Saad-Filho, Alfredo, ed. (2003), *Anti-Capitalism: A Marxist Introduction*, London: Pluto Press.

—— (2010), 'Crisis in Neoliberalism or Crisis of Neoliberalism?', in *Socialist Register 2011: The Crisis this Time*, ed. Leo Panitch, Greg Albo, and Vivek Chibber, London: Merlin Press.

Saad-Filho, Alfredo and M.L.R Mollo (2002), 'Inflation and Stabilization in Brazil: A Political Economy Analysis', in *Review of Radical Political Economics*, **34**, 109–35.

Sanchez, Omar (2006), 'Tax System Reform in Latin America: Domestic and International Causes', *Review of International Political Economy*, **13** (5), 772–801.

Sarai, David (2009), 'The US Treasury and the Re-Emergence of Global Finance', in *Hegemonic Transitions, the State and Crisis in Neoliberal Capitalism*, ed. Yildiz Atasoy, London: Routledge.

Savran, Sungur (2002), 'The Legacy of the Twentieth Century', in *The Politics of Permanent Crisis: Class, Ideology and State in Turkey*, ed. N. Balkan and S. Savran, Huappauge, NY: Nova Science Publishers, Inc.

Schneider, Ben Ross and David Soskice (2009), 'Inequality in Developed Countries and Latin America: Coordinated, Liberal and Hierarchical Systems', *Economy and Society*, **38** (1), 17–52.

Seabrooke, Leonard (2007), 'Everyday Legitimacy and International Financial Orders: The Social Sources of Imperialism and Hegemony in Global Finance', *New Political Economy*, **12** (1), 1–18.

Selwyn, Ben (2009), 'An Historical Materialist Appraisal of Friedrich List and his Modern-Day Followers', *New Political Economy*, **14** (2), 157–80.

Shaw, Edward S. (1973), *Financial Deepening in Economic Development*, Toronto: Oxford University Press.

Shleifer, Andrei (1998), 'State versus Private Ownership', *Journal of Economic Perspectives*, **12** (4), 133–50.

Shonfield, Andrew (1969 [1965]), *Modern Capitalism: The Changing Balance of Public and Private Power*, New York: Oxford University Press.

Sidaoui, José Julián (2005), 'Policies for International Reserve Accumulation under a Floating Exchange Rate Regime: The Experience of Mexico (1995–2003)', *BIS Papers*, **23**, 216–29.

—— (2006), 'The Mexican Financial System: Reforms and Evolution 1995–2005', *BIS Papers*, **28**, 277–93.

Sidaoui, José, Manuel Ramos-Francia, and Gabriel Cuadra (2010), 'The Global Financial Crisis and Policy Response in Mexico', *BIS Papers*, **54**, 279–98.

Smith, Neil (2010 [1984]), *Uneven Development: Nature, Capital and the Production of Space*, 3rd edn, London: Verso.

Soederberg, Susanne (2001), 'State, Crisis, and Capital Accumulation in Mexico', *Historical Materialism*, **9**, 61–84.

—— (2002), 'Deconstructing the Neoliberal Promise of Prosperity: Who Gains from the Maquiladorization of Mexican Society?', *Cultural Logic*, **4** (2): available online: http://eserver.org/clogic/4-2/soederberg. html.

—— (2004), *The Politics of the New International Financial Infrastructure: Reimposing Neoliberal Domination in the Global South*, New York: Zed Books.

—— (2005), 'The Transnational Debt Architecture and Emerging Markets: The Politics of Paradoxes and Punishment', *Third World Quarterly*, **26** (6), 927–49.

—— (2010a), 'The Mexican Competition State and the Paradoxes of Managed Neoliberalism,' *Policy Studies*, **31** (1), 77–94.

—— (2010b) 'Cannibalistic Capitalism: The Paradoxes of Neoliberal Pension Securitization', in *Socialist Register 2011: The Crisis this Time*, ed. Leo Panitch, Greg Albo, and Vivek Chibber, London: The Merlin Press.

Solís, Leopoldo (1997), *Evolución del Sistema Financiero Mexicano hacia los Umbrales del Siglo XXI*, Mexico City: Siglo Veintiuno Editores.

Stallings, Barbara (with Rogerio Studart) (2006), *Finance for Development: Latin America in Comparative Perspective*, Washington, DC: The Brookings Institution.

Stein, Howard (2010), 'Financial Liberalisation, Institutional Transformation and Credit Allocation in Developing Countries: The World Bank and the Internationalisation of Banking', *Cambridge Journal of Economics*, **34**, 257–73.

Steinfeld, Jacob (2004), 'Development and Foreign Investment: Lessons Learned from Mexican Banking', Carnegie Papers, No. 47, Washington, DC: Carnegie Endowment for International Peace.

Steinherr, Alfred, Ali Tukel, and Murat Ucer (2004), 'The Turkish Banking Sector: Challenges and Outlook in Transition to EU Membership', EU-Turkey Working Paper, Centre for European Policy Studies, No. 4, August.

Stiglitz, Joseph E. (2010), 'Contagion, Liberalization, and the Optimal Structure of Globalization', *Journal of Globalization and Development*, **1** (2), 1–45.

Stockhammer, Engelbert (2008), 'Some Stylized Facts on the Finance-Dominated Accumulation Regime', *Competition and Change*, **12** (2), 184–202.

Strange, Susan (1994 [1988]), *States and Markets*, 2nd edn, London: Pinter.

—— (1997a [1986]), *Casino Capitalism*, Manchester: Manchester University Press.

—— (1997b), 'The Erosion of the State', *Current History*, **96** (613), 365–69.

—— (1998), *Mad Money: When Markets Outgrow Governments.* Ann Arbor: The University of Michigan Press.

Taylor, Marcus (2006), *From Pinochet to the 'Third Way': Neoliberalism and Social Transformation in Chile*, Ann Arbor, MI: Pluto Press.

—— (2009), 'The International Financial Institutions', in *Introduction to International Development*, ed. Paul A. Haslam, J. Schafer, and P. Beaudet, Oxford: Oxford University Press.

Teichman, Judith (1992), 'The Mexican State and the Political Implications of Economic Restructuring', *Latin American Perspectives*, **19** (2), 88–104.

—— (2008), 'Redistributive Conflict and Social Policy in Latin America', *World Development*, **36** (3), 446–60.

Tello, Carlos (1984), *La Nacionalización de la Banca en México*, Mexico City: Siglo Veintiuno Editores.

Tezel, Yahya Sezai (2010), *Transformation of State and Society in Turkey: From the Ottoman Empire to the Turkish Republic*, Istanbul: Turkiye Is Bankasi Kultur Yayinlari.

Toms, J.S. (2010), 'The Labour Theory of Value, Risk and the Rate of Profit', *Critical Perspectives on Accounting*, **21**, 96–103.

Tonge, David (1974), 'Progress Abroad: Troubles at Home', in *World Banking 1973–74: Statist 63rd Annual Survey*, London: Investors Chronicle.

Tschoegl, Adrian E. (2004), '"The World's Local Bank": HSBC's Expansion in the US, Canada, and Mexico', *Latin American Business Review*, **5** (4), 45–68.

Unal, Haluk and Miguel Navarro (1999), 'The Technical Process of Bank Privatization in Mexico', *Journal of Financial Services Research*, **16** (1), 61–83.

Vadi, José M. (2001), 'Economic Globalization, Class Struggle, and the Mexican State', *Latin American Perspectives*, **28** (4), 129–47.

Vásquez, Ian (1996), 'The Brady Plan and Market-Based Solutions to Debt Crises', *Cato Journal*, **16** (2), 233–43.

Veltmeyer, Henry (2010), 'The Global Crisis and Latin America', *Globalizations*, **7** (1–2), 217–33.

Vidal, Gregorio (2002), 'Bancos, Fortunas y Poder: Una Lectura de la Economía en el México del 2000', in *Crisis y Futuro de la Banca en*

México, ed. Eugenia Correa and Alicia Girón, Mexico City: UNAM-Miguel Ángel Porrúa.

Vidal, Gregorio, W. Marshall, and E. Correa (2011), 'Differing Effects of the Global Financial Crisis: Why Mexico Has Been Harder Hit than Other Large Latin American Countries', *Bulletin of Latin American Research*, **30**, 419–35.

von Braunmühl, Claudia (1978), 'On the Analysis of the Bourgeois Nation State within the World Market Context: An Attempt to Develop a Methodological and Theoretical Approach', in *State and Capital: A Marxist Debate*, ed. John Holloway and Sol Picciotto, London: Edward Arnold.

Vorkink, Andrew (2005), 'Unleashing a European Tiger: Financial Sector Challenges to Sustain Economic Growth in Turkey', Third International Financial Summit, 1 December 2005, Istanbul: available online: http://go.worldbank.org/ILZ1ULB9C0.

Wade, Robert Hunter (2003), 'Globalization and Development', in *Taming Globalization: Frontiers of Governance*, ed. David Held and Mathias Koenig-Archibugi, Cambridge: Polity Press.

—— (2004), 'Is Globalization Reducing Poverty and Inequality?', *World Development*, **32** (4), 567–89.

Walton, Michael (2004), 'Neoliberalism in Latin America: Good, Bad, or Incomplete?', *Latin American Research Review*, **39** (3), 165–83.

Weber, Heloise (2004), 'The New Economy and Social Risk: Banking on the Poor', *Review of International Political Economy*, **11** (2), 356–86.

Weiser, Teresa (1990), 'Participacion Extranjera en el Nuevo Sistema Bancario, Demanda AMB; Exige Flexibilidad', *El Financiero*, 23 May, Mexico City: 5.

Weizsäcker, Ernest Ulrich von, Oran R. Young, and Matthias Finger (2005), 'Limits to Privatization', in *Limits to Privatization: How to Avoid too Much of a Good Thing: A Report to the Club of Rome*, ed. E.U. von Weizsäcker, O. R. Young, and M. Finger, London: Earthscan.

White, Russell N. (1992), *State, Class, and the Nationalization of the Mexican Banks*, New York: Taylor and Francis.

Wilkin, Peter (1996), 'New Myths for the South: Globalisation and the Conflict between Private Power and Freedom' *Third World Quarterly*, **17** (2), 227–38.

Williams, Heather (2001), 'Of Free Trade and Debt Bondage: Fighting Banks and the State in Mexico', *Latin American Perspectives*, **28** (4), 30–51.

Williamson, John (1990), 'What Washington Means by Policy Reform', in *Latin American Adjustment: How Much has Happened?*, ed. John Williamson, Washington: Institute for International Economics.

—— (1993), 'Democracy and the "Washington Consensus"', *World Development*, **21** (8), 1329–36.

Wood, E.M. (1988), 'Capitalism and Human Emancipation', *New Left Review*, **167**, 1–21.

—— (1999), 'Unhappy Families: Global Capitalism in a World of Nation-States', *Monthly Review*, **51**, 3.

—— (2003), *Empire of Capital*, New York: Verso.

Yalman, Galip L. (2002), 'The Turkish State and Bourgeoisie in Historical Perspective: A Relativist Paradigm or a Panoply of Hegemonic Strategies?', in *The Politics of Permanent Crisis: Class, Ideology and State in Turkey*, ed. N. Balkan and S. Savran, Huappauge, NY: Nova Science Publishers, Inc.

—— (2009), *Transition to Neoliberalism: The Case of Turkey in the 1980s*, Istanbul: Bilgi University Press.

Yeldan, Erinc (2006a), 'Neoliberal Global Remedies: From Speculative-Led Growth to IMF-Led Crisis in Turkey', *Review of Radical Political Economy*, **38** (2), 193–213.

—— (2006b), *Assessing the Privatization Experience in Turkey: Implementation, Politics and Performance Results*, Global Policy Network, available at www.gpn.org.

Yılmaz, Durmuş (2006), Speech by Durmuş Yılmaz, Governor of the Central Bank of the Republic of Turkey, at the Central Bank of the Republic of Turkey, Istanbul, 13 December.

—— (2007), 'The Central Bank of the Republic of Turkey – The History, Recent Developments and the Future of Monetary Policy in Turkey', opening remarks by Durmuş Yılmaz, Governor of the Central Bank of the Republic of Turkey, at the Conference on the occasion of celebrating the 75th anniversary of the Central Bank of the Republic of Turkey, Ankara, 1 June, in *BIS Review*, **57**, 1–5.

—— (2011), 'Recent Economic and Financial Developments in Turkey', opening speech by Durmuş Yılmaz, Governor of the Central Bank of the Republic of Turkey, at the 79th Ordinary Meeting of the General Assembly, Ankara, 12 April, BIS Central Bankers' Speeches, Bank for International Settlements.

Yörüğlu, Mehmet and Hakan Atasoy (2010), 'The Effects of the Global Financial Crisis on the Turkish Financial Sector', *BIS Papers*, **54**, 387–405.

Index

Albo, Greg 13, 14, 33
alternatives in era of emerging
   finance capitalism *see* comparing
   alternatives in an era of emerging
   finance capitalism
Amable, Bruno 18
Argentina 4, 155
   financial crisis 128
Asian crisis 118–19, 128, 138, 147,
   167
Ayhan Kose, M. 8

Baker Plan 74
Bakır, Caner 191
Bank for International Settlements 3,
   128, 205
   Mexico 91, 96, 161–2
   Turkey 106, 121, 184–5
banks and banking 6
   bank-based financial systems 16–18
   bank ownership *see under* bank
      ownership
   central banks 30–31
   changes in 2
   dominant financial institution in
      capitalist development 20
   emerging finance capitalism *see
      under* emerging finance
      capitalism
   exercising political influence 3
   financial crises *see* financial crises
   greater autonomy spurring liberal
      democratization, 16
   labor and workers in *see under*
      labor
   large banks dominating financial
      systems 3
   profit-oriented speculative practices
      2
   rescues/bail-outs *see under* financial
      crises

as social relations 29–31
socialization of financial risk *see
   under* financial crises; Mexico;
   Turkey
state apparatus indispensable in
   emerging capitalisms 3
state interventions a necessary
   feature 1
bank ownership
   in developing countries 8, 21
   in Mexico *see under* Mexico
   qualifying neoliberal bank
      ownership and control 20–24:
      new institutional economics
      22–4; private ownership of
      banks as preferred policy 21;
      quantity theory of bank
      ownership 21–2, 23; state-
      owned banks 21–2
   in Turkey *see under* Turkey
Basel principles 121, 142
   Basel II 170
   Basel III 208–11
   Basel 25 core banking principles
      142, 210
   Basel Committee on Banking
      Supervision Report 209–10
Beck, Thorsten 160
Bottomore, Tom 32
Brady Plan 74–5
Brazil 4, 155
   increased financial volatility and
      accumulation of foreign
      reserves 157
BRIC countries 4

Canada 96
   banks' interest income 148
   see also North American Free
      Trade Agreement Mexico/US/
      Canada

251